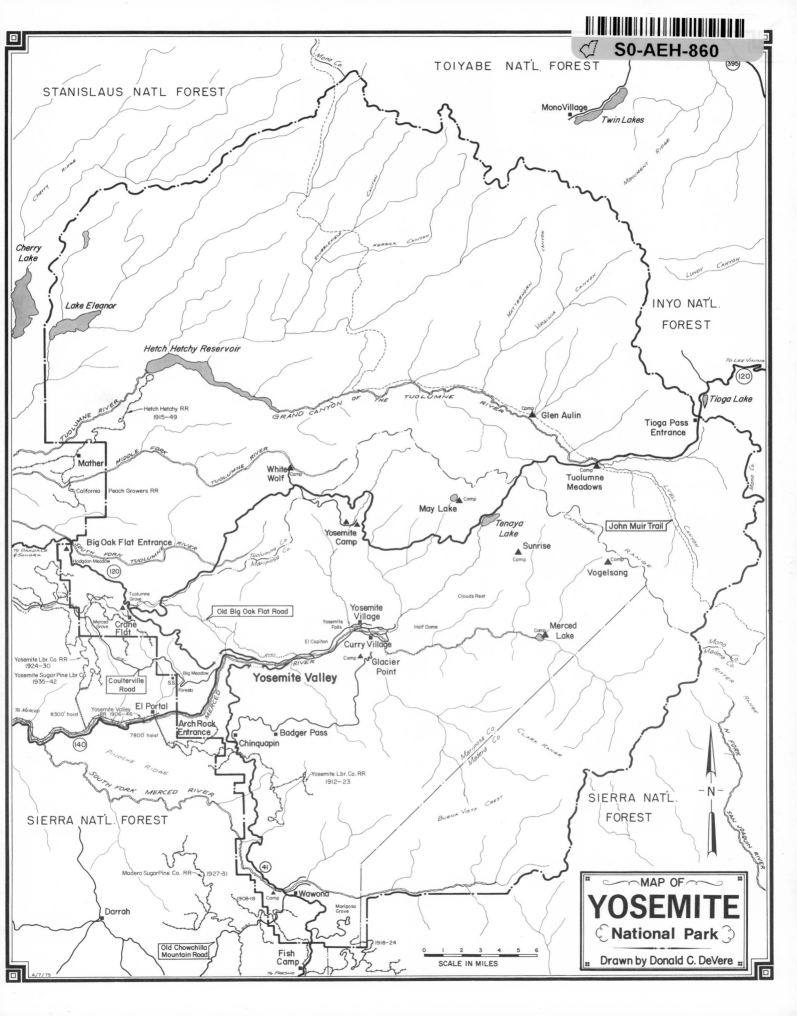

TOIYABE NATL. FOREST

STANISLAUS NATL FOREST

MonoVillage
Twin Lakes

INYO NATL. FOREST

Cherry Lake

Cherry Ridge

Lake Eleanor

Hetch Hetchy Reservoir

Lundy Canyon

To Lee Vining

Tioga Lake

Kerrick Canyon

Grand Canyon of the Tuolumne River

Glen Aulin

Camp

Tioga Pass Entrance

Hetch Hetchy RR 1915-49

Mather

Middle Fork

Tuolumne River

White Wolf

Camp

Tuolumne Meadows

Camp

California Peach Growers RR

May Lake

Camp

John Muir Trail

Big Oak Flat Entrance

Hodgdon Meadow

Tuolumne Co. Mariposa Co.

Yosemite Camp

Camp

Tenaya Lake

Sunrise

Camp

To Oakdale & Sonora

120

South Fork Tuolumne River

Vogelsang

Camp

Tuolumne Grove

Merced Grove

Crane Flat

Old Big Oak Flat Road

Clouds Rest

Yosemite Village

Yosemite Falls

Merced Lake

Camp

Yosemite Lbr. Co. RR 1924-30

Yosemite Sugar Pine Lbr Co 1935-42

Big Meadow

S.S.

Foresta

El Capitan

Half Dome

Curry Village

Coulterville Road

Merced River

Yosemite Valley

Camp

Glacier Point

To Merced

8300' hoist

Yosemite Valley RR 1906-46

El Portal

7800' hoist

Arch Rock Entrance

140

Pinoche Ridge

Badger Pass

Chinquapin

Mariposa Co. Madera Co.

Clark Range

Yosemite Lbr. Co. RR 1912-23

Buena Vista Crest

SIERRA NATL. FOREST

South Fork Merced River

SIERRA NATL. FOREST

N Fork

San Joaquin River

Madera SugarPine Co. RR 1927-31

41

Darrah

1908-18

Camp

Wawona

Mariposa Grove

1918-24

N

Old Chowchilla Mountain Road

Fish Camp

To Fresno

0 1 2 3 4 5 6
SCALE IN MILES

MAP OF
YOSEMITE
National Park
Drawn by Donald C. DeVere

4/7/75

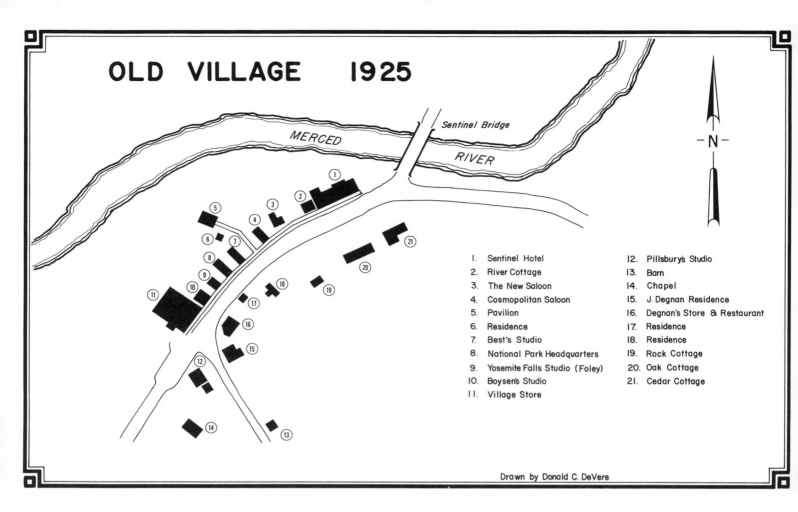

OLD VILLAGE   1925

MERCED RIVER

Sentinel Bridge

-N-

1. Sentinel Hotel
2. River Cottage
3. The New Saloon
4. Cosmopolitan Saloon
5. Pavilion
6. Residence
7. Best's Studio
8. National Park Headquarters
9. Yosemite Falls Studio (Foley)
10. Boysen's Studio
11. Village Store
12. Pillsbury's Studio
13. Barn
14. Chapel
15. J. Degnan Residence
16. Degnan's Store & Restaurant
17. Residence
18. Residence
19. Rock Cottage
20. Oak Cottage
21. Cedar Cottage

Drawn by Donald C. DeVere

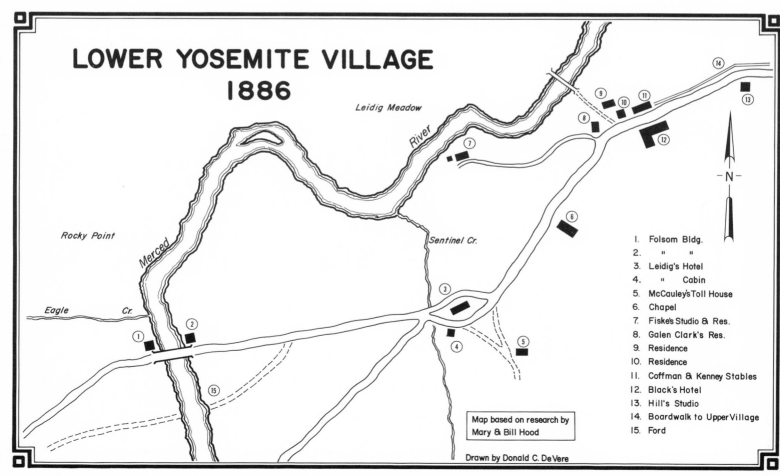

LOWER YOSEMITE VILLAGE 1886

Leidig Meadow

River

Rocky Point

Merced

Sentinel Cr.

Eagle   Cr.

-N-

1. Folsom Bldg.
2.   "   "
3. Leidig's Hotel
4.   "   Cabin
5. McCauley's Toll House
6. Chapel
7. Fiske's Studio & Res.
8. Galen Clark's Res.
9. Residence
10. Residence
11. Coffman & Kenney Stables
12. Black's Hotel
13. Hill's Studio
14. Boardwalk to Upper Village
15. Ford

Map based on research by
Mary & Bill Hood

Drawn by Donald C. DeVere

YOSEMITE'S INNKEEPERS

The story of a great park and its chief concessionaires

Shirley Sargent

Foreword by Horace M. Albright

Ponderosa Press
Yosemite, California

Cover design by Larry Van Dyke

Manufactured in the United States of America

Yosemite's Innkeepers

The story of a great park and its chief concessionaires

by Shirley Sargent

First edition, 1975
Second edition, revised, 2000

LCCCN 99–76229
ISBN 0-9642244-4-5

The front cover photograph

John Muir said it best. In 1889 he commented that the pretentious new Stoneman House, built by the state of California north of where Camp Curry was established later, had "a silly look amid surroundings so massive and sublime." The L-shaped structure was huge for its time: three and a half stories, roughly 125 by 50 feet, with 92 rooms—77 of them guest bedrooms. It boasted toilets (the first in Yosemite, two to a floor), and the sort of city conveniences that pleased moneyed guests. J. J. Cook, an associate of the powerful Washburn brothers, was the hotel's first and only manager, with a ten-year lease. A year before the lease expired, the shoddily built hotel burned to the ground.

This book is dedicated with appreciation and admiration to three men: the late Art Robinson, who insisted that it be written; Dr. Alan Coleman, who made it financially possible; and the late Hil Oehlmann, who aided and guided me throughout my work.

Ponderosa Press
P.O. Box 278
Yosemite, CA 95389

Contents

Photo credits in this book are abbreviated YNP for Yosemite National Park;
YP&CC for Yosemite Park and Curry Co.; SS for Shirley Sargent;
and RCB for Ruth Curry Burns.

Yosemite was still pastoral when a photographer, probably J. T. Boysen, took this idyllic scene about 1900. The cabin and apple orchard in the background had belonged to pioneer James M. Hutchings.
(Los Angeles County Museum of Natural History.)

Foreword

People of every nation in the world know of the extraordinary features of Yosemite National Park—its overwhelming magnificence and beauty that has attracted visitors for one hundred and twenty-four years, but few are aware of the human side. This new book, Yosemite and Its Innkeepers, details the development of both the Park and its entrepreneurs. It was my boss, Stephen T. Mather, first director of the National Park Service. who said, "Scenery is a hollow enjoyment to a tourist who sets out in the morning after an indigestible breakfast and a fitful sleep on an impossible bed."

From 1856 on, Yosemite had had pioneer innkeepers such as Galen Clark, James Hutchings, and the Washburn brothers to provide visitors with beds (usually without bedbugs), meals, and roofs. Even John Muir contributed to the guests' comfort by supplying lumber for buildings. It was 1899 when Jennie and David Curry set up a tourist camp, and quickly became a force in Yosemite Valley. That, too, was a pioneering venture.

When Mr. Mather began to manage the national parks in 1915, two of the thorniest problems were to protect their unique natural features, and find concessionaires who would keep visitors content. In Yosemite we inherited competition between Curry, who was aggressively anti-regimentation, and the Washburn interests, and, unwittingly, fostered turmoil by sponsoring a new concessionaire, D. J. Desmond. Eventually a merger of the opposing forces into the Yosemite Park and Curry Co. made possible a wide variety of facilities and visitor accommodations under the management of Curry's widow, children, and sons-in-law. For three quarters of a century, the beneficial influence of the notable family was indeed great and good. Four generations of Currys not only loved Yosemite, but wanted every guest to love it, be grateful for its preservation, and inspired by its grandeur. Now that family has been succeeded by a conglomerate company which plans to continue the traditions of service and hospitality. This history chronicles not only the concessionaire's achievements, but those of the Park Service in the making of roads, trails, camps, protective and interpretive services. The seasonal urban ills of the 1970s are a far cry from the pastoral conditions of the 1850s, but they, as well as hitherto untold chapters about the depression and World Ware II's effects on Yosemite, are a definite part of this colorful book.

I have had the pleasure of knowing Yosemite National Park and its concessionaires intimately since 1915, and warmly commend this volume as a valid contribution to Yosemite Literature. I have had, also, the good fortune to know and admire Shirley Sargent who has written *Yosemite and Its Innkeepers* after long and diligent research, and rendered it a saga of trials, triumphs, problems, and prestige, with people and nature in surroundings of the greatest beauty and magnitude.

HORACE M. ALBRIGHT
Second Director of the
National Park Service
and friend to Yosemite
for most of his long life
(1890-1987).

Author's Preface

Since my tenure in Yosemite, the world's best place, began as a child in 1936, I have been engrossed with its natural and human history, and that passion has led me to explore, collect, research, interview, and write of it. During the 1960s, I suggested separately to Mary Ellen Degnan, Mary Curry Tresidder, and Hilmer Oehlmann that a history of business development in the Park should be written, but none of them felt objective or energetic enough to tackle it. In January of 1972, Art Robinson, vice president of the Yosemite Park and Curry Co., convinced Alan Coleman, its president, that I should write such a history. After conferring with Mr. Oehlmann, honorary chairman of the Board of Directors, Coleman gave me a grant to enable me to research and write it. Three years, a hundred plus interviews, and five manuscript drafts later, *Yosemite and Its Innkeepers*, the story of a great Park and its chief concessionaires, was finished.

A list of the legion of Yosemite devotees who generously shared memories, pictures, and documentation with me would read like a telephone book, beginning with A for Albright, and ending with Z for Zinser. To them I am everlastingly grateful, and, at least, fragmentary acknowledgment is given them in my source notes at the end of the book. A scattering of other people who gave me aid deserve gratitude here. My thanks to Kay Coffin, Ruth Massey, Louise Woelbing, and Donna Zinser, all faithful typists; Jack Gyer and Leslie Hart, curator and librarian of the Yosemite National Park archives; Ruth Wilson, historian for the Palo Alto Library; Elizabeth Miller, librarian of the *Redwood City Tribune;* Gladys Hansen, former head of the Californian Room of the San Francisco Public Library, and now director of the Museum of the City of San Francisco; Virginia Ried of the San Joaquin Valley Information Service; Dick Dillon, former Sutro librarian, and his assistant, Eleanor Capelle; Richard N. Schellens, Redwood City historian; Nancy Ortiz and Margaret S. Plummer, who helped me on exciting research trips; B. Weiss, Marilyn Fry and Hank Johnston who supplied editing; and Judith Whipple who designed the original book.

Since this book was first published, in 1975, it went through several printings. For each, I updated the last chapter. In this revised edition I have made significant changes, including shortening the title, yet I have retained both Horace Albright's foreword and part of my preface as still fitting and valid.

Many of the people who originally helped me are now dead, but remembered and appreciated. Now, in 2000, I need to acknowledge the skillful efforts of Peter Browning, editor and friend, and Larry Van Dyke, designer of the new cover. The revision has from the assistance of Linda Eade and Jim Snyder at the Yosemite Research Library, who have patiently helped find answers to my questions. Furthermore, Mary and Derrick Vocelka, Audrey Beck Wilson, and Zada James aided me with the multitudinous changes. Sheila Tarvin, my typist and old friend, keyboarded the text into her computer following Peter Browning's instructions for his page-formatting program. That reduced my fairly orderly pages into a formless, unparagraphed, coded mess. I am one of the increasingly rare breed who still type with two fingers on a low-tech electric typewriter and do not understand computers. However, Peter assured me that the finished product would look like a book.

As you see,
he was right!!
SHIRLEY SARGENT
Yosemite, 2000

In 1900, Mirror Lake lived up to its name.
(Herbert Gaytes photo; Courtesy, the Bancroft Library.)

Galen Clark's passion for Yosemite Valley began in 1855 when he first visited it as a member of one of the pioneer tourist parties. *(George Fiske photo; SS collection.)*

1 Welcome to Yosemite

Since 1855, when organized travel began, more than sixty million people have visited Yosemite National Park to absorb the splendor, peace, and antiquity of its unique monoliths, waterfalls, lakes, cañons, meadows, and forested mountains. Since 1967 visitation has exceeded two million a year. Twenty years later that total passed three million and in 1994, four million. Many people, however, come by bus for only a few hours. Few of today's legions, who travel comfortably over paved highways to modern accommodations, have any conception of the hardships endured by early-day visitors or pioneer innkeepers during Yosemite's yesterdays.

Recorded history began in October 1849 when two gold miners, one of whom kept a journal, first viewed Yosemite Valley. Two years later, volunteer soldiers, known as the Mariposa Battalion, rid the Valley of its native Indian inhabitants, and applied place names such as Three Brothers, Half Dome, and El Capitan to its incredible natural features. In 1855, forty-two white men, in four parties, forgot all travel difficulties in awed appreciation of the scenic magnificence. Most of these initial sightseers were miners, and a handful of them realized that Yosemite Valley represented a different kind of gold. One, Englishman James Mason Hutchings, immediately broadcast his account of "luxurious scenic banqueting" via newspaper. His widely reprinted rhapsodic words inspired the beginning of regular tourist travel. In anticipation of increased visitation, Milton and Houston Mann, two pragmatic members of the 1855 parties, wielded axes and shovels in building a trail from Mariposa to Yosemite, a distance of fifty rough miles. It opened in 1856 to footmen, who paid $1.00 in toll, and horsemen, who paid $2.00. Hutchings, in company with an artist, was one of the first to use it.

The midway stopping point on the Mann Brothers Trail was a large meadow, soon known as Wawona, adjoining the South Fork of the Merced River. There Galen Clark, another of the 1855 sightseers, settled in 1856, and, inadvertently, began a wayside inn for overnight guests. In 1857, he and Milton Mann found a grove of giant Sequoia trees six miles southeast of Wawona. Their numbers, size, and age inspired the same kind of wonder and awe as did Yosemite Valley. Clark spread the gospel through newspapers. Mann built a horse trail to the grove, and the Big Trees soon ranked with the Valley as a "must see" spot.

Between 1855 and 1874, when the first stage roads were completed into the Valley, 2,656 visitors arrived afoot or on horseback.[1] These intrepid travelers were served by equally intrepid pioneer entrepreneurs, who provided shelter, beds, and meals. Since every

Ex-cabinet maker James Hutchings captioned this picture "J. M. Hutchings in boat made by him."
(Charles Bierstadt photo; William E. Mills, Jr. collection.)

---

1. Although roofed, Yosemite had stages that differed from stagecoaches in that they were open-sided. Evidently this more open vehicle was adequate for the Yosemite climate from April to October.

The Upper Hotel was photographed soon after it opened, in June 1859. Porches, doors, and windows added later by James Hutchings, who bought it in 1864, softened its exterior. *(YNP collection.)*

piece of lumber had to be whipsawed by hand, and every bit of furnishing from stoves to windows glass had to be transported on mules, accommodations were exceedingly primitive, but nonetheless serviceable and welcome.

In the fall of 1857, four miners built the first Yosemite Valley inn of hand-riven boards near the base of Sentinel Rock. Although known as the Lower Hotel, its function was more that of a saloon until snow crushed it. After rebuilding, it was reopened in 1858 as an inn run by John Neal, a former jeweler, and his wife, Jean Frances. It looked like a barn, and its "rooms" resembled stalls. Windows were without glass, floors were of dirt or pine boughs, and the beds were springless. Mattresses were ticking stuffed with hay, bracken, or some other soft material, and sanitary facilities consisted of a wash pan and a path. Chickens and cows outnumbered wild animals, and meadows had been planted to hay and grain. Comforts were at a minimum, but the surrounding beauty was so great that few lodgers complained.

In the fall of 1856, Beardsley and Hite erected a tent a mile east of Neal's hotel and began cutting timbers for a 20- by 60-foot two-story inn. Soon after the Upper Hotel's opening, in the spring of 1859, James Hutchings, by then the seasoned editor of his *Hutchings' California Magazine,* and a party of friends registered as guests. One of them, Charles L. Weed, was a photographer who took a picture of the graceless structure on June 21 with his forty-pound camera. The resulting photo, in which Hutchings and friends

appear, was the first ever taken of a building or people in Yosemite Valley.

On April 20, 1864, the ubiquitous Hutchings, his young, pregnant wife, Elvira, and his indefatigable mother-in-law, Florantha T. Sproat, took possession of the Upper Hotel, and began the occasional complexities of fitting as many as fifty-seven people into accommodations designed for twenty-eight. Their daughter Florence, who arrived on August 23, 1864, was the first white child born in Yosemite Valley.

Two months after Hutchings established possessory land claims in the Valley and began innkeeping in what was called the Hutchings House, a bill granting Yosemite Valley and the Mariposa Grove of Big Trees—singularly sublime, unique, but widely separated natural features—to the state of California was signed by

Shy, sensitive John Muir was hired by James Hutchings in 1869 to run a sawmill. *(Bradley and Rulofson photo; courtesy the Bancroft Library.)*

President Abraham Lincoln. The date was June 30, 1864, and the Congressional charge was that ". . .said State shall accept the Grant upon the express conditions that the premises shall be held for public use, resort and recreation; shall be inalienable for all time. . . ." This protective act anticipated the creation of national parks, which began in 1872. It also precluded any private ownership of land within the state grant although ". . . leases not exceeding ten years may be granted for portions of said premises." Galen Clark was appointed official Guardian of the new grant. Hutchings, enraged at the prospect of leasing what he thought he owned, instituted suits that dragged on until 1874.

Despite the decade of legal wrangling, Hutchings continued to serve his hotel guests, whose chief complaint seemed to be the lack of privacy between rooms. Most wanted partitions other than the muslin sheets that afforded nightly lantern-lit, piquant shadow pictures. Their host agreed and imported equipment for a water powered sawmill. Boards for partitions and additions were cut in the mill. Tree-lover Hutchings added a lean-to kitchen around a large incense cedar tree, on whose twenty-four-foot circumference pots and pans hung. Inevitably, the addition was dubbed the Big Tree Room, and the building eventually renamed Cedar Cottage. In 1869 Hutchings hired a shabbily dressed, nature-loving Scotsman to run the mill, and the sawyer soon proved to be as ingenious with words as with wood. His name was John Muir. Hutchings' tenure as an innkeeper ended in 1875 after he received $24,000 from the California Legislature in exchange for his land claims. From that time on, The Yosemite Valley Commissioners controlled all structures in the Yosemite Grant, and issued leases for

At Leidig's Hotel, 1869–1888, guests could breakfast on mush, milk, catfish, and ice cream. *(SS collection.)*

Kenneyville commemorated George W. Kenney, who ran an extensive stable business in partnership with William E. Coffman. *(YP&CC collection.)*

their use. G. W. Coulter, for whom the mining town of Coulterville was named, and A. J. Murphy leased Hutchings' former property, and began a big two-story building across the stage road from Cedar Cottage. Part of that edifice, known as the Yosemite Falls Hotel, overhung the river. It was completed by John K. Barnard, who was the lessee from 1877 until 1893, when he was succeeded by A. B. Glasscock who renamed the hotel the Sentinel. After Glasscock's death, in 1897, Jay Bruce Cook took over. By the turn of the century there were six guest units: Cedar, River, Rock, Oak, Ivy, and Locust cottages, plus the main, riverside building, all known collectively as the Sentinel Hotel.

Competition existed down the Valley at both Black's Hotel and Leidig's Hotel, which had succeeded the pioneer Lower Hotel. One guest remarked that the L-shaped Black's resembled a bowling alley. Thanks to roofed porches upstairs and down, Leidig's had a bit more architectural style. Additionally, it had a hot-stove artist in the matronly person of Isabella Logan Leidig, who routinely produced tasty meals and eleven robust children. In July 1884, a hungry man, displeased with food served at the Sentinel Hotel, was delighted with Mrs. Leidig's breakfast menu of catfish, milk, mutton, venison, ham and eggs, and ice cream! That satisfied guest was none other than ex-sawyer John Muir, whose nature writings and conservationist stand were gaining him national fame and influence.

In 1880, the eight-member Board of Yosemite Valley Commissioners was replaced, and Hutchings succeeded Clark as Guardian, only to be unseated himself four years later. Often when a new state governor was elected, he appointed favor-deserving cronies to the Board of Commissioners, and sometimes a political hack was named Guardian. Mismanagement resulted, and the Yosemite Grant was at once a state pride, a public park, and a political mess. Periodically, legislatures responded to demands for more money for trails, bridges, and roads, but funding was neither adequate nor constant enough to meet needs. In 1885, $40,000 was appropriated to build a modern, first-class hotel to accommodate 150 guests. Muir, for one, thought the finished, four-story structure, bulking in the shadow of Glacier Point, had "a silly look amidst surrounds so massive and sublime." Since George Stoneman was governor then, the huge inn became the Stoneman House, and the nearby meadow Stoneman Meadow. After it opened for business, the Commissioners decreed that the old "unsightly" Black's and Leidig's hotels should be torn down. That

Henry, John, and Edward Washburn ran the Wawona properties, and had financial fingers in many Yosemite ventures. Brother Julius is at the left. *(Mariposa County Historical Society collection.)*

4

was done in 1886, and ten years later, the Stoneman, whose interior design was as faulty as the the exterior was ugly, burned to the ground. After that, the venerable Sentinel was the only surviving Valley inn. Its cottages, ice house, laundry, and bath house lined both sides of the road at the east end of Yosemite Village. They were shouldered by the Cosmopolitan Saloon and Bath House, the Guardian's office, several photographic studios, two general stores, a blacksmith shop, barns, a bakery, and employee housing. Lower Yosemite Village, near the base of the Four-Mile Trail, was less compact, but Fiske's Studio, the Chapel, Galen Clark's home, and several houses denoted that settlement even after the destruction of Leidig's and Black's hotels.

A third center of activity, Kenneyville, had sprung up around William F. Coffman and George W. Kenney's extensive stables near the eastern end of the Valley, where horses, shops, barns, and houses mingled. Beyond Kenneyville ranged a wilderness of beautiful spots such as Mirror Lake, Tenaya Canyon, and Vernal and Nevada falls.

Outside the Valley proper there were four hotels of consequence. The biggest and best was the Wawona Hotel, which Henry, John, and Edward Washburn had bought from Galen Clark in December 1874. The New England-bred brothers added buildings, fountains, services, and charm to the place until it ranked among California's finest hotels. The Washburns were self-sufficient, aggressive, and influential businessmen who made money while making guests comfortable.

Peregoy's Mountain View House, on the trail to Glacier Point, was a wayside inn that existed from 1869 to 1878, and was noted for the culinary delights turned out by the innkeeper's wife. Steaks, mutton chops, cakes, and cream pies were Mary Peregoy's specialties.

James McCauley's Mountain House on Glacier Point served guests from 1878 until it was destroyed by fire in 1969. *(Courtesy, the Bancroft Library.)*

Albert and Emily Snow and their daughter, on the porch of the La Casa Nevada inn, which they ran from 1870 to 1897. *(Carleton E. Watkins photo.)*

Irishman James McCauley presided at the unadorned Glacier Point Mountain House from 1878 until 1897. Although unschooled, he possessed native ingenuity, considerable fortitude, and a ready wit. A German-born wife and twin sons assisted him in caring for guests.

Eighteen hundred feet below McCauley's, in the canyon to the east, three picturesque hotel buildings stood within the spray of Nevada Fall. La Casa Nevada, run by Emily and Albert Snow, operated from 1870 until 1897. Its unique location, chalet-type cottages, and cuisine made it popular. In fact, Mrs. Snow's doughnuts, baked apples, bread, pies, and catsup were lovingly described in books written by early travelers. She boasted that they "raised everything

there on the backs of mules." Questioned as to the exact altitude of the inn, her answer was, "About as near to heaven as you'll get." While all the inns served liquor, Snow's was notably free and easy, as testified to by the guests who wrote in the register: "Be sure to try the Snow water," and "No person here obliged to commit burglary to obtain a drink." Even now, well over a hundred years later, broken glass testifies to the abundance of liquor.

All of the nine pioneer hotels fulfilled needs, but because of the problems attendant to the isolated region, six of them closed before 1899. During their reigns, the hardy Irish, Scotch, German, and American innkeepers provided the basic amenities of life to travelers, and in so doing made a significant contribution to the early history and development of Yosemite.

2 "All's Well!"

When the sun beamed out from behind Half Dome on June 1, 1899, H. H. Markham was Governor of California and a member of the Yosemite Valley Commissioners, Miles Wallace was the Yosemite Guardian, and Jay Bruce Cook was the manager of the Sentinel Hotel. All were friends or associates of the powerful Washburn brothers, who not only ran the Wawona Hotel, but had financial fingers in the stage lines, the roads, the hotel on Glacier Point, the Sentinel (through in-law Cook), and even Southern Pacific rates for Yosemite-bound tourists. Scenery and solitude triumphed over commerce, however, so most tourists were unaware of monopoly or politics, though they were sometimes vocal about prices charged for stages, rooms, meals, and mules. Complaints fell on deaf Washburn ears. On the whole, their services and prices were reasonable for the time, but Valley sightseers who could not afford the Sentinel Hotel's minimum charge of $4.00 a day plus tipping had no alternative other than to camp in primitive campgrounds spread along both sides of the Merced River. On June 1, 1899, however, the Sentinel's supremacy was challenged by a couple of men erecting a handful of tents for public rental at the pine-studded base of Glacier Point.

"Camp Sequoia" was the innovative brainchild of David Alexander Curry, a dynamic, ex-Indiana schoolteacher, who planned to offer visitors inexpensive accommodations in an unstructured atmosphere. Because he and his wife Jennie were teaching school in Redwood City, California, they could not participate in either choosing the camp's site or superintending its opening, and so delegated three of Mrs. Curry's numerous cousins—Rufus L. Green, a Stanford professor, and two of the Thomson brothers, journalist Will and farmer Austin—to begin the camp. Aged, alert, former Yosemite Guardian Galen Clark had guided the men around Yosemite Valley, and strongly advised against the location they liked as too shady, cold, and isolated from the Village for a successful business venture. Despite Clark's disdain, the cousins decided upon the place between the site of the ill-fated Stoneman House and the cliffs, partly because of the marvelous views of Half Dome and Tenaya Canyon, and partly because platforms and tent frames were already in existence.

These structures, Clark explained, were remnants of a family camp established the previous summer by William Thomas, a prominent Bay Area attorney. In 1973, his daughter recalled that the summer camp had been a substantial one with a number of tents for family and guests, a bathhouse, a cook tent presided over by a Chinese chef, ". . .and a pig to take care of the garbage."

The cousins regarded the abandoned camp as a ready-made labor saver and obtained permission from the Yosemite Valley Guardian to use it. Among the initial guests at the new camp were Mrs. Rufus Green, daughters Helen and Hazel, three Stanford professors, and several people from out of state. A photograph of the assemblage was taken to mark the historic founding of Camp Sequoia, the name picked by David Curry to commemorate the monstrous trees and Sequoia High School, where he was principal.

That night the campers gathered around a roaring fire, thus beginning a tradition of nightly campfires and attendant programs that continued for decades. So, too, began the informality and guest participation that gave the camp its ultimate success. "An ideal camping spot is Camp Sequoia amid the big cedars at the base of Glacier Point," reported the *Yosemite Tourist* of June 8, 1899, "There are a dozen or more tents in the camp and many young people, in fact they are all young. . . Even the professors from Stanford, usually calm and dignified, join in making Camp Sequoia other than a Sunday School recital."

Editor Daniel J. Foley printed the four-page *Yosemite Tourist* several times a week between May and October. A page or so was devoted to news and names of campers and Sentinel Hotel guests, while historical articles and pictures were the standard format for the inside pages. News of Camp Sequoia was a curiosity to residents, who considered it transitory and certainly not competition to the Sentinel.

During the first weeks of existence the camps welcome mat was of pine needles, the tent flooring of burlap, and the furnishings makeshift. Washstands were simple cracker boxes covered by oilcloth and faced with calico, and bedsprings were supported by chunks of wood. Mattresses, however, were new and the bedding was clean. There was no ice house, so meat was hung on a cross piece between trees. Mrs. Babb, the

By 1899, the Sentinel Hotel had outlasted all rivals. *(SS collection.)*

Rufus L. Green, professor of math at Stanford University, was a cousin of Mrs. Curry. He and Will and Austin Thomson, also cousins, set up Camp Curry on June 1, 1899. *(Thomas E. Green collection.)*

cook, was the sole paid employee. Austin Thomson's wife, Eva Mary Thomson, stayed behind to assist with the cooking, and college students acted as general flunkies in exchange for tent and board. Bathing was provided by washbasins or the Merced River, and the sanitary facilities were outhouses. Conveniences were few, but the scenery was grand and the price was right. For $12.00 a week and no tipping, guests of Camp Sequoia had Half Dome, a tent, a good table, and a clean napkin at every meal!

On June 14, David Curry left Redwood City for Yosemite Valley accompanied by his wife and their three children, Foster, eleven, Mary, five, and Marjorie, four. Their trip, via boat across San Francisco Bay, then by wagon and stagecoach, consumed three days. On June 17, David A. Curry shook off the Coulterville road dust and surveyed Camp Sequoia. In its two weeks of existence, it had achieved entity and a casual leisure. After Curry's arrival, it had identity! Within a short time it became known as Camp Curry, and its flamboyant host the "Stentor of Yosemite." Almost instantly,

8

Yosemite changed Curry's life and style, for its magnitude thrilled, awed, inspired, and relaxed him. For fifteen years in classrooms he had tried to subdue his ebullient spirits and booming voice. Now the piney air, breezy days, and magnificent surrounds made him expansive, his words echoed from cliffs, his eloquence delighted guests, and his ingenuity, taxed by the challenges of his enterprise, blossomed. According to Mrs. Curry, the camp had an immediate and steady growth, largely because of her husband's personality. "Big in body, mind and soul," she said, "interested in life and people, simple in his ways and habits, absolutely without any affectation, his friendly spirit and genial whole-souledness appealed to people and made him the perfect host."

Neither Jennie nor David Curry was business-oriented nor a Californian. They were Hoosiers by birth, and pioneers by heritage and inclination. David, the first-born of ten children, had begun life February 15, 1860, in a farm house near Bloomington, Indiana. In 1869 his Irish-born mother, Mary Kerr Curry, and farmer father, William Renwick Curry, settled permanently on 640 acres near Winchester, Kansas. Eventually "Ren's" parents, brothers, and sisters moved to the same area, and family ties, always close, were strengthened. By the time David was six, his mother recalled, he was earning his board and keep "running errands, feeding stock, plowing the land." In between chores, he attended country schools, and in time became valedictorian of his high school class. After graduation, he earned money toward college by working on the railroad.

His parents indoctrinated him with the Puritan ethic of industry, thrift, and sacrifice, reinforced by the Scotch Presbyterian Covenanter's zealous, high-principled religion. In the fall of 1879, David entered non-sectarian Indiana University. Then nineteen, he was a tall, stocky young man whose goal was to become a minister. During his freshman year he met Jennie Etta Foster, a wraith-like classmate whose gentle appearance obscured a strong intelligence. Her birth on October 12, 1861 had taken place in a a log cabin three miles from Rushville, Indiana, where she was welcomed by a brother and their parents, Margery McKee and Robert A. Foster. The Fosters were southerners by birth, but slavery was anathema to them so they had moved west. Like David, Jennie grew up on a farm, "sharing in its labors and pleasures," she said "in a family . . . where there were few luxuries . . ." but "a sufficiency of the necessities."

Education was considered a necessity, and Jennie attended Greensburg High School, about twenty miles south of Rushville. A favorite cousin, Rufus Lot Green, was her classmate there and later at Indiana University. Jennie had dozens of cousins, since her mother was one of seven sisters and her father was one of three children. Invariably, family love and loyalty were binding.

Their senior year, 1882–83, was the turning point in Jennie and David's lives, for then they enrolled in Dr. David Starr Jordan's geology class. His encyclopedic knowledge, uninhibited informality, and a vocal enthusiasm altered their futures. The climax of the class came

For $2.00 a day, Camp Curry's initial guests had a tent, good food, and a clean napkin at every meal! *(YNP collection.)*

David Starr Jordan, an evolutionist, naturalist, and outstanding educator, greatly influenced Jennie Foster and David A. Curry. *(Stanford University archives.)*

in the spring, as Dr. Jordan recalled in his autobiography:

> It was then the custom for Western colleges to grant the senior class a vacation of three weeks at the end of the academic year, in order that they might prepare their graduating orations. . . .
>
> As the eighteen members of the class of '83 were all students of mine in Geology, we arranged to utilize the special vacation for a geological tramp across southeastern Kentucky from Rock Castle Falls to Cumberland Falls and Cumberland Gap, returning by way of Mammoth Cave—a total distance of two hundred miles across a region wonderfully picturesque, through noble forests intersected by sparkling springs and all instructive from every point of view.

David Curry had a sociable nature as well as organizational ability, and proved that in making arrangements for the party's food and lodging. "Jordan, and the trip, imbued us with a love of . . . God's great outdoors," Jennie said, "and taught us the art and pleasure of hiking. . . ." Jordan led his suntanned, exuberant class back to Bloomington in time to dress up for graduation. Afterwards David Curry asked Jennie to marry him, and she accepted with the understanding that they both work first to repair their finances.

His first job was exciting and immediate, for right after graduation, he and a classmate, Joseph Swain, traveled abroad assisting Dr. Jordan in an excursion that introduced students and teachers to European cultures. They traveled, largely on foot, through Holland, Belgium, France, Germany, Switzerland, Norway, and Italy, staying at inexpensive inns where Curry and Swain arranged accommodations and meals. After that, Curry was imbued with concepts of European civilization and history, as well as a strong sense of public service.

Consciously or unconsciously, he emulated his mentor Jordan. Six feet two inches tall, with a barrel-chested physique, he sported a brush-like mustache like Jordan's. His voice boomed, echoing his mentor, and he was eloquent, argumentative, positive, and high-principled. Jordan's influence helped mold Curry into a liberal, thus unacceptable to the Covenantors, who did not believe in voting or participating in government.

That fall Curry taught Latin at his alma mater, to which he and Jennie had immense loyalty. His next teaching job was at Greensburg High School where Jennie taught the three R's and baseball! They were married in Bloomington on March 6, 1886. In 1888, after the May 19th birth of David Foster Curry, they traveled east so Curry could take Latin and Greek at Harvard Graduate School. After that the family moved west to Xenia, Ohio, where he studied for the ministry in the United Presbyterian Theological School, but only remained, he said, until "the professors could no longer agree with him." Eventually, Jennie wrote, he "found his place in the Congregational Church where he was a faithful member with the liberty of conscience he desired." One of the Congregational Church's interests was the Ogden Academy, founded in 1887 in Ogden, Utah.

In 1891 Curry was hired as its principal, and his wife as a teacher. Yellowstone National Park, in neighboring Wyoming, was a magnet. Its geysers, petrified and living forests, waterfalls, canyons, and wildlife were famous, and they determined to visit it in the summer of 1892. "When word of this proposed trip spread," Jennie remembered, "several other teachers came to us asking if they might go along as paying guests."

Recalling his experiences aiding Jordan, David Curry was confident that he could lead a successful tour. He hired a cook and arranged to take a covered wagon as a kitchen; tents and camping equipment would be carried by team and wagon. His gregarious nature was well-suited to filling wants and needs. Soon

Jennie, too, developed a philosophy of "What do the people want?" and "How can we give it to them?" The excursion was so popular that it was repeated in succeeding years.

After the Yellowstone trip of 1894, Mrs. Curry said, "We went to California particularly to visit the Yosemite; when we got there we found that we did not have half enough money for one of us to go." The cost for train, stage, food, and lodging for the trip that could not be made in less than three days one way amounted to over $100. A railroad strike further complicated travel. Crestfallen, they returned to Ogden, but not before succumbing to California's charms and climate. Before departing, they presumably saw Dr. Jordan, who by then was president of the infant Leland Stanford University at Palo Alto.

Besides teaching and assisting with the annual Yellowstone excursions, Jennie Curry bore two daughters: Mary Louise, on November 29, 1893, and Marjorie Lucile, on April 11, 1895. Both were born in Ogden and named for grandmothers and aunts. In 1895, the Currys took thirty-nine teachers from Denver on a twenty-five-day tour of Yellowstone. Shortly afterwards, they moved to California, ostensibly for postgraduate work at Stanford, but Jordan had been alerted and had promised to aid them in finding teaching positions. San Mateo County officials were in the process of selecting a name and a principal for their first high school, and Jordan recommended his former student. On September 5, Curry was elected principal of Sequoia High School at a salary of $75 a month, and his wife hired as a teacher at $50 a month.

Neither had time to attend Stanford that year, since they were too busy with school, civic, and church activities in their new community. Her parents, the Fosters, lived with them to care for the children. Although Yellowstone authorities had received several complaints against Curry of "unfulfilled promises, unnecessary delays, insufficient food and bad cooking, . . ." he was awarded permits to conduct groups through the Park in 1896, '97, and '98. While his wife remained in California, Curry hired her cousin, Brower Elliot, as his assistant.

Despite pacifist leanings, Curry became more aggressive and even abrasive, which accelerated his disputes with the school board and its president about the school's operations. So controversial was he that, later, a San Jose County historian judged him as:

". . . a big, boisterous importation from the middle west, one of the hegira of educational characters

In 1891, Jennie and David Curry and their son Foster moved to Ogden, Utah, where they taught school, conducted tours of Yellowstone National Park, and had two daughters. Presumably Foster's hair was cut after they arrived. *(RCB collection.)*

crossing the Rockies in the wake of David Starr Jordan. . . . From the beginning to the end of his career as principal of the Sequoia High, it was evident to all that Professor Curry was not endowed by nature to fit himself to the needs of the position.

By 1898 the Currys were considering quitting the educational field because of politics and finances. Their savings had been lost in the failure of an Ogden Building and Loan Association, and a teaching future held little promise of security. Therefore, they discussed abandoning the Yellowstone tours in favor of establishing a Yosemite camp that would offer reasonably priced tent accommodations. Luxuries and tipping would be non-existent, but beds and food good and service would make every guest feel at home. They consulted Jordan and Rufus Green, who had followed him to Stanford. Both men approved, and Green helped the Currys obtain a $500 loan from the Palo Alto bank. Further, since Stanford closed for the summer before the Redwood City schools did, Green and cousin Will

Thomson offered to go to Yosemite, begin the camp, and run it until the Currys arrived. Advertisements were inserted in the *Redwood City Democrat*, and supplies were ordered. Since a good cook was a necessity, Curry recruited a Mrs. Babb, who managed a college boarding house, and guaranteed her $100 for the summer's work, and double that if the camp was successful. Tents and staples were packed into horse-drawn wagons, and the pioneering venture launched.

As already noted, once Curry took over, in mid-June, the camp had character, and his energies were absorbed in its operation and improvement. He had a loading platform built for stage passengers, ordered more tents, erected them, and improved the water system, which tapped a large spring. He arranged to buy milk from John Degnan, who had a dairy herd below the Village where his wife ran a popular bakery. Produce was freighted in from Merced and Coulterville. In time, meat and berries were supplied by George Meyer and James McCauley, pioneers with ranches adjacent to Big Meadow, twelve miles west on the Coulterville Road.

Daily the open stages swept in, and "there would be a warm welcome for the travelers—with much flourishing of feather dusters," Mary Curry remembered. "Ladies had their hats tied down with heavy veils, and unfortunate was he or she who didn't sport a linen dust-coat." Curry said his guests arrived covered with "pulverized scenery." As stages arrived, he shouted, "Welcome to Camp Curry," and echoes bounced back from the cliffs. When the four-horse stages wheeled off with a crack of the driver's whip, dust and Curry's voice rose. Cupping his hands to his mouth to form a megaphone, he would boom, "FAREWELLL!" Campers a mile away could hear him and the echoes. It wasn't long before they were answering his "FAREWELL" and "ALL'S WELL" with ragged shouts of "LIKE HELL!"

Often young Foster would emulate his father calling, "Foster Curry greets you!" and "FAREWELL" with all his might. At eleven, he carried wood and water, ran errands, and did all kinds of camp jobs. Camp life, high boots, casual work clothes, and a straw or cowboy hat suited him fine. Watched by their Foster grandparents, his little sisters played in the pine needles, but Foster had work and, better yet, fishing to do. A local Indian, Captain Sam, taught him to fish, and that became a practical obsession, for trout were desired by Mrs. Babb and the guests.

Sunday was the only dreary day in Foster's life, for it meant church services in camp or the Yosemite

Big in bulk, ambition, and vocal prowess, Curry was soon famed for his stentorian shouts of "WELLLCOME," and "FARRREWELL." *(Hensleigh Family collection.)*

Chapel, far down the Valley, and a confining list of parental "don'ts." No card playing, no games, and worst of all, no fishing. His energy spilled out in teasing his sisters and various frowned-upon pranks. While his family gave thanks on the Sabbath, Foster was grateful only when it was over. Sunday newspapers never arrived until later, but that was just as well since the Currys would not allow them to be read on the Lord's day. A relative felt that "Foster was badly handled as a child. Cousin David would tell him he couldn't have something, and Cousin Jennie would give it to him. Cousin David would send him to bed as punishment and she would go read to him." Furthermore, his parents were so occupied in satisfying guests that they had little time for him.

Most of the guests worked in the educational field. They were teachers, professors, and administrators who spread the good Curry word on the educational grapevine, so many came. Prominent people such as Fred T. Steinway of piano fame, Yosemite pioneer James Hutchings, William Jennings Bryan, and John D. Rockefeller, who visited the Valley in 1890, stayed at the Sentinel Hotel. "The idea of a camp did not appeal to Easterners," Jennie Curry recalled. "They thought they had to sleep on the ground and eat from tin plates. Those who did come were usually quite happy, but it took so many venturesome souls to make the break. The Southern Pacific and the Washburn boys were well established; the Wawona stage line connection and the Currys were sort of interlopers." An old timer agreed, ". . .you can just be sure that Curry did not get any guest that came in from Wawona on the Wawona road."

Camp operation was far from placid. Transportation was the biggest problem. ". . . It would be difficult to indicate all the embarrassing moments," Mrs. Curry said, "that occurred when, for instance, the stages which brought perishables daily and any other freight they had room for . . . arrived perhaps with a canvas for tents but no poles; . . . or late." Sometimes meat arrived spoiled and eggs scrambled, or freight wagons didn't arrive at all, and the Currys had to improvise their own version of the "loaves and the fishes." Perishables, such as meat, butter, eggs, and vegetables, arrived on daily stages, but canned goods, staples, tents, furniture, and other supplies came on freight wagons whose four-horse teams had to be changed every ten miles.

During the pioneer summer, Curry had "booked a party of school-teachers, a large windfall for us," daughter Mary recalled. "They were due to arrive, shepherded by him, but, alas, the freight wagon was overdue and the supplies were running low. Mother (Mrs. Curry) was practically desperate about it; all the possible beds were already made up in secluded spots under the trees, and still the number was short, and the food on hand was decidedly short rations. However, the freight arrived just in the nick of time, with the explanation that the mule-skinner had broken his leg—kicked by one of the mules. . . Imagine driving a heavily loaded freight wagon down the old Coulterville grade with a broken leg!"

Foster Curry delighted in the informal camp life.
(RCB collection.)

June was the month of heaviest visitation, and the Fourth of July the peak, after which travel declined steadily. When the snowpack in the high country had melted, several falls, inevitably Yosemite, dried up while the others diminished in volume and grace. As the falls disappeared, so did the visitors. Sequoia High School began its fall semester on August 15, 1899, but David A. Curry was not present as Latin instructor as he had agreed to in July. Camp Curry's popular and financial success had decided him on continuing his new career, so he severed all scholastic ties, not without rancor, with Redwood City.

According to the *Yosemite Tourist*, 4,500 people visited Yosemite Valley in 1899, 2,669 at the Sentinel, 1,500 camping out, and 290 at Camp Curry. Since the majority of the visitors either spent one night en route at the Wawona Hotel, were Sentinel Hotel guests, or used some other service supplied by the Washburn brothers, they hardly noticed the competition. To them, 290 guests was a minor figure, but to the Currys it was major, particularly since many of that number had

Captain Sam kept both the Sentinel Hotel and Camp Curry supplied with tasty trout. His eager and increasingly able assistant was young Foster Curry. *(YP&CC collection.)*

remained a month or longer. By Labor Day, the season's end, twenty-five tents stood at Camp Curry, and, when they had been full, the family had slept out in the woods. To them, crowding was a measure of success, and their hospitality, even to relinquishing beds, had insured that success. All was well in Yosemite and with its innovative interlopers, who gladly paid Mrs. Babb $200, repaid the bank loan, and pocketed some profit before departing reluctantly from the Valley. Both Mrs. Babb and Eva Thomson were asked to return as cooks for the following year.

3 Yosemite's Stentor

During winters, snow and solitude blanketed Yosemite Valley, and few tourists braved the elements or snow-blocked roads to see the alabaster wonders. Only the ten-member Degnan family and a handful of other residents remained in their Valley homes. Caretakers shoveled snow off roofs at the Sentinel Hotel and Kenneyville, and attended to other essential maintenance work. Between storms, woodcutters cut fuel to fill the summer appetites of wood ranges and heating stoves, then doubled as ice cutters when ice on Mirror Lake thickened. Because of weather and minimum population, the school was closed during winter, but sometimes a private teacher gave lessons to the eight Degnan youngsters, usually the sole juvenile residents. So little was law and order needed that the Yosemite Valley Guardian moved out for the season, and only two civilian "rangers," representing the U.S. Army, superintended the enormous surrounding area of Yosemite National Park. Often the Valley was virtually snow free by March, but the three stage roads, descending into it from higher altitudes, were not cleared until April or early May. Winter isolation was not ended until stages could roll.

Between mid-September 1899 and late April 1900 Curry was a dynamo of purposeful energy and enterprise, much of it directed toward expanding and improving Camp Curry. Once he had moved his family and the baby-sitting Foster grandparents to Palo Alto, he bought half interest in a furniture store, invested in oil property, and helped organize a salt company. Additionally, he and Jennie gave classes in mathematics and Latin to college-preparatory students, and he bicycled to the Stanford campus for advanced math courses. The major part of David's money, time, and vigor was expended on Camp Curry and three similar tent camps, two to be set up at Lake Tahoe and a third in the Mount Shasta region. Each was to be called Camp Curry, and all, he boasted in a sixteen-page promotional brochure, would

provide "good beds, good meals and courteous treatment. . . . my camps are designed for those who, whether from necessity or inclination, wish to make their money go as far as it will."

Brower Elliot, who had assisted in the Yellowstone excursions, was to be "managing partner" at the Lake Tahoe Glenbrook Camp, and good old cousin Austin Thomson, "managing partner" at the Lake Tahoe Rubicon Park Camp. Cousin Paul Green was to run the Shasta or Sweet Briar Camp. The title "managing partner" gave notice that Curry would keep an eye, if not a hand, on the new camps. Additionally, he stated, "Mrs. Curry, who was in charge of the Yosemite Camp, during part of last summer, will be managing partner this summer."

To insure patronage, Curry advertised in the *Palo Alto Times* that his furniture store would reward the biggest buyer in May and June 1900 with a ten-day all-expense-paid trip to any one of the camps. No further documentation of the Tahoe or Shasta camps has been unearthed, and, after 1900, Curry devoted himself

Jack-of-all-trades John Degnan, his wife, Bridget, and their children were among the handful of year-round residents in Yosemite Valley in the 1890s. *(YNP collection.)*

single-mindedly to the Yosemite enterprise. Commercial success was critical for him, but he regarded the original camp as a public service.

Yosemite and Camp Curry were synonymous in his mind, and the camp's first six years were successful ones. Each season, roughly May 15 to September 1, drew larger and more enthusiastic registrants. Each season more tents, improvements, and student-help employees were added. Mrs. Babb returned as cook, as she did for years, but her salary was upped and she had plenty of assistance.

A major portion of what the Currys grossed each season financed expansion the following year. State control of the Valley, administered by the Guardian, featured a myriad of regulations, but enforcement was as scant as manpower. What money was allowed by the State Legislature was speedily expended, and thousands of dollars more were needed to build roads and bridges and to install even rudimentary sewage facilities. The biggest single improvement provided by the state was the building of a power plant at Happy Isles in 1901. By 1903, stores, the Sentinel Hotel, and presumably Camp Curry were electrified. The cost was 65¢ per light, so illumination was not overwhelming. For example, it cost $150 a month to light the Sentinel Hotel. As early as 1901, a telephone line ran between the Sentinel and Valley camps, but it was 1908 before extensive service was provided throughout the Park. Telegraphic service had been in existence since 1872. Mail arrived daily during tourist season, and three times a week the balance of the year. The Post Office, telephone switchboard, and Wells Fargo office stood near the Sentinel Hotel, as did laundries, a blacksmith shop, stables, and a number of photographic studios. Photography was such a rage with visitors that the Yosemite Valley Commissioners had a darkroom built solely for their use. Professional aid was available, however, in Foley's Yosemite Falls Studio, established in 1891, Boysen's Studio, begun in 1900, and Best's Studio, started in 1902 by landscape artist Harry Cassie Best. In 1903 Hallet-Taylor Co. built still another studio there which was purchased four years later by Arthur C. Pillsbury—who proved to be the most enthusiastic and creative of the photographers.

David Curry had little direction or interference from the Guardian as he constantly improved camp services. Beginning in 1901 he did have competition, for two summers of observation had persuaded the Washburn brothers that Camp Curry was a revenue producer. In the late spring of 1901 they established Camp Yosemite, near the base of Yosemite Falls. Sentinel manager Jay B. Cook ran the new camp as well as the hotel. Camp

At the turn of the century, the general store and Boysen's Studio were two of the many businesses in Yosemite Village.
(J. T. Boysen photo; YP&CC collection.)

Ideal, operated in connection with a stage line, had lasted only for the 1900 season, but Camp Yosemite flourished from its inception. Its creek-cut, oak-and-pine-shaded site, its proximity to thundering cascades, and its "host," pioneer Galen Clark, aged eighty-seven—Mr. Yosemite himself—made it a success.

Despite the rival, Camp Curry prospered. By April 12, 1900, ads in the *Palo Alto Times* proclaimed that the camp provided 40 to 50 rooming tents and two 28- by 48-foot dining tents. Additionally, Curry's brochure advised that "Camp Curry is on the driest spot in the valley, and therefore freest from mosquitoes." "Ladies unaccompanied by gentlemen may make the trip with ease and comfort." "The smaller the grip the happier you may be." "Conventional customs of dress are laid aside in Camp Curry. The camp is a place for the enjoyment of Nature and the necessary incidentals of eating and sleeping." "Extra charges at summer resorts are frequently equal to the regular rates. In my camp, baths only are extra. Bathing in the river is free."

Tourists thronged in by stage, in private conveyances, on horseback, by bicycle, and on foot. In 1900, 410 people registered at Camp Curry, in 1901, 715. Travel statistics show that more than ten percent of all Yosemite visitors stayed at Camp Curry.

	Park Visitors	Curry Guests
1902	8,023	800
1903	8,376	1,300
1904	9,500	1,300

When Curry asked the Southern Pacific agent in Merced for reduced train and stage rates for Camp Curry employees, the man "in a determined manner stated that Yosemite Valley was adequately accommodating all guests and that no rates would be made." Curry saw the Washburn hand in the agent's refusal, and soon associated himself with the D. K. Stoddard stage line, which gave a lower rate on tickets for employees and concessionaires. Stoddard ran a fast stage—eleven hours from Raymond, the last railroad station, thus cutting out an overnight stay at the Wawona Hotel.

Each season was marked by special happenings. The big excitement of 1900 was the chugging advent of the first automobile at Yosemite. Portly Oliver Lippincott piloted his 850-pound, two-cylinder, ten-horsepower Locomobile into the Valley on June 24, making dust and history. "Whatever the new style of conveyance," he commented, "it cannot detract from the sublimity of the great valley. . . ." In July a second automobile snorted in. Until 1908, when horseless

The first automobile to enter Yosemite Valley was this Locomobile piloted by portly Oliver Lippincott, on June 24, 1900. *(Los Angeles County Museum collection.)*

carriages were prohibited from entering the park, several arrived every year. All were objects of great curiosity, foreboding, and/or admiration, and rated front page coverage in the *Yosemite Tourist*.

Tragedy marked 1901, with the death of the famed geologist Professor Joseph at Camp Curry on July 6. At seventy-eight, he was on his eleventh trip to Yosemite Valley. His first epic visit, in 1870, partly in company with John Muir, had resulted in the book *Ramblings Through the High Sierra*, a classic that is still in print. Besides informal lecturing in 1901, and meeting a host of admirers, LeConte rode horseback around the Valley and up to Vernal Fall, but suffered a heart attack July 5, and died in his tent the following morning.

A committee of influential Sierra Club members was organized to raise $5,000 for an appropriate memorial in the Valley, and LeConte Memorial Lodge, a rough-hewn picturesque granite structure, was the result. The site was a knoll directly under Glacier Point,

Joseph LeConte, revered professor at the University of California, died in his tent at Camp Curry in 1901. *(YNP collection.)*

In memory of "Professor Joe," the Sierra Club built LeConte Memorial Lodge on a knoll back of Camp Curry. *(Virginia Best Adams collection.)*

about 1,000 feet back of Camp Curry. More than 200 members attended the July 3, 1904 dedication. Among them were LeConte's son, Joseph N., and Muir's daughter Wanda. Sierra Clubbers began camping near the new lodge, which served as a meeting place and library, and used Curry facilities such as the restrooms. In time this caused friction, but in 1904 the Currys welcomed the Memorial and any club members who came down for meals. To further commemorate LeConte, Curry and geologist François E. Matthes collected rocks from various glacial moraines and built a cairn beside the tent in which the professor had died.

A happier event of 1901 was the building of the camp's first permanent structure, to house the dining room and kitchen. "It was a tall, bleak building later softened by the addition of porches which, in summer, were roofed with fir bough for overflow dining," Mary Curry remembered. "They were usually the most popular places to lunch or dine, but were sometimes the scene of a hasty exodus when a summer thunderstorm threatened. . . ."

After a sewer was installed, in 1902, restrooms and a bathhouse were built. Wooden tent platforms were added that year also, and tennis nets and a croquet court were set up. About 1904 an office with wide covered porches and a cobblestone fireplace were built. Stage passengers unloaded at a mounting platform in front of the new building, which still exists. Porters applied feather dusters, while Curry supplied the "Wellllcome" shouts and personal greetings.

Once the office was built, his favorite spot—indeed, his outdoor office—was a corner of the porch, where he settled into an Indiana-hickory rocking chair. His vest and pants were invariably rumpled, his hair tousled, and his manner affable. When he added a suit coat and hat, the whole camp knew he was going on a trip. Daytimes, a money bag serving as a cash register was at his side. On one occasion he asked a guest who was leaving for Palo Alto, "to carry this little package to the bank."

"What's in it?"

"Three thousand dollars," Curry replied casually.

Day or night he would discourse to guests and employees about Yosemite geology, trails, history, and Camp Curry's own story. In these informal talks, and others around the campfires Curry was at his best. His thirst for knowledge kept him studying and learning, and what he learned, he imparted enthusiastically. At times dramatic, always entertaining, he was also educational and anticipated later interpretive programs by naturalists.

Tennis and croquet were available for non-hiking guests.
(RCB collection.)

In those early years Curry did much of the heavy labor around camp himself, especially in setting it up and dismantling it. One observer remembers seeing him bent over under the weight of two mattresses he was carrying to a tent. It wasn't unusual to see him packing furniture, swinging a hammer, or moving rocks with a pry bar.

Already he was an institution, his stentorian calls a tradition. His morning call was rousing. He began it gently—"Have you used your Pears soap?"—and ended aggressively: "It is now 7:30 in the morning; those who do not rise for breakfast by 8:00 a.m. will have to postpone it till tomorrow. At eight o'clock the cook gets *hot* and BURNS THE BREAKFAST!" Not even a sound sleeper could miss that warning. Since bath facilities were limited, sign-up was necessary, and Curry's public announcement of "Mrs. Jones, your Bawth is ready," was amusing if not embarrassing. Once, a family of five registered for baths, which kept Curry busy stoking the wood-fueled boiler to provide hot water. At appropriate intervals, he would shout, "The second Garthwaite bawth is ready," etc. By the time the last child was bathed, the Garthwaites were clean, decent, and red-faced!

While James McCauley was running the Mountain House on the ridge back of Glacier Point he had built a big fire on the edge of the cliff and pushed it over. The resulting fire fall so delighted onlookers below that he

Not only was a clean napkin provided at every meal, but pretty waitresses were there to serve.
(J. T. Boysen photo; YP&CC collection.)

The firefall, begun by pioneer James McCauley in 1872, was made a nightly spectacle by showman Curry early in the twentieth century. *(SS collection.)*

experimented with kerosene-soaked gunnysacks, fireworks, and even bombs for spectacular fire falls. His occasional blazes were a fringe benefit of schooling for his twin sons, Fred and John. To attend school, open from April to October in the Valley, they rode burros down their father's Four-Mile Trail. After school, campers and hotel guests gave the boys money to insure a firefall.

After McCauley's departure from Glacier Point, in 1897, a firefall was rare until drama-loving David Curry determined to reestablish the custom. He sent employees up to the Point to build a bonfire and push it over at a designated time. So intrigued were the guests

that thereafter Curry ordered firefalls for special holidays and to honor prominent guests. At the end of the nightly entertainment around the campfire, he would alert assembled guests to the treat by an introduction that many memorized. "The original Stentor was a captain in the Greek army in the days of Homer and the Iliad. It was said of him that he could command 10,000 troops by the use of a megaphone. But the modern Stentor lives at Camp Curry in Yosemite Valley, and his voice is heard at Glacier Point, eleven miles distant—by the long trial!" Then he would throw his head back, cup his mouth with his hands, and shout to the fire-tender on Glacier Point, "Is the fire ready?"

Campers breathlessly awaited the faint answer, "The fire is ready," followed by Curry's roar of command, "LET 'ER GO GALLAGHER!"[1] Slowly, glowing embers fanned over the cliff in a shower, and then a flow of red. For several minutes, thrilled spectators watched the fire cascade pour downward to a granite ledge where the embers died harmlessly.

Yosemite's epic event in 1903 was the visit of President Theodore Roosevelt. Residents, Yosemite Valley Commissioners, and California politicians planned a gala welcome, featuring banquets and fireworks—which was disdained by "The Rough Rider," who preferred a camping trip with John Muir and succeeded in avoiding crowds except for one afternoon in Yosemite Valley.

None of the Currys so much as even glimpsed the president, for a typhoid epidemic in Palo Alto had so affected the girls that they spent a quiet summer recuperating at Hazel Green, which Curry was negotiating to buy.

Hazel Green, elevation 6,000 feet, had long been a stage stop on the Road, and, after purchasing it, Curry utilized the eighty acres of sugar pines, springs, meadow, orchard, barn, and log cabins as a tourist camp. By 1906 Hazel Green was advertised in Camp Curry brochures as "restful. . . The table will be kept at the high standard adopted by Camp Curry and cottage rooms and numerous tents are available for guests. . . ."

While David regained strength after an attack of typhoid, Cousin Austin Thomson took over as camp manager. One of his three preserved purchase orders to the Sun Sun Wu store in Coulterville requested "2 sacks cabbage, ½ sack carrots, 1 sack beans (string), 1 sack

---

1. It is assumed that the pioneer fire-tender was named Gallagher.
   In later years the call was changed to "LET THE FIRE FALL!"

peas, 2 doz. heads lettuce, 3 doz. chicken, and some parceley."

In 1904 and 1905, increasing numbers of guest arrived and settled in for stays of days, weeks, or the season. They "did" Yosemite by foot or astride a horse or mule. George Kenney, of Coffman and Kenney's stables, boasted that he specialized in providing appropriate steeds:

> . . . when a tourist comes and wants Rebecca, I give him Rebecca. I never refuse. Sometimes I have three Rebeccas on the trail. . . When an animal carries a tourist safely over a trail, that tourist never gets over recommending that particular animal to all his

friends and relatives. . . Some days every passenger on the stage wants Rebecca and every passenger on the stage is under the delusion that mules are safer than horses. I had a lady who insisted on a mule or nothing. They had all the mules already promised. . . So I went on calmly leading out the mules according to my book. When it came to her turn, I had a horse in the barn which had been roached, which means that its mane had been clipped, so I gave him to her. She mounted triumphantly. "There" she says, "I knew I'd get a mule if I stuck out for it."

Daytimes, the camp atmosphere was quiet, for most of the guests were up and off soon after breakfast. "Most of the guests were walkers," an employer of the

In this 1903 photograph, entrepreneur David Curry is shown presiding at his campfire clean-shaven. His mustache had been shorn while he was ill with typhoid. Daughters Marjorie and Mary are in canvas chairs at the extreme left. *(YNP collection.)*

day wrote. "It was Mirror Lake early in the morning and the Happy Isles in the afternoon with the Falls, Glacier Point and sometimes Telescope Peak for the younger folks. There were enough horses for the elderly (anyone over forty), and few stayed in camp—or fished—unless it was to allow foot-blisters or sunburn to heal." These guests who remained frequented the croquet court, hammocks, rocking chairs, or sunny rocks where they read, wrote letters, or sketched. While guests enjoyed leisure, college students washed dishes, peeled vegetables, made beds, and scrubbed floors, often accompanying their chores with rollicking songs. After the stage had come and new arrivals settled, employees headed for the woods or cliffs, dashing breathlessly back just in time for the next camp duty. They were an attractive, idealistic, loyal group who loved Yosemite, the camp, and the Currys, who took real interest in everyone they hired. Local Indians, who knew discrimination, always had fair treatment and jobs at Camp Curry. "Even if we were dirty from working," one man remembered, "we sat down for meals right with the guests. Curry didn't believe in separate tables." Another oft-told antidote concerned an irate guest who complained that he couldn't tell the help from the guests. Curry loved to tell that as proof of the camp's democratic spirit.

"Smiling" Jim Barnett and one of his biggest customers, David Curry.
(J. T. Boysen photo; SS collection.)

4　Earthquake!

On April 18, 1906, an earthquake in which more than 3,000 people were killed gravely damaged much of northern California. The resultant property damage and job losses were so enormous that many businesses and banks were closed. Although Yosemite escaped physical damage, its businessmen were affected for months. In 1905, for the first time, visitation had exceeded 10,000; in the earthquake year, only 5,414 people came. Camp Curry fared well nevertheless: 1,200 guests stayed there in 1906, but another earthquake-like event in 1905–6 upset it more seriously.

That was the recession of the State Grant to the federal government, a bitter battle spearheaded by John Muir. After the area surrounding Yosemite Valley and the Mariposa Grove became a national park in 1890, there were frequent conflicts between the Army, which supervised the Park, and the Yosemite Valley Commissioners regarding care, control, and fire fighting. The recession bill was not signed into law until June 11, 1906, but Army cavalry units were selected to extend their jurisdiction over the State Grant in 1905. Headquarters was "Fort Yosemite," southwest of Yosemite Falls. Shorn of its name, Camp Yosemite became Camp Lost Arrow.

Concessionaires soon found that Army officers took their administrative duties far more seriously than had the politically oriented Guardians. Curry's first confrontation with the government occurred in the fall of 1907 when the chief hydrographer recommended that Camp Curry's concession not be renewed at its site because of inferior sanitary facilities. Curry protested any change of site, but agreed to reduce the camp's capacity to 200 rather than expanding to 500. This written promise induced the hydrographer to recommend that Camp Curry continue until an adequate sewage disposal system was installed. Camp Lost Arrow had similar problems, since its sewage disposal unit was nothing more than Yosemite Creek! When that dried up in mid-summer, the camp closed.

Earlier in 1907 the completion of a railroad from Merced to a terminus named El Portal, twelve miles west of Yosemite Valley, signaled progress and a rise in tourism. After its initial run, on May 5, thousands of visitors took the train to El Portal, and horsedrawn stages on to "paradise." In retrospect, Jennie Curry said that the rail service "increased the number of visitors very largely but decreased the length of their stays from two weeks or more, as it had been in the earlier days, to two or three days."

David Curry welcomed the railway, not just for the guests it carried, but for the freight it could haul cheaply. Freight wagons, however, still had to be hired for the last twelve miles of road, and at times, that freight bill was as much or more than what the railroad charged for its seventy-eight mile journey.

Surprisingly, all invoices, bills, and canceled checks for Camp Curry's 1908 season survived the years. Curry was buyer, bookkeeper, accountant, and bill-payer, and each check bears his flourishing signature. R. Barcroft & Sons of Merced sold Curry $155 of hardware that season. Everything from kegs of nails to claw hammers and butcher knives were included in their delivery. Merced Lumber Co. was paid $635 for lumber, doors, and windows, and another $338 was expended on sewer materials. A total of $413 was spent on seventy-five tent flies, twelve hammocks, eight chairs, and hammock spreaders. A single tent fly was $6.45.

Hickory furniture was ordered direct from La Porte, Indiana. A dozen chairs, ten rockers, two stools, two

Fort Yosemite, southwest of Yosemite Falls, was Army headquarters from 1905 until 1914. (*J. V. Lloyd photo.*)

In 1907, the "Shortline to Paradise" was completed from Merced to El Portal. *(Hank Johnston collection.)*

settees, and five table tops cost only $101, but freight on the 950-pound load was $40.26. A kitchen range and bake oven cost $200, a dough scraper 45¢, four dozen teaspoons $1.88, four granite ladles $3.00 each, and a copper-bottomed, twenty-five gallon vegetable boiler, $4.50.

Food was a major expenditure. General groceries in 1908 amounted to $2,951 plus railroad freight of $226 and wagon freight of $129. In addition, John Degnan supplied about twenty gallons of fresh milk a day at 20¢ a gallon, and rancher Fred McCauley provided 154 pounds of pork at 8½¢ per pound. Fresh meat for the season totaled $1,112, including 25¢ a pound to pay for the 262 pounds of trout caught by Indians.

Fresh produce was shipped mainly from Merced. One sack of carrots weighing ninety pounds cost just 45¢! Two boxes of lettuce weighing ninety pounds cost $2.27. Ten sacks of "spuds" weighing 1,000 pounds cost $3.10, and freight was $4.00. Cabbage was 50¢ a box, rhubarb the same, and freight on them more than either. Eggs were shipped from Merced by the case, and Curry paid one butter bill for $523. At the beginning of the season, E. Poppleton delivered 300 pounds of that indispensable regulatory fruit the prune, for which he charged $18.00 plus freight.

The increase in guest turnover signaled more work and problems at Camp Curry. While David Curry was busy in the office or meeting guests, "Mother" Curry was everywhere in camp. Although her work was mainly supervisory, she admitted "I did a little of everything, one time or another. I have made soap and put up tents. I have been baker and headwaitress, postmistress and pantry woman. I've put up lunches and looked out for the babies and it didn't hurt my pride, any of it."

"Where he was hale, jovial, and dramatic in every movement," author Frank J. Taylor wrote, "she was quiet, retiring, and efficient. He was satisfied with a camp big enough to accommodate five hundred guests, but Mrs. Curry saw that Camp Curry had to grow year by year or else fall by the wayside, as other resorts in the park had done."

Once Curry was persuaded that whatever guests wanted, and his wife quietly pushed for, was right, he fought for that improvement. After the recession, Curry received yearly leases from the Department of the Interior, and had to travel to Washington, D.C. every year to argue for a renewal as well as for each new service of his camp. For years he agitated for a long-term lease so as to allow him to obtain loans large enough to insure significant improvements. Time and again he was refused. Invariably on these trips he stopped at Winchester, Kansas, to see his family, and often borrowed money from his father and brothers to finance camp improvements. Rufus Green's son recalled Curry's other source of capital: "If it hadn't been for the Bank of Palo Alto," he told the author," Camp Curry could never have kept going."

"He often consulted me about his business in Yosemite," banker George Parkinson remembered in 1917, ". . . and went over his plans at length and asked for my opinion. If my suggestions did not suit him, he would frankly tell me so, and do as he pleased. Whether one agreed with him or not, one could not help admire him, for he was always ready to defend his opinion, and defend it vigorously. . . ." Both in Yosemite and Palo Alto, Parkinson observed that Curry "was his own boss and manager, his own teamster and delivery boy, his own plumber and helper. I have seen him blacking stoves in front of his store, and it seemed he got as much blacking on his hands as on the stove. He was his own janitor when one was needed, or used, his own bookkeeper and clerk. His visible equipment for accounts was a daybook and a short pencil, poorly sharpened. His real equipment was his brain."

Curry was town trustee for Palo Alto, a charter member of the First Congressional Church, and the leader and life of the Bible class. "There was never a dull moment when he was present," the Reverend O. L. Elliot recalled. ". . . Our discussion could never take refuge in generalities. . . . He could denounce in strong and plain language, and he was always ready for an argument."

By 1909, when the Currys built a twelve-room, two-story house on Hamilton Street in Palo Alto, both of Jennie's parents had died, and Foster, who loathed military school, had left it and run away from home. Jennie, his invariable champion, welcomed him back when he returned with the announcement that he wanted to work at Camp Curry but would never return to school. His sisters annoyed him, partic-

Camp Ahwahnee, established in 1908 by Will Sell, Sr., provided competition to Camp Curry. *(SS collection.)*

ularly Mary whose studiousness merited parental approval.

Both girls attended Castilleja, a select college-preparatory institution in Palo Alto. Although discipline

Despite competition from rivals, Camp Curry expanded every season. *(RCB collection.)*

was rarely invoked, they were raised strictly. "We didn't dance," Marjorie wrote the author, "until I was sixteen, as dancing was `hugging set to music.'" Her greatest delight was to take the reins of the four-horse stage and drive it from Camp Curry to the stables. One of the stage drivers, with whom she was popular, taught her to drive, but her favorite place was astride a horse. She was a vivacious extrovert, whereas Mary was a book-loving introvert. Despite their contrasting personalities, the two sisters were close.

All of the Currys were happiest in Yosemite, where action and beauty mingled. Some summer events there were predictable, such as the annual Fourth of July festivities, which included human and horse races; others, like real-life stagecoach robberies, were almost annual. Curry himself was involved in a stage holdup on the Big Oak Flat Road, but his wife said that "he only lost a little, a small amount, because that was all he carried in those days."

Curry invariably supported educational or instructional programs. For example, when naturalist Charles

D. Kellogg was in camp, Curry arranged for him to give a show of "movie and stationary pictures of birds, reptiles, and animals" at LeConte Memorial Lodge.

Whenever possible, the family explored the high country. On a 1905 pack trip, ten-year old Marjorie was the champion fisherman. "I caught 49 trout in about two hours in Tuolumne Meadow, thinking the limit was 50, but it was 30. So the seven of us hurriedly ate them all." Foster was the guide on the 1907 outing, and in 1910 there was another family trip to Cathedral Peak and Lakes. All three younger Currys were imbued, as were their parents, with the love of all natural things, and they became ardent boosters of the high Sierra. Mary hiked, but Foster and Marjorie preferred riding horseback.

Pictures saved by Foster show him atop Clouds Rest, Half Dome, and the Overhanging Rock, alone and with Mary. His dress alternated between that of a cowboy and a white-suited, self-confident young businessman. Either way, he was attractive, and had long since discovered both girls and liquor. Drinking was considered ruinous by the ultra-conservative religious Curry family. On the basis of one preserved letter, well-typed but poorly spelled, it is presumed that Foster promised reform and made a fresh start. In Panama, on October 8, 1910, he wrote his mother from the Isthmus, saying that he was employed on the Panama Canal building force as a civil "cervice" man at $100 per month. By the following spring, however, he was back in Palo Alto ready to become manager of what the newspaper ads called "Yet another Camp Curry." This one was located in Lyndon Glen, south of Los Gatos, "amid groves of alders, sycamores and redwoods." Rates were $2.00 per day, $10 to $12.50 a week, and "kitchen, dining room, and office are patterned on Camp Curry, Yosemite."

Postcards prove that the camp had a tree-shaded beauty. Envisioning year-round financial returns, David Curry attempted to keep it open all winter, but tent life during winter months, even in an equable climate, held little appeal for Californians, and the camp folded. After that experience, Curry remarked wryly, "You can only pick cherries when cherries are ripe!"

For a couple of subsequent summers Curry turned the camp over to a charitable institution that operated it for disadvantaged children from San Francisco under the name of "Happylands." Rufus Green acted as agent and took care of arrangements.

Meanwhile, Foster had picked a Cherry for himself—one Mary Cherry, whom he married in May of 1912. Her parents were Clarissa Markham (a relative of Poet Edwin Markham) and Frances Halleck Cherry, an engineer and former minister. They had given their

This is the only known picture of Mary, Foster, and Marjorie Curry together. *(Hensleigh Family collection.)*

Foster Curry tried his wings in Panama and Los Gatos, but returned to Yosemite. *(RCB collection.)*

daughter every cultural advantage—she was interested in art and photography and learned to develop as well as to take pictures. Foster's mother and sisters were present at the Palo Alto wedding, but his father was in Yosemite. In David Curry's mind, not even the marriage of his only son came before the welfare of Camp Curry.

5   David and Goliath

While Foster was trying his wings, his father was doing battle with the United States Army, the Southern Pacific Railroad, and any other authority brash enough to set foot on Camp Curry's pine needles. He sold his furniture business in June of 1910 to devote full time to the prospering Yosemite camp. A year earlier, he had persuaded postal authorities to establish a seasonal branch post office at Camp Curry, which was a great convenience to guests and staff. Curry's mail was particularly heavy in 1910 as he fought a threat to the camp's expansion from Major W. W. Forsyth, who was acting superintendent of Yosemite. Sanitation, or its lack, was once again an issue since the camp's capacity had increased beyond that of the sewage system. From available evidence, Forsyth must have threatened Curry with closure or transfer by action of the Department of the Interior.

Curry retaliated by bombarding Forsyth and congressmen with letters of protest about the Army's own pollution of the Merced River. Moreover, he galvanized his supporters into letter-writing action. Never guileless, he had been making friends for years. At campfires he spoke bluntly of his problems with the Army and his need for a long-term concession agreement. He wanted to provide more services for guests, he said, but was stopped by the Department of Interior, acting on the recommendations of Major Forsyth.

"The camp's very existence hinges on the whim of one man," he would explain, "but that man could be appealed to by you, the audience, you who love Camp Curry, you who want to see expansion and improvement here."

Among his audience were people of status and profession who were impressed by his initiative, candor, and courage. Many viewed him as David, the Army as Goliath. When he alerted them to the threat against the camp, they rallied to his support with letters such as the following:

> I learned that it is proposed by the military authorities in charge of Yosemite Valley to remove Camp Curry to an inferior and intolerable location.

> As a result of a prolonged visit in the Valley last summer, I desire to state my opinion that the management of the Valley is a disgrace to the nation and a reproach to California's Congressional delegation. This feeling is so constantly obtruded upon the visitor that a full and hearty enjoyment of the Valley is impossible. The constant annoyance and disgust swamp all other sensations.

> To all this, the one glowing exception is Camp Curry, ideal in location, perfect in every detail of management. To abolish Camp Curry or limit its usefulness, is the crowning outrage. Let all the rest go, keep the dusty roads, the filthy military camp, the government pig pen on the banks of the river, spreading its balmy odors half a mile around, keep up the prices of the livery monopoly, let the brush and rubbish grow denser till the last view disappears, let the public be dammed generally, but spare us Camp Curry, and we shall have something to be grateful for.

Congressman James C. Needham, of the powerful Ways and Means Committee, responded to that and other protesting missives by addressing a long letter, part of which is reproduced here, to Forsyth on March 7, 1910.

> I have received about two hundred letters from various people who have visited the Yosemite and who have stopped at Camp Curry, protesting against the way in which the proprietor of this camp has been treated. These letters breathe a unanimous spirit in favor of Camp Curry and protest against what they charge to be the disposition of the authorities to discriminate against the camp. A large number have also reached the Secretary of the Interior and I think it is the general opinion that the Camp has not been treated fairly. . . .

> It seems to me that there ought to be some method of enforcing fair treatment as between the different concessionaires. It is reported there that some of the other concessionaires deliberately endeavor to do all they can against Camp Curry . . . the people of Camp Curry are subjected to petty annoyances, etc., by others. It is alleged that the use of the telephone, etc., is so hinged about as to show a petty spirit. . . .

Forsyth's response has not been found, but closure did not materialize, and Camp Curry remained firmly in place for the 1910 season. Some of the flavor of the era is reflected in a nostalgic reminiscence written by

May Ballantyne, who was twenty when she applied to David Curry for a job and was accepted:

> . . . On the fourth of May I left Palo Alto with Mrs. Curry, her daughters, and several other girls who were going to work there for the summer. We went by Southern Pacific Railroad to Merced at night, where our car was switched over to the Yosemite Valley Railroad for breakfast. . . We then boarded a horse-drawn stage. . . and in due time arrived at Camp Curry. . . I'm sure no tourist ever got more of a kinked neck than I did from craning to see the tops of the tall cliffs. . . .

May had a tent in "Jungletown," as the employee area was known. Conveniences there consisted of chamber pots, a couple of showers, and "telephone booth" outhouses. "I had been hired to wait tables," May said, "but I was absolutely no good at that whatsoever, so I went to work in the laundry, eight hours a day, six days a week, for $25 a month. . . ."

Days off were strenuous: May and her friends climbed most of the surrounding heights. "We could go on any hike we wished except the Ledge Trail," May said. "It had been closed as too dangerous. Mr. Curry informed us that he had no way of stopping us from going, but if we did, he would have to fire us!"

In 1911 Curry was arguing with the Southern Pacific about commissions paid for tourists carried by the railroad. "I have not had fair treatment ever from the S.P. offices," he complained in a scrawled letter to Will Sell, Jr., manager of Camp Ahwahnee, which had been set up in 1908 near the site of Leidig's Hotel. Curry was willing to "try the non-commission business one year" if the other Yosemite concessionaires and the three railroads, Southern Pacific, Santa Fe, and the Yosemite Valley Railroad, could reach a satisfactory agreement.

Upon his return from Washington, D. C., where he had once again been refused a long-term lease, Curry was dispirited, weary, and ill. After medical tests, a doctor diagnosed diabetes as the cause and ordered a strict diet. Body and foot care in particular were stressed by the doctor, since sores, infections, and even gangrene could result from vascular degeneration. Documentation of his incapacity, and activities at Camp Curry, were supplied to the author via letters and in an interview with Dr. Emile Holman, Stanford emeritus professor of surgery. Holman received his B.A. from Stanford in May 1911. He and his sisters, Esther and Lillian, who had been interviewed and hired by Mrs. Curry on her annual hiring visit to the campus, traveled to Yosemite. Shortly after he arrived, the future prestigious surgeon faced official expulsion.

"The first thing I did," he reminisced, "was to immerse myself in trouble."

We arrived at Wawona by Tallyho and I started up the trail, and encountered two girls from Oakland, which was my home town at the time, carving their initials in the stump of a fallen tree. They were having a difficult time, because they had no decent knife with which to do it, so I offered my services and my jack knife, and started whittling on the initials. Along came a game warden, or whatever they called them in those days, who arrested me and took me over to the Commissioner at Yosemite Valley to explain myself—but he didn't accept any explanations. He said, "You're going out of the Park area," but I succeeded in getting Mr. Curry interested in my plight, and he got me free of the Commissioner's clutches.

David Curry's breakfast call was as loud and clear as was his opposition to the Army and the Southern Pacific Railroad. *(RCB collection.)*

Naturalists Vernon Kellogg and John Muir near Camp Curry in July 1912. (*SS collection.*)

As soon as Curry discovered that Holman had done secretarial work for David Starr Jordan at the University, "he assigned me to the 'Front Office,'" and began using me as his secretary. It was customary for Mr. Curry to dictate letters and discuss the day's work sitting at a small table in a large room where guests assembled at night to sit around the fire and listen to the various entertainers...." Curry himself provided entertainment, since "he delighted in transacting his business in full public view, dictating his letters in his large voluminous voice," Holman said. "It amused him to let them in on some of his deals, even. He was full of deals. I remember one statement he made that he never thought he was prosperous unless he was $50,000 in debt." Holman recalled that the Stentor

had a bad sore toe, which accompanied his diabetes but he was very adverse to carrying out the strict diet for this disease. He would come in and take all the chewing gum for sale in the office because he was in search of sugar. I don't know whether he recognized that fact, but he certainly chewed an awful lot of gum, and that, I am sure, kept up his diabetes. This was before the days of insulin, when one controlled diabetes largely by diet, but he was a tough man to handle on that score.

Sometimes Curry had to stay in bed, and I'd have to go to the tent to take his dictation there, but usually he was up and around. Mrs. Curry, greatly

concerned about her husband, tried hard to keep him on his diet, but she didn't keep him away from gum.

Holman was paid $25.00 a month for secretarial duties, working at the reception desk, and carrying baggage after the stages arrived. His sisters, who worked as waitresses, made more money than he because they collected tips. Although not customary, it was possible for pretty and efficient waitress to collect as much as $500 in tips during a season.

Curry was frequently at loggerheads with the Army administration. "Some of us couldn't understand why the officials permitted him to go on." Holman said. "We thought he'd lose his concession. The main Army and guest complaint was the smell of the outflow of Camp Curry. It was a submerged sewer, but it would seep out of the ground and had no place to go. The odor wafted over the camp at night, but it wasn't constant, so we put up with it."

Despite Curry's problems, his supervision and that of his wife helped the camp to have a successful summer, with 3,622 guests. The October 2, 1911, *Palo Alto Times* noted that "D. A. Curry had returned to town smiling after a $50,000 season in Yosemite." Business had increased twenty-five percent over previous years. On October 18 the Curry Camping Company was incorporated, with all stock owned by the family.

One of the camp guests during July 1912 was the aging John Muir, along with Scripps-Howard publisher F. W. Kellogg and party. Since autos were not allowed beyond Wawona, the party rode to Camp Curry on a stage. They stayed for five days while Muir revisited old haunts. Dr. Vernon L. Kellogg, an eminent entomologist, was also in camp, and one night Curry persuaded the pair to talk informally on Yosemite subjects. The Muir-Kellogg party left Camp Curry the morning before a fire that threatened its very existence.

While lunch was being served, flames broke out in the laundry building just east of the dining room and kitchen and spread to the ice house, bakery, and tents. Chairs were overturned as most guests raced off to grab their belongings or fight the fire. A few continued to eat, prompting an observer to comment in the *Mariposa Gazette*, "Men sipped bouillon while women and girls, dripping wet, carried pails of water to the men on the firing line.... I marveled at the power appetite wields over majestic man."

Since the telephone line was out of order, Marjorie Curry vaulted onto a horse and galloped off bareback to report the fire. Editor Foley recorded the aftermath:

By 2 o'clock the fire was over, and as the stages left for El Portal, Curry was there, as usual, calling off the names of the outgoing visitors and giving them, as the coaches speeded out of the smoking camp his famous "Farewell." He then addressed the guests, assuring them that the camp was still able to take care of them. "We have lost 75 tents," said he, "but we still have 200 left, enough to care for 300 people." His assuring talk quieted the more timorous and within a short time the "refugees" from the burnt section were comfortably tented in the other part of the camp. A few nervous ones sought the hotel or other camps, but nine-tenths of them were game and stayed put.

At first Mr. Curry thought his loss would be about $20,000 but after careful examination, loss to building, tents, and equipment was set at $12,000. None of that was covered by insurance as Curry had thought rates too high, so he had to finance the building which began the following year.

A 40 by 90 foot swimming "tank" between the laundry, which is still used, and the dining room, and the 64 by 86 foot auditorium, west of the camp entrance, were built in 1913.

As usual, Curry's sewage system was overtaxed by summer's end, and there were complaints. Fly nuisance, too, was "becoming intolerable," according to the acting superintendent's report for 1912, especially in Kenneyville, where the stables proliferated insects. Despite such annoyances, Camp Curry entertained 3,516 guests that season, compared to 1,162 people who stayed at Camp Awahnee and 954 at Camp Lost Arrow. The sewered and fly-less Sentinel Hotel entertained 2,615 guests, but because of hotel overflow the Merced River was grossly polluted below it.

By 1913 there was political, if not public, demand that the various national parks needed full time supervision and well-defined status. The first step in rescuing the Army's foster children was the appointment of Franklin K. Lane, a Californian, as Secretary of the Interior, on March 4, 1913. He persuaded Adolph C. Miller, an economics professor at the University of California, to become an assistant secretary. Among other jobs, Miller was to give the national parks a unified direction, and he cajoled his able economics class reader, Horace M. Albright, to go to Washington, D. C. as his confidential clerk. Four years of college had changed young Albright from a Bishop-raised farm boy to a broad-minded, capable, and eager pre-law student with an amazing memory.

Mother Curry surveying fire damage. (*Lillian Holman collection.*)

Several months after Albright's arrival, on May 31, 1913, he witnessed a confrontation between Miller and David A. Curry. Sixty years later, Albright recalled the details of that meeting:

The Stentor's entrance was dramatic. He strode in flanked by two United States senators and two congressmen, sat down in front of Mr. Miller's desk and proceeded to outline in his loud voice what he wanted, i.e., a long-term contract and certain new privileges. The Congressional representatives supported him in a general way. They said they felt it was time (since Mr. Curry had proved himself) he be given a chance to expand, and he could only do that with an assurance of a longer term.

Miller listened attentively to all that was requested, then looked directly at the big self-confident concessionaire and said, "Mr. Curry, I am very familiar with your operations. I have stayed at your camp. I know how you conduct it, and I know what you do in the evenings around the campfire. You have made it a practice to abuse the Department and the Secretary of the Interior. You have been very uncooperative and, as far as the Department is concerned, I see no reason why anything should be done for you.

"We are not going to do anything for you. I'm not going to give you anything you ask for. Furthermore, I'm going to take something away from you. I hope you will learn from what we are going to do here, because you just can't go along the way you are now and expect to be a concessionaire." Miller glanced at the silent inscrutable congressmen, then back to Curry, and continued deliberately, "I'm going to take the Firefall away. There will be no Firefall."

The Stentor. (*Hensleigh Family collection.*)

Curry wilted visibly, while the congressmen remonstrated at the drastic action, but Miller was inflexible. Curry had strode in like a conquering hero. He left quietly, dazed and disbelieving.

On April 30, 1913, Army troops cantered back into Yosemite Valley, commanded by Major William T. , who was replacing Forsyth. Littlebrant was Army from polished boots to uniform slouch hat, and, before many campfires had died, Curry was telling his guests of the foibles of Major "Littlebrain!" Despite official admonitions, Curry continued to complain to, and enlist the support of, his campfire audiences. When they clamored for firefalls, he told them bitterly that Washington had canceled the event.

No death or serious accidents occurred in the Park that season, despite the fact that automobiles were finally permitted to enter the Valley, beginning August 23. They were allowed passage only on the Coulterville Road, and only if drivers observed sixty-five restrictive

regulations. For example, any autoist reaching the Merced Grove entrance station after 3:30 p.m. was not allowed in the Park until the following day. Guests could park in front of the hotels or camps to unload passengers and luggage, IF time did not exceed five minutes and IF a driver remained in the vehicle. Maximum speed was ten miles per hour on straight stretches, with a six-mile-per-hour limit at all other points. Rule number 53 commanded, "When teams, saddle horses, or pack trains approach, automobiles shall stop and remain at rest until the former have passed, or until drivers or riders are satisfied regarding the safety of their horses. If the approaching animals manifest signs of fear, the engine must be stopped."

Campers faced segregation. They, and what Muir termed "blunt-nosed mechanical beetles," had to stay in a special auto camp. All other autoists had to leave their vehicles at a specially built garage opposite Army headquarters. It was equipped with everything from bench tools to a complete blacksmith shop, and averaged $25 worth of business for every car that came into Yosemite. Anti-auto Littlebrant hated the noisy garage and its nonesquestrian occupants. He berated the managers, E. Lounsbury and Dick Shaffer, and once cursed them, threatening that "he would see to it that the objectionable garage business would be eliminated from the park." Despite regimentation and the lateness of the season, 127 autos were admitted into Yosemite Valley, and Littlebrant commented in his report covering 1913, "In the light of the experiences gained . . . in handling automobile traffic, it is believed that some of the causes of irritation will be removed from next year's traffic." His prediction proved true—he did not return to Yosemite in 1914!

While national parks were still stepchildren, Secretary of Interior Franklin Lane and his assistant, Adolph Miller, were trying to give them better administration in anticipation of the creation of a special guardianship bureau. In 1914 civilian employees called "rangers," under Acting Superintendent Mark Daniels, were slated to administer Yosemite. One Army holdover was likable, capable, Polish-born Gabriel Sovulewski, the Park's premier trail builder, who remained as a civilian supervisor to help organize management. Another ranger was Forrest S. Townsley, a young Nebraskan. Like the Currys, Sovulewski and Townsley were to be identified with Yosemite until their deaths.

For twenty-two years an average of 200 soldiers had supervised Yosemite National Park each spring and summer. Their most notable achievements were in ridding the place of sheepmen and and their devastating charges, trail making, and mapping. Now, in contrast, a band of seventeen men were to guard the Park against fire and man, enforce laws, regulate auto traffic, and oversee concessionaires.

David Curry, always an individualistic, anti-control entrepreneur, must have expected a good, unhampered year. Indeed, 1914 was the last of the booming, non-competitive tourist seasons for him. Hat in hand and temper under control, he returned to Washington,

Polish-born Gabriel Sovulewski came to Yosemite with the U. S. Army in 1895, and remained as a packer, supervisor, and trail-builder for the Park Service until he retired in 1936. Here he is pictured on an inspection trip near Hetch Hetchy with a contemporary Dodge.
(J. V. Lloyd photo; YNP collection.)

Mary Curry was happiest on the trails.
(Hil Oehlmann collection.)

D. C. early in April to negotiate a new contract with the establishment. Not even his non-belligerent attitude won back the firefall, although a study of the cliffs to determine damage was promised. "Curry's privilege of saying `good night' in stentorian tones, so as to be heard from one end of Yosemite Valley to the other, remains untouched," was the comment of the supportive *Palo Alto Times*. The new contract also enumerated concessions bestowed or prohibited by the powers: Curry was not allowed to open a film studio but might be permitted to sell fishing tackle; he could not sell fresh fruit, but permission was restored to sell candy, postcards, and guidebooks; if a guest wanted film or fruit, he or she could walk a mile to the Village to buy such. For his concession, Curry was charged $2,000 a year, $1,500 more than in 1906, the year the government took over the state grant.

Camp Curry's opening on April 28, 1914 was prefaced by months of planning and ordering and weeks of cleanup. Either Curry himself or Bill Lewis, the maintenance foreman, supervised removal of snow, rock slides, fallen trees, branches, and pine needles, repair of tent frames and buildings, erection of tents, and myriad other details. During the winter, blocks of ice had been cut on Mirror Lake and stored in the ice house.

There were two ways to secure one of the fifty jobs at Camp Curry. One was to fill out an application form, which warned prospective employees that "It is a waste of postage for anyone from a distance to apply unless they make a strong appeal with photographs, testimonials of character, experience, hustling ability and intention to please both the employer and guests." Each

spring, Mrs. Curry visited both Stanford and the University of California to interview and hire students.

However, if a capable looking All-American type boy or girl showed up at the camp itself, with a note of introduction from some Curry friend or relative, employment usually resulted. So it happened in the spring of 1914 when a lean, handsome Hoosier lad of twenty appeared in camp with a note from Rufus Green. Green had met Donald Bertrand Tresidder in Bakersfield, where flood-stalled trains had stranded them. After graduating from high school, and a year of school teaching in Tipton, Indiana, Don Tresidder wanted to enter Stanford University. He told Green that both of his parents and an uncle were doctors, and that he was determined to work his way through Stanford and its medical school. Green gave him directions to Yosemite and a letter of recommendation to Curry, who couldn't resist the Indiana-born, Stanford-bound combination, and put Tresidder to work as a porter. Thus began a Horatio Alger story. Don's hustle, looks, charm, and enthusiastic response to Yosemite's wonders earned him tips, favor, and, eventually, an executive position. Only the boss's elder daughter received an unfavorable first impression, because he set her trunk wrong side to against the tent frame.

Marjorie Curry became the first official hostess at camp that year. "I remember getting about fifty little firs and having them on the dining tables," she said. Earlier, when she and Mary had waited on tables, they had been "terribly disappointed" because of the lack of tips. Marjorie was known as the gal who drove stages from Camp Curry to , but her wildest feat was swimming across the Merced during high water by hanging on to a horse's tail.

Soon after Foster's marriage, a steadying influence in his parents minds, he had begun calling his wife "Cherry," partly because having two Mary Currys at Camp Curry was confusing. His reaction to the news that Cherry had produced a daughter rather than a son on April 9, 1913, was "Oh, rats!" but he soon succumbed to being a proud father, and on August 14 superintended an unusual ceremony on a ledge below the top of Vernal Fall. There Katherine Cherry Curry was christened by an Episcopalian minister with Yosemite waters as witnessed by her parents and four grandparents. In subsequent summers a pony cart, tea table, toys, and a cat named Yosemite, were provided for Katherine's entertainment. In time, the Cherry grandparents moved to camp to care for her while "Cherry" worked in the gift store.

As always, Mother Curry, as she was widely

known, was unobtrusive but indispensable to the camp's operation. She instituted outdoor church services for the employees by having a student minister or two whose only duties on Sundays were to preach, somewhat to the resentment of the hardworking porters, waiters, and other employees. In August a song by vaudeville performer Walter DeLeon was published and dedicated to her and her husband. "I'm Strong for Camp Curry" soon became a regular feature of the campfire. Its chorus ran:

Oh, I'm strong for Camp Curry, because
    there's no worry,
No hurry, no flurry is there;
The location's immense, there's no boundary
    or fence,
It's all common sense,
And the life is intense,
You accumulate tan,
And you eat all you can.
Every night there's a campfire and ball;
You can hear Curry yell.
Oh it's: "Hello, All's Well,"
Oh Camp Curry's the best of them all.

Inevitably the student help concocted a parody:

I'm off this Camp Curry, where there's so
    much worry,
And hurry and scurry is there;
The location's all right, but the boss
    is a fright,
We work day and night,
    and his wife is a sight!
Well, you work and you sweat, and you eat
    what you get,
And sometimes you get nothing at all;
I can hear Curry yell, "ALL IS WELL,
    but it's hell–
Oh, Camp Curry's the worst of them all.

DeLeon's song and the "The Stentor March," by a Stanford orchestra leader, were recorded in New York. "Curry was present himself, of course," reported the *Palo Alto Times*, "and gave the same calls he gives every evening. . . . His voice is so tremendous that he had to turn his back to the phonograph receiver to keep from spoiling the record. Calling *Hello Glacier!* against the back wall, the sound rebounded into the receiver and gave just the desired effect." Four of his calls were interspersed amongst the martial music.

During 1914, Curry introduced a new

service, furnishing camping equipment to those people who wanted to see the high country. "Compared with these mountains, Curry says the cliffs of Yosemite Valley are mere foothills," the *Palo Alto Times* stated. "He was so enamored with the alpine areas that he wanted to share them with others and was responsible for introducing the joys of mountaineering to many people." To achieve this goal he became a motion picture producer, directing and financing Arthur C. Pillsbury in the filming of "dizzy cliffs and canyons, stupendous sparkling waterfalls and glaciers" of various places and seasons.

Curry was confident that the film would attract good reviews and perhaps a thousand or more visitors the following season. Soon after his camp closed for the winter, the film was readied for showing, and went on

Don Tresidder with the ones that didn't get away.
(Hil Oehlmann collection.)

the road. His first two showings, in Redwood City and Palo Alto, attracted enthusiastic audiences. Admission was a quarter for adults and a dime for children under twelve. "Curry's big voice boomed," said the *Palo Alto Times,* "through an hour and a half of comment on two hours and a half of reproduced mountain loveliness."

Curry shared his pleasure with his mother:

I am not going east now but may do so later. Took in $44.10 Friday at Redwood City and $104.10 yesterday in the Marquee here. Show for a full week in the Savoy Theater next week, seating capacity 1300. If successful in SF and Los Angeles will go east for a month or two. People like the pictures and my talks. What won't it be next?

Even now, more than one hundred years after Camp Curry's founding, this archway is a treasured fixture. *(Hensleigh Family collection.)*

6 David and the Park Service

One of Yosemite's 15,154 visitors in 1914 was forty-seven-year-old Stephen T. Mather, the Chicago-based business tycoon of "Twenty Mule Borax" fame. Born, raised, and educated in California, he was a perpetual Bear Flag waving booster, even when he resided elsewhere. After noting rough, potholed roads, inadequate accommodations, and other deficiencies in both Yosemite and Sequoia National Parks, he wrote a letter of complaint to Interior Secretary Franklin K. Lane, a fellow alumnus of the University of California. "If you don't like the way the national parks are run," Lane replied tersely, "come on down to Washington and run them yourself."

With politically seasoned Horace Albright as his right-hand man, Mather began overall management of the thirteen parks and eighteen national monuments on January 21, 1915. Part mountaineer, part dynamo, the free-wheeling, intense Steve Mather was a man of constant action who charmed and cajoled others into motion. Repercussions were soon felt in every park, but especially in Yosemite, his acknowledged favorite.

One of his first official acts was to set up a three-day National Parks Conference, beginning March 11, on the University of California campus. State and national officials, members of the Sierra Club and the auto clubs, and many park superintendents and concessionaires attended. They discussed the needs and problems of the parks and monuments, for, as Mather remarked, "Scenery is a hollow enjoyment to a tourist who sets out in the morning after an indigestible breakfast and a fitful sleep on an impossible bed."

Concessionaire monopolies were considered, to the indignation of one intent listener. "I see Mr. Curry sitting patiently up here," moderator Mark Daniels said. "What are your problems in Yosemite National Park, Mr. Curry?" Curry's answer was immediate and emphatic.

> I believe we need some hotels, and we ought to have better hotels also, but I want to begin with an answer to something that was said yesterday regarding hotels in national parks—that they should be handled under one management in the interest of the tourists. It was proposed that we go into a monopoly and put somebody in charge of each park and have all of the tourist business in one park done by one company or one person. I am very thoroughly against that proposition. If you want to put all of the hotels in a park under one company, I have no objection to that, but if you combine hotels and camps and private camps, I am bitterly opposed to it, and I believe it is opposite to anything that is democratic in the American people. I have seen the effect of combining hotels and camps belonging to the same parties. I do not believe in it. I believe we should have camps that are made as good as people can make them, and the hotels should be just as good as hotel men are willing to make them. There is a cry all the time that we ought to have a four or five or six dollar a day hotel. The camp men do not care if there are a dozen such hotels in Yosemite Valley. I would not care if there were such hotels all through the national parks, but the trouble with such hotels is that they will not pay expenses.
>
> . . . I am going to talk about our own park, the Yosemite Park. The reason we do not get business to Yosemite is on account of the high charges to get there. It is not due to the Southern Pacific Railroad nor to the Santa Fe, but it is due to the Yosemite Valley line. . . .
>
> What I would like to get is lower rates for trips to our parks. I do not believe any other park in our county has as exorbitant rates as we have to Yosemite. It is a side trip that costs too much. I want lower rates.
>
> What we want in our parks are business men who will go into the business and stay in the business, and will be willing to put the last dollar they make into the business. . . .

Mather missed half the sessions; he was away, searching for a man, or men, who had vision and courage enough to add accommodations, especially a first class hotel, in Yosemite. Such a man would have to be something of a gambler, having faith that better services, roads, and publicity would insure growth and profit. Allegedly Mather's insistence on a hotel had begun when a titled Englishwoman disdained the accommodations of the Sentinel Hotel as primitive, and left the Park. Mather was stung, and instituted a building campaign. Not only did he want a new concessionaire, but he was seeking funds to buy the unused trans-mountain Tioga Road from the mining company

Steve Mather, first director of the National Park Service. *(YNP collection.)*

Mather's right-hand man and successor, Horace M. Albright. *(YNP collection.)*

that had built it in 1883. Ultimately he donated half of the $15,500 needed for the purchase.

To celebrate the completion of the Panama Canal, San Diego and San Francisco were hosting lavish expositions, and Mather was confident that a large number of the spring and summer exposition visitors would also visit California's national parks. To prepare Yosemite for the influx, Secretary Lane and Mather urged immediate construction of additional guest facilities in Yosemite Valley.

Laurence W. Harris, who ran a tent and camp equipment business in San Francisco, suggested Daniel Joseph Desmond as a good man to head the new service. At that time Desmond was operating a restaurant and a number of ornate kiosks on the San Francisco Exposition grounds, where he pioneered the sale of hot dogs on the West Coast. He was backed by such prestigious San Franciscans as Harris and A. B. C. Dohrmann, operator of a hotel supply business, who had organized to sell stock in the Desmond Park Service Company. In Merced, for instance, the businessmen pushed sales by explaining that new Yosemite facilities would mean increased business for San

Joaquin Valley towns. An "Abstract of Operations and Activities of D. J. Desmond, . . ." prepared by Park Service officials in February 1923, stated that:

> . . . after an extensive consideration of the matter and a careful investigation of individuals and concerns that were suggested as financially able and intelligently capable . . . a temporary permit for a period of one year from June 1, 1915, was granted to D. J. Desmond of San Francisco. Although Mr. Desmond had had no previous experience in hotel, or hotel camp operations, he had had extensive experience in the operation of construction camps operated in connection with the construction of the Los Angeles aqueduct, in organizing and handling the work of feeding and caring for the San Francisco earthquake refugees, and in operation of certain concessions involving the supplying of food at San Francisco. He was successful in all of those.

"Joe Desmond's work was efficient," a Merced businessman commented, "but not very satisfactory to workmen (on the aqueduct) who called him Desperate Joe Desmond, the belly-robbing son-of-a-bitch!"

True or not, Desmond had the capital, the ambition, and the drive required to launch a tourist camp in a short time. A Los Angeles native, and a graduate of that city's St. Vincent's College, he was thirty-eight in 1915, and had known both success and failure in business. He had six sisters and one brother—C. C. Desmond, who ran the well-known Desmond's clothing store, founded by their father, in Los Angeles. Joe Desmond was a big, bluff Irishman who dressed smartly, drove sporty cars, enjoyed sports, and had a beautiful wife and one son.

Within a few months, he leased the four-and-a-half acre former Army camp site in Yosemite Valley from the Park Service for $40 per acre. Included with the land were two large barracks buildings, two bath house and lavatory buildings, and 156 tent frames. Some of the acreage had been cleared for a parade ground, but the rest was shaded by pines and cedars. Desmond hired the San Francisco construction firm of Gutleben Brothers to convert the barracks into a lounge, dining room, and storehouse, and to build a laundry, dairy, tennis court, garage, and employee housing. Some of those projects were not completed until 1916. Since the Owens Valley aqueduct camps had been abandoned, Desmond bought a quantity of the twelve-by-fourteen prefabricated cabins and had them dismantled for rail shipment to El Portal. From there they were trucked into Yosemite Valley and reassembled as rental units, some of which were still in use in 1999.

In the spring of 1999, 100 similar buildings were constructed as "temporary employee housing" to replace those lost in the 1997 flood. Those built at the western edge of Curry Village are shaded and are pretty well hidden by pines. The other forty were built in the parking lot between the post office garages and Degnan's dorm and are in full sun—miserable to inhabit and miserable to look at.

Work on the camp began before the lease was signed, on June 1, 1915. Gutleben had the barracks moved end to end, added a long, low porch on the front, a kitchen on the back, and partitioned the interior into a dining room and lounge. "That was very temporary—very temporary," he stated decades later.

Editor E. D. Coblentz, businessman Larry Harris, and poet George Sterling in front of Yosemite Lodge, circa 1915. *(Arthur Pillsbury photo; L. W. Harris, Jr. collection.)*

"I understand it was temporary for years!" Troubled by the desert-like appearance created by marching soldiers, Gutleben bought over $100 worth of wildflower seeds to plant around carefully placed paths, benches, and rocks. Although construction continued throughout the summer, the instant camp was ready for guests by June 12, 1915. Lane and Mather were delighted with Desmond's achievements and urged him on. Gutleben considered Desmond to be a good promoter, but impatient and extravagant. For example, Desmond ordered sixteen White touring cars and had them shipped in by express rather than at the cheaper freight rate. He set up offices in San Francisco and Los Angeles, and leased hotels in Stockton and Merced.

On June 26, the *Mariposa Gazette* quoted Desmond's announcement that a hotel would be built on the grounds of public Camp Five of his Yosemite Falls Camp. On July 17 he was again quoted as saying that Park Service officials were studying plans for a hotel on Glacier Point. Desmond's byword was "hurry." He had his auto fitted with train wheels so that he could whiz between Merced and El Portal at will, and for several

D. J. Desmond and a famous guest—Douglas Fairbanks—circa 1916. (*D. J. Desmond, Jr. collection.*)

months he his wife and son, Joe, Jr., lived in Yosemite Valley while he pushed construction projects and instituted a jitney service in the Valley.

The resident manager and vice president of the company was C. R. Renno, who supervised the work when the boss was away and, according to the *Gazette*, saw that no expense was spared. At first the new resort was called Camp Desmond, next to Yosemite Falls Camp, and eventually, as now, Yosemite Lodge. (To avoid confusion, it will be referred to as Yosemite Lodge throughout this book.)

The adjacent "Soapsuds Row," the former residences of Army officers, were reserved for Park Service administrators such as George V. Bell, park superintendent in 1915. Bell, Mark Daniels, general superintendent of all parks, and Mather himself kept close tab on the frenetic activities at Yosemite Lodge. So did David A. Curry, but he had activities of his own during the spring of 1915, and in April won a victory against the railroads.

From its inception the Yosemite Valley Railroad had routed trains on its "Shortline to Paradise" so that travelers arrived in El Portal too late in the day to continue on to Yosemite Valley. Thus, a night had to be spent in the railroads' huge Del Portal Hotel, and, similarly, another on the way out. Lodging and meals there added considerably to trip expenses. Curry sued the Yosemite Valley Railroad, Southern Pacific, Santa Fe, and the Yosemite Transportation Company for through service—and won! The Railroad Commission ordered the Yosemite Valley Railroad to change its timetable "so as to make trains leave Merced at 1:45 p.m., on the return trip to arrive at Merced by 12:10 p.m. . . ." This meant that San Franciscans could reach "Paradise" within a day, and Los Angeles area passengers could count on a twenty-four hour trip instead of forty.

Jubilation swept over David Curry, but it was short-lived. Partly because of the Department of Interior, through service was instituted only one day a week. "This compromise had to be made on account of the opposition of the Department of Interior to permit the operation of automobiles on the floor of the Valley after 7 p.m. which would always be necessary when trains were late," Curry told a reporter. "My spirit will never be quiet until there is through service either way, which service would redound to the good of all transportation interests as well as the public requirements. I maintain that transportation interests should give service everywhere better and cheaper, to withstand the tide of competition about to overwhelm them, both in passenger and freight service, from the use of automo-

Yosemite Lodge's lounge was a remodeled Army barracks.
(Arthur Pillsbury photo; L. W. Harris, Jr. collection.)

biles and trucks. Business is not increased by stiff terms and slow timetables."

As had Mather, Curry anticipated crowds that season, and had his business stationery emblazoned with a "Panama-Pacific International Exposition" emblem. The return address on his envelopes proclaimed "A MESSAGE from THE STENTOR of Yosemite Camp Curry, California."

Permission had been granted the Curry Camping Company to build 300 more tent frames, increasing the camp's overnight capacity to 1,000. Foster Curry was in charge of the expansion, and his crew consisted of carpenters, an electrician, a plumber, and student laborers. One of the "chain gang" was John Fahey, a medical student who, with a classmate, had walked from Stockton to Yosemite Valley to seek adventure and jobs. Foster put Fahey to work leveling rocks with dynamite to make room for the tent platforms, and, later, building trails through the boulder-strewn camp. "We were given cots and a dresser," Fahey wrote the author, "but no tent so I found a large space between two tents, and we obtained a big canvas to make a roof. That make-

shift shelter was our home for the next couple of months."

On May 13, 1915, another University of California student, with close-cropped blond hair and a winning smile, reported for work at Camp Curry. Hilmer Oehlmann had been interviewed and hired by Mrs. Curry in Berkeley. That his summer job would lead to a half-century of loyal service and eventually the top executive position with the company was not conceived of by either employee or employer. However, Hil Oehlmann was instantly impressed with Mrs. Curry's keen eyes, ready smile, and graceful composure. "Gracious lady," was his characterization of her at first encounter, and he never changed that opinion.

Hil donned a short-billed cap and became a porter under David A. Curry whom he described as:

. . . a large impressive man by all standards . . . intensely proud of Camp Curry and its loyal following of guests and employees. He loved to wander about the Camp, and conducted daily trips to show interested groups the "back of the house," which

41

Hil Oehlmann, at right, began work as a porter in 1915.
(Hil Oehlmann collection.)

volunteered by guests and employees of the Camp, among whom were Jim Barnett, of the stables at Kennyville, and Wallace Curtis, chief clerk of Camp Curry, who usually sang his "Burglar Song." Mr. Curry always started the show with his "Welcome to Camp Curry, where the Stentor calls and the fire used to fall." He would describe the many activities which Yosemite offered the visitor, often telling thrilling experiences of going to Glacier Point by the Vernal-Nevada Trail and returning down the Four-Mile Trail. He announced that there was a daily mule trip over this route, and said that, "if you walk, you'll wish you'd ridden, and if you ride, you'll wish you'd walked." When he talked of the trip to the Merced Lake High Sierra Camp, he would proclaim that "the trout are so plentiful and hungry that you'll have to climb a tree to bait your hook."

Once, Oehlmann continued, a young woman was discovered circulating among the tents in a decidedly questionable manner. Curry, who invariably called a spade a spade, erupted, "Get that flaxon-haired whore out of here!"

included the laundry, kitchen, bake-shop, and other facilities requisite to a self-sustaining resort.

It was my feeling that Mr. Curry was a stern but kind and fairminded individual. His mien, which, doubtless appeared austere to some, was tempered by a droll sense of humor. I can still picture him expressing some pleasantry with a slight droop of the eyelids and the flicker of a smile. I recall him, too, in some moments of anger, and his wrath was a fearsome thing to behold, as the following incident may suggest.

A lady who had been staying at Camp Curry missed the bus out of the Valley, and was greatly upset on learning that she would have to wait until the next day to leave the Park. She accused the management of having given false information as to the departure time of the bus. The dispute was referred to Mr. Curry, and the guest accused the front office of deliberately misinforming her in order to obtain another day's revenue by the enforced delay of her departure. The argument grew heated, voices were raised, and finally the guest said: "You're no gentleman. You are talking back to a lady!" At that Mr. Curry's voice boomed out, "I'd talk back to God Almighty if he dared to impugn my motives."

In the years when I worked at Camp Curry the firefall had been discontinued, and Mr. Curry had no hesitancy in averring that its loss was due to pressure by the rival Desmond Park Service Co. upon the Park Service. He used to preside nightly over the entertainment, which consisted chiefly of magic and tales

Foster was a good worker with innate warmth and charm, but overfond of liquor. One time he was entrusted with several thousand dollars with which to purchase supplies for the camp in the Bay Area. After several drinks en route, he convinced himself that he could double the money in Reno, drove there, gambled and lost everything, including his automobile, and had

Foster Curry was affable and personable. *(RCB collection.)*

42

to hitchhike to Yosemite. He tried to enter camp without notice, but his sharp-eyed father spotted him and alerted everyone by booming, "Behold the son of David." Foster was forgiven upon contrite apology, and promised again to quit drinking.

Fellow porters Hil and Don Tresidder struck up an instant and enduring friendship. "Hil immediately established himself as a lover of the out-of-doors, an indefatigable hiker, mountain climber and camp cook of no mean proportion," Don recalled. "The memory we both cherish the most is a hike up the Ledge Trail after a day of work at Curry, overnight in a couple of blankets at Glacier Point, up for the sunrise, down the Pohono Trail to Yosemite Valley where we arrived about noon, on to Vernal and Nevada Falls, and Half Dome for the second night, down to Camp Curry in time for breakfast the following morning."

Night after night every one of the 540 tents was full. In fact, by the end of the 1915 season, 11,715 guests had stayed at Camp Curry; the Sentinel Hotel had hosted 8,323; 2,611 had stayed at Camp Lost Arrow; 1,426 at Camp Ahwahnee; and 2,851 at the new Yosemite Lodge. Another 5,090 people had pitched tents in the public camps. Mather had been right: travel to Yosemite had more than doubled because of the exposition and the increased use of automobiles.

Although Yosemite Lodge had not detracted from Camp Curry's business, its existence was a threat, and David soon discovered a valid reason for complaint. His letter to Interior Secretary Lane was reprinted in the *Palo Alto Times*.

I wish formally to protest against the maintenance of the bar at the Yosemite Falls Camp, as a direct violation of the rule in regard to saloons and bars in national parks, including the Yosemite valley interests.

I am told that the permission to have this open bar is granted in the lease of the above-mentioned camp. I cannot understand how this may be true, and if not true this action is in direct violation of the law.

I wish to state that Camp Curry has had more trouble in the matter of its employees drinking in the past two months than it has had in its entire sixteen years previous.

Two excellent workmen were sent out of the valley on account of drunkenness and rowdyism caused by liquor obtained at this bar. One of our most trusted

employees, who has the handling of several thousand dollars during the season and who has been with us for three years and has never before occasioned any trouble at the Camp Curry on this account, has been drunk twice within the past week. Other employees have been under the influence of liquor at various times. The general character of the Camp Curry employees is very much superior, as we believe, to what will be found in the ordinary place of this kind. . . .

It is my belief that every concessionaire in the valley feels the same in regard to his employees and the liquor situation as I do, but they may not all be willing to say so thus plainly.

Furthermore, the feeling of the guests at Camp Curry, as expressed to me by those who have known the facts, is to the effect that they consider that the valley loses much of its desirability as a place of resort through the introduction of liquor. They feel that drivers, guides and employees in general are

Big Chief Curry and his squaw posed, in a rare moment of comedy, with Mary, a Yosemite Indian. *(John F. Fahey collection.)*

As Muir said, "The snow is melting into music." *(Vernal Fall, by Ansel Adams.)*

much less safe persons to whom to entrust their lives and property if they at any time indulge in the use of liquor. The introduction of drunken men is also a menace to the private campers, many of whom are unprotected women and who have hitherto felt that the Yosemite was a place perfectly safe from drunkenness, rowdyism and all such evils as accompany the sale and use of liquor.

For the above reasons, Mr. Secretary, I beg that this bar may be closed and that the sale of liquor by the drink or in quantity may never again be allowed in the Yosemite valley.

Respectfully,
DAVID A. CURRY

That Mather had deliberately allowed the Desmond Park Service Company to sell liquor was verified by Horace Albright years later. "The idea was to give them as much money as they could, to give them every opportunity to bring in a good income so as to build a concession which would warrant a hotel."

Mather and Lane considered Desmond and associates the right men to construct first-class hotels at Glacier Point and in the Valley, plus three Swiss chalets in the high Sierra. By September of 1915 Secretary Lane proposed a supervised monopoly in Yosemite. If finalized, "Desmond would control all hotels, camps, stores and photographic rights in the valley," reported Bay Area newspapers. "The proposal was that Camp Curry and other Yosemite concessionaires give fifty percent of their net profits to the Desmond Company, the Desmond Company in turn to give fifty percent of its net revenue to the federal government."

Such "Desmondizing" was "monopolistic, undemocratic, unjust, unrighteous and iniquitous," Curry telegraphed Secretary Lane. His anger led him into Desmond's San Francisco office on Saturday, Sept. 27, which encounter was reported the following day by the *San Francisco Chronicle.*

. . . About thirty seconds later things began to happen. There is a dispute as to just what did take place, but Curry emerged with a bruise over his right eye, and he admits he got the worst of the encounter. He says Desmond made an unprovoked assault . . . struck him in the face with his fist five or six times, knocked him from a chair, hit him again after he was down, and called him names.

Pacifist Curry sought a warrant for Desmond's arrest, and both men were cited to the warrant clerk's officer, but no judges were at work on the weekend, so a warrant could not be issued. According to Joe Desmond, Jr., the rivals had tangled physically earlier in Yosemite Valley. Curry was older, larger, and more aggressive, but no match for Desmond who had once sparred with Jim Jeffries and kept himself in shape at an athletic club.

Meanwhile, Lane telegraphed that the contract with Desmond had not been signed, and that "he had been waiting to see Curry in a personal interview." An

Chief Ranger Townsley, at right, with the ranger force. (*H. R. Sault photo.*)

October 15 hearing in Washington, D. C., was scheduled for all embattled parties. As was his custom, Curry first aired his grievances publicly so that he could show support to the "establishment." Well in advance of the new showing of Yosemite pictures, he ran an advertisement for them with the promise that "Curry will also tell what 'Desmondizing' Yosemite would mean to the public, and how he proposes to thwart monopolistic plans in this Democratic age. Help him mold sentiment in 300 lectures this winter." Between the two showings at the Varsity Theater in Palo Alto, he elaborated on "Desmondizing," and then called "for all those in the audience who had ever acted as help at Camp Curry to come forward and sing, `I'm Strong for Camp Curry.'" Twelve responded with the song and then it's parody, at which Curry's laugh was the loudest.

The next blast in his campaign was a paid ad in the *San Francisco Chronicle* of October 10.

ALL CALIFORNIANS INTERESTED IN KNOWING YOSEMITE

Please write or telegraph Secretary Franklin P. Lane, Washington, immediately, protesting monopolization of Yosemite by Desmond blanket concession, including transportation, hotels, camps contrary to the vested interest of the present concessionaires, making us tributary underlings, subsidiary to Desmond's management and tributary in part of net earnings at rates of $15.00 per week to our overlord competitor, thus making up his deficiency for five to ten dollars per day, hotels and accessories for nine or ten months annually. Granting transportation and hotel facilities together effectively kills competition in hotel or camp lines.

Interlocking transportation with hotels and camp facilities has proved a curse to the public in National Park Service. Protest present demand for a bar selling liquor indiscriminately to guides, rangers, hotel and camp help, chauffeurs and all comers contrary to law. No drinking saloon or barroom should be permitted on government land in the park. I hold affidavits of sale throughout the season. Ask restoration of firefall, denied the public without reason.

Ask, properly regulated, to use your own automobile on floor of valley, now allowed some while denied others. Such has been the almost universal complaint from two thousand machines the past season. Ask parking garage for Camp Curry, not inconveniently located more than one and a half miles from present garage.

I am asking all old concessions for all concessionaires on competitive basis only for old and new concessions with no favors to Desmond or old concessionaires, and I know all my requests are just and equitable for the best good of Yosemite and the public

whom we concessionaires and the Department of Interior should serve. Will editors of California papers copy this appeal and comment thereon?

DAVID A. CURRY

When the meeting in Secretary Lane's office began, the Currys, Desmond, Will Sell, Jr., A. C. Pillsbury, E. T. Huffman of the Yosemite Transportation Service, storekeeper William Thornton, Clarence A. Washburn, Merced businessman Richard Shaffer and two lawyers were present. Mather made an earnest and lengthy discourse on the need for improved facilities and a regulated monopoly to take over all business interests in Yosemite, then asked for reactions. Instantly Curry bellowed opposition. Eyewitness Shaffer stated later that both Mr. and Mrs. Curry "were most outspoken in condemning the deal as unfair, an outrage, and that they would see Steven Mather, Joe Desmond, and his self-seeking San Francisco merchants in Hell before they would go along with such a plan. Other concessionaires tried to be more diplomatic, and said they could and were financially able to take care of any increase in business, had done so in the past, and felt entitled to go on until found wanting. Also they claimed an understanding of the Yosemite problems and love of the place that would be better to serve the tourist needs than any `regulated monopoly' scheme. . . ."

Discussions continued for the better part of two days, until most of the smaller businessmen were persuaded to sell to Desmond. Eventually, his company bought out Camp Awahnee, Camp Lost Arrow, Thornton's general store, the meat market, Coffman's stable business, the transportation business and the assets of the Sentinel Hotel, and the old Mountain House on Glacier Point.

David A. Curry did not capitulate. Documentation for his actions was included in a lengthy "Report on the Franchise Situation," which was not issued until March 27, 1923. That was coauthored by Horace Albright, who was involved throughout and had access to all official records. According to the report, at the October 1915 meeting, Curry "confined himself to abuse of D. J. Desmond . . . in trying to prove by pictures and affidavits that Mr. Desmond was a saloon keeper by reason of the fact that certain alcoholic beverages were sold . . . in his temporary camp . . . Mr. Curry wanted to give all kinds of service to his American plan guests in Camp Curry, including transportation, and cared nothing about the public that did not choose to avail themselves of his service. Had Curry possessed a calmer temperament, and broader vision, the official view was that he

Mrs. D. A. Curry.

**Publisher Harry Chandler, Superintendent W. B. Lewis, Mather,
A. B. C. Dohrmann, and other VIPs are seated around the campfire,
but only David and Foster Curry are readily discernible. Mother Curry
liked the picture so well that she had it made into calling cards.** *(RCB collection.)*

would have been permitted to undertake new development and handle all Park concessions. In short, Curry, not Desmond, would have been offered the long term franchise." Secretary Lane vehemently criticized the Stentor "for his obstructive tactic and abuse . . . of officials," and granted Desmond a twenty-year franchise.

Even with his immoderate words and deeds, Curry had exhibited a love for Yosemite and dedication to serving his guests. That, backed up by numerous letters and telegrams, influenced Lane, if not Mather, to grant Curry some consideration. After several weeks of study, Lane announced that Camp Curry would continue to operate independently of Desmond on a year's lease. "The Stentor Says Farewell to Trouble When Lane Speaks" headlined the Palo Alto paper. What the press did not state, but official reports did, was that Curry had been restricted to operate only on the American plan enterprise for housing and feeding guests, with such incidental services as these guests might require in 1916. No new privileges were granted, and the f was not restored.

Degnan's Bakery, Best's, Boysen's, Foley's, and Pillsbury's Studios, all of them small, personally managed businesses, were allowed to continue operation for the lifetime of their owners. Desmond's takeover did not directly affect the Washburns, since their Wawona business site was outside Yosemite National Park. After the deaths of A. H. and Edward Washburn, in 1902 and 1911, the surviving brother, John, and his son, Clarence, concentrated on their extensive Wawona buildings, and relinquished their dominance of the valley interests.

Curry, that "big, boisterous importation from the middle west," pocketed his slingshot, broadcast his triumph, and took to the road. Daughter Mary wrote that her father "went to and fro in the land preaching Yosemite as a gospel . . . he backed Arthur Pillsbury in making his early mountain and flower movies, and toured the schools and clubs of California and more distant places with them, not just as a business promotion, but with the truly religious sense of what the mountains held for people."

Early in 1916 Curry took some time off to accompany his family to Hawaii. Typically, he was photographed shouting "FAREWELLLL" from shipboard. Both Mary and Marjorie went along. Mary had graduated from Stanford in three years and was taking graduate work for her master's degree.

Preparatory work toward opening Camp Curry was begun soon after the travelers' return. Curry's brochure was twelve pages long and boasted that "the camp served ice cream daily, chicken every Sunday, had two pianos, a barber shop, the only swimming tank in the Valley, and the largest and best hardwood dance floor in Yosemite—experts say it is not surpassed in California—all for $2.50 a day or $15.00 per week. All roads formerly led to Rome. All roads now lead to Camp Curry."

Along with the new season there was new supervision for the Yosemite concessionaires, in the person of Washington Bartlett Lewis, who arrived there in March of 1916. Handpicked by Mather, ex-engineer "Dusty" Lewis, thirty-two, was capable, progressive, and handsome. His tenure was to be long and firm, though complicated by opposition, experimentation, and lack of funds.

Both Don Tresidder and Hil Oehlmann were waiters in the 1916 season, but they were sometimes diverted from their duties. One evening they rushed outside to see alpenglow on Half Dome. "Heedless of our guests," Hil recalled, "we watched enraptured as the light faded . . . my companion exclaimed, `By George, I love that mountain!' Besides the magnificence of Half Dome, there were other distractions in those days. . . . In being helpful and attentive to the comely waitresses we were not always mindful of our patrons,

and occasionally there were gentle admonitions from Mother Curry."

Father Curry was much less gentle when he discovered that Don had taken Mary up the hazardous ascent of Half Dome, even though Mary explained that she had persuaded Don to let her go. Curry fired the youth, who went to work assisting photographer Pillsbury. Besides working in the studio, Don was the star of movies that Pillsbury made interpreting Indian legends. Make-up and a breech clout turned the Indianian into an Indian.

Among the new faces at Camp Curry in 1916 was Grace Rogers Jilson, a sixty-eight-year-old widow. She was trim, small, brown-haired, and vivacious. During the daytime she was a typical fond grandmother, who loved to brag about her six children and grandchildren. At night she was transformed into a comic! For years she had done impersonations and character skits for charity and church affairs in the East.

In 1915 she had bought a six-month round-trip ticket to California to see the exposition and, while staying in a San Diego hotel, met friends who persuaded

Mary Curry, Don Tresidder, W. B. "Dusty" Lewis, his wife, and Arthur Pillsbury picnic beneath the pines. (*Arthur Pillsbury photo; YNP collection.*)

her to give some readings. David Curry heard her and signed her up as an entertainer for Camp Curry. On the outdoor stage, *American Magazine* explained, she gave monologues, "such old-fashioned stuff as Finley Dunn's "Mr. Dooley," James Whitcomb Riley, Eugene Field, Opie Reed, Kate Douglas Wiggen, and Dorothy Dix—Irish, Negro, Yankee, and Indiana farmer dialects."The audience laughed, loved, and applauded her, and she became a Curry institution second only to the Stentor himself in popularity.

That summer the office force consisted of a bookkeeper, an assistant bookkeeper, a postmistress, Celeste Curry, the secretary, and George Henry McKee, the cashier. Celeste was the second cousin of David Curry, and McKee was a cousin of Mrs. Curry. Relatives were invariably given jobs and, if they proved able, retained.

"I was very fond of cousin David," Celeste Curry told the author. "He was very nice to work for but was determined to give me a word I couldn't spell. He couldn't stump me until he dictated the word 'eleemosynary,' and I hadn't ever heard that before . . . I had learned shorthand, but he wouldn't let me use it. He wanted to dictate direct and would lean over me to watch his words come out of the typewriter. And maybe you don't think he didn't write angry letters! One time, I recall, in a letter to Washington, he wrote about Desmond, something about how he would last as long as a snowball in Hell! Cousin Jennie tried to keep him on a diabetic diet, but he liked to break over. . . . He wasn't allowed potatoes, and the office force had a table to itself in the dining room. Sometimes after he finished his dinner with Cousin Jennie, he would come over and sit down at our table, reach down for a small potato, put butter on it and eat it."

Dancing was the big thing evenings, but George McKee, who was courting Celeste, couldn't go until after the office closed at 9:30 and the day's receipts were counted. To hurry things, Celeste would help count "all those beautiful gold twenty dollar pieces in stacks." Guests left their valuables too—rings, watches, and other jewelry, to be stored in the safe, and when its door broke, the staff was in a dilemma. "The safest place in camp is in our tent," Mother Curry decided. "Nobody, not even a mouse, could enter that without waking me up, so you just put the sacks under our bed at night, George." Night after night McKee would walk into the Currys' tent, place money and valuables, under the bed, and leave—without either Jennie or David as much as stirring!

One young man who didn't share Celeste's regard for David Curry was James V. Lloyd, one of the new

The star of Arthur Pillsbury's films of Indian legends was Indianan Don Tresidder. *(John F. Fahey collection.)*

Park Service rangers. Before he had time to acquaint himself with Yosemite Valley, he was told to go to the aid of an injured hiker on the Ledge Trail back of Camp Curry. Upon reaching the camp, Lloyd asked directions from a burly, rumpled-looking man. Instead of answering, showman Curry stepped up on the porch and bellowed, "Folks, here's a *ranger*— a *ranger* who doesn't even know where the Ledge Trail is! What kind of a *ranger* is that?" Lloyd did his best not to encounter the Stentor again!

His experiences with Foster Curry were similarly embarrassing but less public. One of Lloyd's jobs was to patrol the east end of the Valley and, after a big lunch at the Sentinel Hotel, he would mount his mare, pull his broad brimmed hat over his eyes, and snooze while the faithful horse plodded along the gravelled road. Several times Foster drove past him in his auto, then hit the brakes, so as to pepper horse and rider with the sharp pebbles.

By 1916, Foster had wearied of tent life and wanted more privacy for his family, so he chose a sloping site backed by a jumble of boulders under Glacier Point, and had an ingenious two-room bungalow built. It was constructed of cedar poles and slabs, with a wide, roofed porch on the front. Three sides of the large, living-sleeping room were screened and covered by striped canvas on curtain rollers. The fourth side, against the talus slope, consisted mainly of a cavernous fireplace built against a huge rock. Foster spent $1,000 on the tile and fixtures for the bathroom. His collection of Indian rugs and bear skins carpeted the floor, others served as bedspreads on the hand-carved cedar bedsteads, and Indian baskets and miner's lamps added charm. Foster felt that his rustic cabin should be the

prototype of rental units—which would replace tents—but his father was unconvinced.

Desmond was expanding all over the Park in 1916. He had tent camps and Alpine-type lodges built at Tuolumne Meadows and at Tenaya and Merced lakes, and a fourth camp erected just west of Yosemite Lodge. These were built quickly and at reasonable cost, but the two hotels under construction at the same time swallowed money. Estimates had called for $35,000 to be spent on a hotel at Glacier Point, and $150,000 for the Grizzly Hotel on the Valley floor, but expenditures were reversed. After $35,000 had gone to pay 200 men to excavate an enormous basement and 1,500 feet of rock foundation walls, Desmond ordered work halted on the Grizzly, and pushed it on the elaborate, three-story Glacier Point inn.

While Mather was satisfied with Desmond's energy

SRO prevailed at Camp Curry's evening entertainment.
(SS collection.)

For years Camp Curry's most popular entertainer was mild-appearing Grace Rogers Jilson.
(*Charles H. Petersen collection.*)

Curry ordered enough paper from the *Palo Alto Times* to print 75,000 advertising folders for Camp Curry. Soon afterwards he left for Southern California to give more film lectures. Jennie accompanied him, since Marjorie was at Stanford and Mary in New York doing graduate work at Columbia. An eager young man named Robert Tatum Williams drove the car. "At that time," he told the author, "I was attending Stanford and trying to get in strong with the parents of Marjorie, and when they invited me to drive them around California (as far south as San Diego) while Mr. Curry went to the people by hiring local halls and giving his side of the Yosemite story, I accepted gladly."

When the Currys returned to the Bay Area on March 8, they heard that Secretary Lane had granted the Curry Camping Company a five-year lease! Increases in rates were allowed. Pictures and postcards could be bought at the camp, and the Ledge Trail would be improved. Best of all, Lane said that the firefall could again be reinstated as a nightly feature. David A. Curry was exuberant, and confident that his campaign of offense, and Desmond's instability, had been responsible for the concessions. Actually, Horace Albright, who was particularly sympathetic to Mrs. Curry and well aware of her large part in the camp's operation, had been a prime mover in the new concessions.

Desmond was so near bankruptcy that he had to appeal to Harris and Dohrmann for an emergency loan of $17,000. Both men were shocked, supportive, and thereafter actively involved in direction of the faltering

and purpose, official personnel in the Valley felt that he was extravagant, impulsive, and arbitrary. The well-known Desmond-Curry feud was heightened by the merest rumor. To fuel it, Desmond broadcast that his contract was monolithic and inferred that "it was the eventual intention of the Department of Interior to absorb all the operations in the Park, including Camp Curry." That kind of statement inspired a new spate of vitriolic letters from Curry. Many—intercepted by Jeannie Curry—were never mailed. Others added documentation to the Park Service's opinion of Curry as abusive, vituperative, and obstructive.

After Desmond's camp closed, Foster took rolls of pictures of privies, makeshift bathhouses, and anything else that looked disreputable, especially at the Yosemite Lodge. The film was intended as anti-Desmond ammunition with the Park Service. Curry's behavior was more and more unruly, and because of his hostile, anti-regimentation attitude, officials tended to forget his large innovative and progressive contributions to business development in Yosemite. On January 2, 1917

One of Ranger Jim Lloyd's multitudinous jobs was painting the 26 fireplugs in Yosemite Valley.
(*J. V. Lloyd collection.*)

company. All of the directors paid a voluntary 60 percent assessment on their stock shares to quiet creditors.

While Curry was in Southern California, a car door had slammed on his foot, but the hurt was soon forgotten. Weeks later, he complained of pain, and X-rays taken on April 15 revealed that a bone in one toe had been shattered, and was decaying. ". . . there is absolutely nothing to be done but to amputate the little toe," Jennie wrote David's sister, Ida. "It is the healing that will be the question." David scrawled a postscript, "Dear Mother, sisters, brothers, and friends. I hope to come through O.K. and it would not be worse than a cut finger were it not for my diabetic condition. My love and affection to all."

He was operated on in San Francisco's German Hospital on April 16, and convalesced slowly, fretting about opening Camp Curry. Jennie took over, helping Foster with buying supplies, and dictating business letters to Celeste Curry McKee. In an April 2 letter to Ida, Jennie showed concern. ". . . When I think how long it has sometimes taken a little hurt to heal on his foot, I cannot imagine how long it will take such a wound as this. . . . He had expected to open Camp May 1st as usual, but there is still so much snow that we have decided to postpone opening until the 10th. . . . Of course David and I cannot get up at the first, probably, but Foster is quite capable of starting things and running them for some time. With almost the same office force as last year; with Mr. Kussman and several other former employees in the kitchen; with Louise Logue as

head waitress and more than half the old force back in the dinning room; with the same head porter and several of the old—or should I say former maids on the job, the work ought to start off like clockwork. We shall be doing little or no expansion or building except necessary repairs. A big oak fell on Foster's bungalow, almost demolishing it—we rejoice no one was in it—our keeper says we will have plenty of wood as trees are down all over camp. Suppose electric wires will be down too.

"We were fortunate in having about three thousand dollars worth of provisions left last fall. They are worth far more now. Also we have bought pretty advantageously this spring so we think we shall pull through if the war doesn't keep people away too much and indications are that business will be good.

"But isn't the war the most awful thing that ever happened? I hope it isn't too selfish to hope the other people will drive the Germans home so we won't have to get any deeper into it."

Two days later Jennie wrote a gloomy, fearful, confidential letter to say that tests indicated Bright's Disease, and "his toe developed a little gangrene. . . Woe is me for our David." He was not told of either complication, but was nervous. When his granddaughter, Katherine, was brought in to see him, David asked her to sing "There's A Long, Long Trail A-Winding," and tears were close among her listeners. Within a few days blood poisoning set in, and the Stentor died on the last day of April.

A memorial service at Palo Alto's Congregational Church was not held until Sunday, May 6, to enable Mary Curry to travel from New York and Grandmother Curry and Ida Curry Hensleigh from Kansas. Chancellor David Starr Jordan, the Reverend O. L. Elliot, and banker George Parkinson gave eulogies praising David Curry's uprightness, personality, and forthright spirit. Parkinson concluded his tribute by saying, "Devoted to his family, his home, his business, his religion—a just man, an honest man, a Christian man—one of God's noblemen."

No taps sounded as the scores of friends and relatives filed out of the church, but even the most reverent must have thought of what was missing—David Curry's "FAREWELLLLLLLL!"

7   Foster Curry Greets You

The Yosemite show must go on! Although the showman was gone, he was replaced by a slimmer, better-looking, better-dressed replica who had the big smile, glad hand, and charm that made him an ideal front man. Behind the scenes, Mother Curry continued to run the camp, but the showman, in the scenic show place of the world, was Foster Curry. He boomed a good imitation of the traditional calls, but he couldn't glance at a guest and astonish him by recalling his name, the year he had been in camp, and the number of the tent in which he had stayed. His father's memory had been prodigious, and he was keenly missed by family, staff, and repeat guests. Nevertheless the camp ran smoothly, and more than 10,000 guests were entertained during the 1917 season.

Foster and his mother were supported by a loyal band of returning employees and equally faithful and helpful relatives. Cousin Celeste and George McKee were on the office staff. Cousin Will Thomson, who had helped pick the camp's site, was using his journalistic talents to write and publish the daily *Stentor's Call*, which David Curry had established the previous year, in the new printing plant. David's sister, Ida, and his aging mother visited and gave moral support to Jennie Curry. Mary and Marjorie were part-time workers and full-time companions to their mother. Reliable Rufus Green, always supportive with counsel and loans, shouldered so much of the business direction that he was put on the payroll. Back in Palo Alto, bankers George Parkinson and P. M. Lansdale negotiated with Green and continued to finance Camp Curry's operations of wholesale buying, advertising, maintenance, insurance, taxes, and administration.

The highlight of the summer was the reintroduction of the firefall. "My greatest thrill was being given the assignment of throwing the first firefall from Glacier Point," John Fahey reminisced. "Another fellow and I climbed the Ledge Trail to gather pine cones, start the fire, and at 8:30 p.m., when the lights were out in the camp below, we heard the Stentorian voice of Foster Curry shouting, `LET 'ER GO GALLAGHER.'" Once more, glowing embers spilled over the granite cliff, fanned out in a crimson veil, and died harmlessly on a ledge far below. Spectators held their breath, then expressed thrill in gasps or muttered adjectives.

Although Steve Mather had been appointed as the first director of the National Park Service, in the spring of 1917 he had a nervous breakdown and was only on the job a few weeks that year. His capable assistant, Horace Albright, acted as director, making him cofounder of the NPS, and it was he who saw to it that the five-year contract and firefall restoration was transferred to Mrs. Curry.

Desmond interests were upset at the reintroduction of the firefall. It was a great attraction to visitors and, since it could not be seen from Yosemite Lodge, was often a deciding factor in a guest's selection of where to stay. Desmond had hired entertainers for his camps and the Sentinel Hotel, but never achieved the well-executed entertainment and special features provided at Camp Curry. Despite reorganization of his company, Desmond's finances were still shaky, and his personal drive and abrupt management changes caused dissension and turmoil among his staff. According to the August 4, 1917 *Western Hotels and Travel* newspaper, "He `drove' his men to distraction and, in turn, they threw many of the public patrons into a state of being `knockers' instead of `boosters.'"

Desmond was driven by the threat of bankruptcy. Because of the United States' involvement in World War I, he could not purchase building materials for the Grizzly Hotel, and its rock foundations and yawning basement in the Valley floor must have been a nagging torment to him.

From the day the Glacier Point Hotel opened, in 1917, it was a white elephant. Rates were high, and most guests stayed only one night. Yosemite Valley was always and forever where most visitors wanted to stay—amid nature's wonders, and with the interaction of people and the opportunity for diverse recreation.

No correspondence of Desmond's has been unearthed, but numerous letters written by Harris and Dohrmann to Mather and Albright exist, to reveal the Desmond Park Service Company's problems in 1917, as well as the close cooperation between the company and the Park Service. While Mather was recovering from a nervous breakdown, Albright was in complete charge. Joe Desmond, too, was suffering from stress, and was hospitalized for observation in February of 1917—his basic ailment was diabetes.

At the peak of the tourist season, Desmond's Yosemite manager, C. R. Renno, quit because of conflicts with his boss; his replacement was a former stenographer for the company! The final blow was the destruction by fire of the year-old El Capitan Camp, immediately west of Yosemite Lodge, on June 23. "Rebuilding will begin at once," announced the *Mariposa Gazette.* Instead, Desmond resigned, and left for several months of travel to recover his health.[1] His collapse was headline news in San Francisco, Los Angeles, and in the weekly *Western Hotels and Travel.*

A comprehensive abstract of Desmond's operation, prepared by Park Service officials and dated February 2, 1923, shows that reorganization efforts directed by A. B. C. Dohrmann, whose son, Bob, and Joe Desmond, Jr., ran a business together decades later, and Larry Harris, succeeded in finding a mighty array of backers but little capital by stock subscription. War conditions made the raising of money almost impossible.

Thomas E. Farrow, forty-one, who had directed resorts in Yellowstone and Glacier national parks, was appointed as manager of the Yosemite concessions, but it was too late in the season to influence profits. Desmond "luck" struck again on October 27, 1917, when the huge Del Portal Hotel in El Portal was destroyed by fire, and Farrow was so severely burned attempting to save company records that he had to be hospitalized for weeks.

Earlier that month Foster Curry had talked to Dohrmann about the possibility of the Curry Camping Company taking over the Desmond interests. Dohrmann was encouraged at the amicable spirit, but Albright responded negatively to the news. "Of course, it is entirely proper to discuss the possibilities of the absorption of the Desmond interest by the Curry Camping Company, but you will understand, of course, and I know that Mr. Dohrmann

will, that we could not, under any circumstances, consider the approval of the transfer of the property of the Desmond Company nor its franchises to the Curry interests. However, I do not think there is any likelihood that Mr. Curry and his associates could secure the necessary financial support to even negotiate seriously. . . ." Dohrmann's attempt to eliminate antagonism by creating friendly feelings between the rivals was misunderstood by Foster Curry, who talked exuberantly of what he would do with the Desmond concessions. Harris related that apologetically to Albright, adding ". . . apparently to become friendly with our late enemy we unconsciously have piled up a little trouble for the

Foster Curry and his mother posed under the gateway he designed.
(YNP collection.)

---

1. Despite financial difficulties and increasing health problems, Desmond remained optimistic and was negotiating for the commissary contract on the Hetch Hetchy dam project when he died on March 11, 1920, at age forty-four.

Next to Half Dome, the firefall, a manmade attraction, was the most famous feature of Yosemite Valley.
(YNP collection.)

Department. . . ." Finally, a lease, covering the months between April 1 and October 1, 1918, with an option to buy the Desmond company, was given to Richard and Harold Shaffer of Merced, since Harris and Dohrmann had become so involved in Red Cross war work that they could not give the company the necessary intensive direction.

Meanwhile, Camp Curry ran smoothly. Foster's energy and enterprise were responsible for most of the guest entertainment. In August he organized a lavish four-day pageant depicting the history of Yosemite Valley. Among the spectators were the Japanese Ambassador, fifty-five members of his party, and Mayor Rolph of San Francisco. Mrs. Jilson, Glen W. Hood, Bill Lewis, and about fifty other employees and guests acted in the pageant. A week earlier Cecil B. DeMille had directed a movie starring Geraldine Farrar and Wallace Reid, using Yosemite Valley scenes as

settings. Camp Curry was headquarters for DeMille, and, at other times, for several other movie companies.

Real life drama starred Jennie, Marjorie Curry, and young John Fahey one stormy night. First, a fire flamed outside the camp gateway, and then it was discovered that the main hydrant had been turned off. Arson by Desmond's employees was suspected because the hostility between the two camps had been manifested in minor but destructive acts. Coincident with the Curry fire, Mother Curry received word that postal authorities were about to close the camp's branch office. This meant that all mail would go through Desmond hands at the Sentinel Hotel post office, and stages would not continue on to Camp Curry. Mother Curry counter-attacked by giving John Fahey a loaded gun to guard the camp all night while she and Marjorie drove through wind and rain to reach San Francisco in time to persuade an influential congressman to intercede. He was successful, and the Camp Curry post office was retained.

During the season. Foster discovered that one of the office girls was a Desmond "spy," fired her, and talked a guest, Ruth Higgins, whom he knew to be an expert legal secretary, to fill in during the remainder of her vacation. Before she left, she arranged to return the following summer since, she said, "that was the only way I could get a month's vacation in Yosemite."

After the camp closed, Jennie Curry traveled east with her daughters to keep house for them while they both attended Columbia College. Mary was still in graduate school, and Marjorie remembers that "I took courses in cooking, sewing, household administration and home decoration, and saw sixty-five New York shows in four months." In February 1918 they all boarded a train to Quincy, Illinois, where Marjorie married Bob Williams in the home where he had been born. Like his bride, Bob was an extrovert, an enthusiastic, warmhearted, good-looking young man, and a newly commissioned lieutenant in the 69th Balloon Company.

That winter Foster went to Washington, D.C. to lobby for more concessions and, like his father, showed Yosemite movies in eastern cities. Later, Park Service officials stated that he "proved himself not to posses any of the virtues of his father, but all of the faults. . . ." Foster was a fighter, singlemindedly advancing Camp Curry's cause in the tradition of both his father and mother.

Mother Curry's sweet nature was notable, but thirty-one years of marriage to David Curry had inspired some aggressiveness in her too. After David's death she filed suit against the State Compensation

Insurance Fund, claiming that his death resulted from the car door hitting his foot, and asked compensation of $5,000, based on his salary for a year. Conversely the State claimed that Curry had died from diabetes—not induced by the accident. Ultimately the claim was denied. Curry's estate of $60,000 had been willed exclusively to his wife, but it consisted chiefly of stock in the Curry Camping Company—paper wealth.

In 1918, as in other seasons, Camp Curry was largely staffed by tried-and-true employees. Mrs. Jilson was back as well as Chef Kussman and head waitress Louise Logue, Bill Lewis, camp superintendent, and his right-hand man, Al Littell, who came in early to open camp. Foster's father-in-law, F. H. Cherry, had a fancy title, chief engineer, to operate the boiler, and George McKee was cashier and chief clerk. Cherry Curry ran the Studio, which consisted of a gift shop, candy counter, and the popular soda fountain where wild strawberry sundaes were a specialty. This money-making Studio was Foster's "baby" and listed on company records as his department. From childhood, Cherry had done photography work, so she enjoyed working in the Studio darkroom.

Yosemite's spectacular beauties were the lodestone that drew student employees back summer after summer, but they had developed a love and loyalty to the Currys too. "Old Dave," or "Dad Curry," had been a favorite; Foster was popular and Mother Curry venerated. She was an advisor, counselor, and a strict yet gentle summer mother for students. She earned their

Interesting Outdoor Men

A. B. C. Dohrmann, President of the Yosemite National Park Co., Says the High Sierra Is a Great Asset

RALPH O. YARDLEY, Artist   O. VAN WYCK, Jr., Biographer

"ALPHABET" DOHRMANN BELIEVES THAT THE CALIFORNIA SIERRA IS ONE OF THE GREATEST UNDEVELOPED RESOURCES OF THE GOLDEN STATE

A. B. C. (Alphabet) Dohrmann was the subject of a 1924 *Stockton Record* cartoon. *(SS collection.)*

A REVIEW OF HOTELS, CLUBS, STEAMSHIPS, TRAVEL, CATERING AND PURVEYORS THERETO

Western Hotels and Travel

Published Weekly By Irvin C. Keeler

With Which is Incorporated "The San Francisco Hotel News" and "The Culinarian"

VOL. X. No. 31.   SAN FRANCISCO, AUGUST 4, 1917.   Terms: $3.00 a Year; 10c a Copy.

YOSEMITE ALPS SENSATION

Stunning Collapse of the Government-Concessionnaire Park Service Corporation — Two Months' Veiled Rumors Escape as Staggering Facts—Causes and Consequences of the Toboggan Thud!

Desmond's downfall made headlines. *(YNP collection.)*

In 1920 a news cameraman photographed the second airplane to do stunts and land in Yosemite Valley. The first one landed there on May 27, 1919. *(Matilda Sample collection.)*

I was only fourteen, but was so husky-looking, nobody asked my age." Herman H. Hoss, a law student, began work as a Camp Curry room clerk that same summer, and was identified with the business for the remainder of his life.

Still another important new employee was Charlie H. Petersen, who in 1918 became the company's first auditor. He was a stenographer for the Fleischacker firm in San Francisco, but had typed and interpreted so many statistical reports for the Price-Waterhouse accounting firm that he had a real grasp of bookkeeping. After an interview, Mother Curry hired Petersen and agreed to pay him $100 per month plus room and board for his wife and self. Before reporting to work, he studied accounting books, then discovered that the Currys "had never had anybody to set up a set of books for them. It was just done on those big government report sheets. They listed all the expenses on one side, revenue on the other, and they had a place for capital outlay. That was it!" Petersen assembled everything into an accounting system which, later, met the approval of an auditor from Price-Waterhouse. "Bookkeeping took ten to twelve hours a day then," he said. "It was a lot of steady work, because there was always some guest arriving or leaving." Mother Curry was his boss, and "she was tops! . . . a great businesswoman and person." Many of Petersen's detailed records were used as documentation for this book.

There were myriad cost entries for Petersen to make that season for there was $36,000 worth of new construction going on at camp. Foster Curry had persuaded the Park Service to allow the addition of bungalows, a new Studio building, a combined bowling alley and social hall, and other minor additions. Despite the war, the Currys were able to secure materials because their orders were modest and they utilized local labor and their own sawmill, which had been built just east of the camp. Like Foster's cabin, the bungalows were rustic in design but modern in detail, and scattered in a grove of cedar and pine trees. Each had a bathroom, electric lights, hot water heater, a clothes closet, and one roll-up canvas side. The first fifteen were such an immediate success with guests that more were planned.

The largest cottage was built to Mother Curry's specifications, faced and sided with cedar bark slabs,

admiration, and they repaid her with conscientious work, well-seasoned with innocent hijinks.

Thirty male employees were away serving Uncle Sam in 1918. Hil Oehlmann, Don Tresidder, and John Fahey were among the absent. All were represented by stars on a giant flag Mother Curry had had made to fly over the camp. Gold stars represented two men killed. A Red Cross booth, in the middle of the camp, was run by fund-raising Mrs. Jilson, and the *Stentor's Call* gave news of the men in service. Even though he had never worked there, Bob Williams's status as son-in-law and serviceman earned him a star on the flag. Because of the Camp and family responsibilities, Foster remained a civilian.

A leg injury kept Herbert Earl Wilson, who had dramatic training, out of uniform, and Foster hired him to put some zip in the firefall. Wilson made bigger fires, which created longer falls, and soon established a record in climbing up the Ledge Trail from camp to the point in fifty-four minutes. He was so enamored of Glacier Point that he wanted his fiancee, whom he met there, to marry him on the Overhanging Rock, but she refused the pleasure. Wilson's Yosemite tenure was to last for fifteen years. Al Littell and Alex Beck were other notable fire builders.

Two teenage boys, whose Yosemite careers were to endure for decades, pitched camp in the Valley that summer. After their "dollars got thin," Syd Ledson recalled, "George and I applied for jobs at Camp Curry.

with an attic, a fireplace, and roofed front porch. After nineteen seasons of tent life, she had a real home—called Mother Curry's bungalow—which was usually overflowing with her daughters and visiting relatives.

Despite emphasis on the comfort and convenience of the new bungalows, the 1919 brochure for Camp Curry boasted that tenting tonight on the fairly new campground had class. All 550 tents were of 10-ounce white duck (a heavy canvas material) . . . "set on board platforms and carpeted with grass rugs." Each had iron beds with "excellent bed springs, floss mattresses, dressers, washstands, and chairs." Each was given "the same service as in a first class hotel." "No consumptives" was another claim in the brochure. Did that mean that anyone with a bad cold would be cross-examined before registration? The brochure's boast of a white kitchen crew betrayed a racist attitude.

Foster made a point of meeting and talking to all guests and, if one possessed some talent, he or she was usually asked to perform in the evening entertainment.

Best of all, the nightly campfires were "the largest and the jolliest in the world. . . ." Like his father, Foster was the chief entertainer and master of ceremonies around the campfire. He gave short informative talks, made graceful introductions, and at 9:00 called for the firefall.[2]

Entertainment was provided by the paid professionals. Mrs. Jilson continued to please with her amusing recitations, and Eddie Horton played classical or popular music on the piano by request. Besides playing piano and organ, he was a race-car driver and soon became the camp's champion fisherman! He played accompaniments for baritone Glen Hood, who sang ballads at night and operated the bowling alley and billiard and pool tables by day.

A youthful San Franciscan with musical ambitions was caretaker of the LeConte Lodge in 1918. "Once Mother Curry asked me to play the piano for her," he said. "Several times I attended some of the evening entertainment; they were occasionally good." Exposure

After Mother Curry's bungalow was built, in 1917, Mrs. Jilson, Foster, Mrs. Curry, Marjorie, and Mary casually posed in front of it. *(YNP collection.)*

2. The time for the firefall varied as the days grew longer.

Arthur Pillsbury and Hil Oehlmann piloted a new Studebaker to Tioga Pass in 1919, a month before the Tioga Road was opened for the year. Logs, bogs, a collapsed bridge, and snowbanks caused two broken springs in the auto and aching backs for the men, who surmounted all obstacles by brute strength.
(Arthur Pillsbury photo; Hil Oehlmann collection.)

in 1919. First, M. Hall McAllister, an influential member of the Sierra Club, donated $5,000 to erect a safe and lasting cableway up the last and steepest 450-foot pitch of Half Dome. Phil Gutleben supervised the installation of parallel steel cables raised on pipe supports, with a plank step every ten feet; then erected an ornate rock and timber gateway at the cable's base. The second event occurred on May 27 when Army Lt. A. S. Krull landed an open cockpit airplane in Leidig's Meadow. Yosemite residents flocked to the site, and W. B. Lewis and Foster Curry were photographed with the daring pilot. A year later a civilian airplane landed, and "A huge delegation of guests from Camp Curry greeted the boys enthusiastically, and a banquet was tendered to them," according to the *California Advertiser*. The following day two flights were made, one with Mother Curry as passenger, and the other for the purpose of taking movies. Before long the Park Service made a ruling prohibiting the landing of airplanes in Yosemite Valley.

The Shaffer brothers operated the defunct Desmond Company's Yosemite concession from April 1 to October 1, 1918. They netted $16,000 in those five months and planned to exercise the option of buying the company, but Dohrmann asked $450,000 more than the Shaffers could manage. Early in 1919 Dohrmann and Larry Harris reorganized, sold stock and signed a twenty-year lease with the government for all the former Desmond concessions in Yosemite.

Mather was still so anti-Curry and pro-hotel development that he aided the new Yosemite National Park Company politically and financially. Although it was contrary to law, and Lane and Albright advised him not to, Mather loaned the company $200,000! "He excused it by taking the position he wasn't charging more than five percent interest, which in those days was nothing in the way of income," Horace Albright told the author. The loan was made secretively, though the Currys heard of it, but not even Foster Curry leaked it to reporters, for Mather's integrity was unquestioned.

Beginning in 1919 the Yosemite National Park Company ran the Sentinel Hotel, Yosemite Lodge, various stores, the High Sierra Camps, and the transportation business. T. E. Farrow was the resident manager in Yosemite, but A. B. C. Dohrmann, sometimes called "Alphabet" Dohrmann, was in charge. He believed in

to Yosemite altered his life, at the same time insuring enjoyment to millions of people, for Ansel Adams became a professional photographer instead of a pianist. Besides nature's attractions, he was beguiled by pretty Virginia Best, daughter of artist Harry Cassie Best, who ran a studio in the Old Village.

The once isolated LeConte Lodge stood in the way of expansion. The Currys wanted to build bungalows around it, to which plans the Sierra Club objected. Mother Curry settled the problem by paying the Gutleben Brothers Construction Company $3,500 to move the memorial to a new site a half mile to the west. In 1919 Phil Gutleben found the stone wall impossible to remove intact, so he took the roof and some of the stones to utilize in a replica. The walls, floor, and steps remained in Camp Curry, providing a picturesque spot for romance.

Funds were finally appropriated in 1918 to rebuild the Ledge Trail. It had been blazed by James Hutchings in the 1870s, and climbed by scores of intrepid mountaineers who ascended over 3,000 feet in a steep, slippery mile-and-a-half staircase way. Even after repairs, it was the most dangerous trail in the Park, and many deaths have marred its history. It is now closed.

There were two notable historic events in Yosemite

Foster Curry happily cooperated with Arthur Pillsbury's desire to photograph a Studebaker on the Overhanging Rock at Glacier Point. (*RCB collection.*)

competition but not hostility, and kept on friendly terms with the Currys. But the Currys were suspicious, for they were the little guy against the monopolistic giant, and they felt that they, the pioneers, were more deserving. "Toot your horn for Camp Curry" was their widely distributed placard and "I'm Strong for Camp Curry" their song and motto.

Continuing in his father's tradition of pressuring the government by demands, propaganda, and outside influences, Foster barraged the infant Park Service for additional concessions. Finally, on February 17, 1920, he was successful in having a new nineteen-year contract signed to run concurrently with the Yosemite National Park Company's already-in-effect twenty-year contact. Broad privileges were granted to the camp, but Foster chafed that it still was not allowed to operate a service garage for repair work, gas, oil, and parts. Before the ink was dry on the contract, he was making himself obnoxious to the Park Service by his complaints and repeated demands.

On the other hand, Foster, like his father, was an earnest student of geology and natural history. In 1920 he supported the pioneer interpretive program instituted by the Park Service. At that time, Harold C. Bryant and Loye H. Miller, eminent naturalists, conducted nature walks and gave illustrated evening talks, anticipating the later, more extensive educational work led by Ansel F. Hall and Carl P. Russell. Both of the latter men authored meaty books about Yosemite's flora, fauna, and human history; in fact, Russell's *One Hundred Years in Yosemite* is still the bible of the plethora of books about Yosemite. Hall began a pioneer museum, and Russell carried on that important project.

Another of Foster's passions was autos. Soon after they were allowed in the Park, he began sponsoring annual economy runs from Los Angeles and the Bay Area to Camp Curry. Winners' names were inscribed on a large silver loving cup that stood on the mantel in the Curry office. In 1915, for example, Arthur C. Pillsbury won the Oakland-Yosemite race via the Big Oak Flat Road, in eight hours and forty-four minutes in his Studebaker Six. Foster was a booster for the much-discussed All-Year Highway, which was begun in 1920. It would run from Merced to Mariposa to Yosemite Valley, partly via the Merced River Canyon.

In 1920, $27,462 of new construction went up at Camp Curry. Electric rates were so low, thanks to the government's new power plant below the Valley, that the camp was completely electrified. No longer would ice have to be cut from Mirror Lake, stored, and used sparingly. Two new bungalows, a bath house, movie booth, an addition to the sawmill, and the long desired garage were also built.

At 10:00 a.m. on June 17, 1920, a significant wedding took place amidst the remnants of the original LeConte Memorial Lodge. Foliage, flowers, and ferns covered the walls, and pine needles carpeted the rock floor. While violinist Carol Weston played Bach's "Air for the G String," Mary L. Curry and Donald B. Tresidder entered unattended to exchange vows. After the ceremony there was an informal reception, and a sumptuous Kussman-prepared breakfast featuring everything from fruit cocktail to creamed chicken, marshmallow sundaes, and wedding cake. Ever-shy, mountain-loving Mary had not wanted a big wedding, so only a few close friends, her mother, sister, brother and family, and Don's mother and sister were present. Part of the honeymoon was spent at Miami Lodge, Ed Huffman's rustic retreat southwest of Fish Camp.

In 1919 Mary had been made Phi Beta Kappa at Yale, then began work toward her doctorate. After her oral, an examining professor said, admiringly, "We have tried to find out everything you know, and everything you don't know, and have failed utterly. You have passed your oral examination not only magna, but summa cum laude." Marriage interrupted her studies but Don's were to continue in the fall at Stanford Medical School.

Oliene, Don's sister, stayed on at Camp Curry as a waitress. She loved to sing, and eventually her rendition of the "Indian Love Call" was established as a feature after the Firefall. Her mother, Sarah Tresidder, was a camp fixture too. She and Mother Curry became such good friends that they wintered together in San Francisco. During summers Mrs. Tresidder shared a bungalow with Oliene in Camp Curry.

Even without Mary, Mother Curry's bungalow was full, for the Williams family was with her—toddler Bobby was underfoot and Marjorie was again pregnant. Bob, who had graduated from Stanford the preceding June, was on vacation.

Foster was extremely well paid for that time, about

VIPs such as Senator Knowland and his wife were guided through the Park by Foster Curry. (*RCB collection.*)

$15,000 yearly, and spent it on hotels, cars, and travel. One winter he and Cherry sailed to Australia and the South Pacific, returning with reels of movies. Katherine said that he helped Don Tresidder through school with loans but felt ill-paid, for he thought that Don was undermining him with Mother Curry.

Foster's sidekick was Wallace Curtis, the camp's associate manager, whose looks and fine voice stirred romantic interest among female employees. Baritone Glen Hood and burly maintenance man Bill Lewis were among Foster's faithful supporters, as was his brother-in-law, Bob. "Foster did a lot for Camp Curry and Yosemite," Williams reflected. "He built up a simply tremendous support with newspapers which resulted in copious publicity."

In 1921, 91,513 people visited Yosemite, and 18,803 of them stayed at Camp Curry in one of the 650 white duck tents, or in the new bungalows, which were advertised as the last word in charm and comfort. Lodging in tents for two was $4.00 per day, while two in a cabin cost $6.00. There were plenty of places in camp to spend money, for there was a beauty shop, which consistently lost money, a barber shop, the bowling alleys and pool hall, and the Studio, where anything from an apple to a fishing license could be purchased. People spent lavishly—the war was only a bad memory, wages were good, and the future promising. Petersen's monthly income statements show that profits were approximately $19,000 in May, 1921, $70,700 in June and $75,300 in July.

Pay varied according to time and responsibilities. For example, in September of 1921 head waitress Louise was paid $56.00 plus tips, while janitor John Powell received $138.70; entertainer Grace Jilson, $381.67; Chef Kussman, $192.27; maintenance superintendent Lewis, $624.23; associate manager Wallace B. Curtis, $225.00; and handyman Alex Beck, $202.00. Bus boys, porters, maids, and the like earned about $45.00 a month and tips. Managerial staff commanded larger salaries. In September 1921, Jennie Curry received $699.67 while Marjorie Curry Williams, who worked regularly, received $1,000. Neither of their husbands was employed at camp. Don was in medical school, and Bob was working in the construction business in San Francisco.

Despite the fact that they were in business to make money, the Curry family's love of Yosemite, and desire to have guests share that feeling, continued to express itself in support of all outdoor activities. In 1921 Foster helped sponsor a program of distinguished lecturers at Memorial Lodge, and urged people to take advantage of the lectures and field trips offered by the Park Service. Both the annual Fourth of July celebration and Indian Field Days were sponsored by Camp Curry, and Foster and Bob competed happily in the latter.

Neither Cherry nor Foster behaved conventionally, and Mother Curry alternatively begged or threatened them to reform. Remonstrations only made Foster defensive and angry; his drinking increased and his conduct deteriorated. Worse, guests were involved. One time he turned a fire hose on a noisy group who had lingered around the campfire. Inevitably, complaints were filed against Foster, and he was warned by Superintendent Lewis that he must reform or face eviction. The superintendent had the power to evict undesirable people from the Park for a year, and only an order from the Secretary of the Interior could countermand him. Several times Foster's contrite promises, and his mother's apologetic distress, persuaded Lewis to give him another chance.

At one time Foster fled family and duties on a sort of "see how you manage without me" strike, then wrote an apology. In answer, his mother assured him, "There's no one I love better on earth . . . and forgetting the things that are behind, let us press forward . . . to make Camp Curry not only the biggest but the best camp on earth."

Foster's vows were negated when he physically abused a frightened driver whose stopped car blocked

Marjorie Williams tamed her wild horse, Pico, so well that she was able to ride him the length of the John Muir Trail, accompanied by her husband, Bob.
(Williams Family collection.)

Foster on the narrow zig-zags above Glacier Point. Afterwards, the tourist filed a complaint with Superintendent Lewis, whose patience promptly ended. Not even Mother Curry could dissuade him from evicting Foster, but she did gain promises of time and no publicity. Foster could finish out the season, and his departure could be explained in any way she liked, Lewis said, so long as Foster left for good when the camp closed.

During the remainder of the summer, stormy family councils were frequent. Since Foster owned a one-fourth interest in the company, he couldn't be fired summarily. Attorneys were consulted, and Foster's stock was eventually purchased by family members. Since Bob Williams had recently sold his factory in Illinois, he furnished the cash to buy in for himself, Marjorie, and Don Tresidder, who repaid him later. Green and Mother Curry borrowed heavily to cover the reminder of the $100,000 due Foster in payment of his quarter interest.

Camp Curry closed September 30, 1921. Four days later Mrs. Curry issued a press release that was picked up by many California newspapers.

> Mr. Foster Curry and Wallace B. Curtis are no longer connected with the management of the Curry Camping Company.
> Camp Curry will continue, as heretofore, under the management of Mrs. D. A. Curry, who has been in control since the death of her husband, David A. Curry five years ago, and who was associated with him in the organization and management of the camp twenty-three years ago.

Several newspapers added that Bill Lewis, foreman of Camp Curry, had also tendered his resignation and that the future management of Camp Curry was to be in the hands of Mother Curry and Rufus L. Green.

Of all the clippings supplied by a press clipping bureau, and saved by the family, only one contained an original comment, and that was in the *Oakland Tribune* of October 11. Since publisher Joseph R. Knowland had stayed at Camp Curry, and had been guided to the Mariposa Grove by Foster, it may be assumed that he or someone on the staff contacted Foster for first hand information;

> Foster Curry states that his withdrawal from the company, together with Curtis and Lewis, became necessary because of the dissension among some of the minority stockholders. Curry will take a three months' vacation, after which he will enter the hotel business in California.

He did not exit gracefully from the place he loved, and where he had spent twenty-two of his thirty-three years, but bitterly—denouncing his family and vowing never to return to Yosemite.

Washington B. "Dusty" Lewis, the first superintendent of Yosemite National Park—1916 to 1929. *(YNP collection.)*

8   The Last Battles

Less than two weeks after the announcement had been made of Foster's "resignation," a number of newspapers carried news of a much happier event at Camp Curry, which showed the sympathy and regard that local residents had for Jennie Curry.

> One of the most notable social events of the season occurred this evening when the residents of the Yosemite Valley extended their best wishes and congratulations to Mrs. D. A. Curry on her birthday at a reception held at the studio at Camp Curry. The reception was largely attended by the older residents, the government officials and staffs of the other hotels and camps in the valley, and numerous messages of congratulations were received from other parts of the state. The heads of departments and the other employees of Camp Curry, were the hosts of the evening and arranged the party as a surprise to Mrs. Curry.
>
> Mrs. Curry has resided in the valley for twenty-three years, and is the senior in service of those engaged in public camping business in Yosemite. Her kindliness of character is shown from the fact that all her employees and many residents of the valley constantly refer to her as "Mother Curry," and her vigor and strength are shown by the fact that, at the close of the busiest season of her life, she is now actively superintending improvements, running into many thousands of dollars, in preparation for next season. Mrs. Curry ranks as one of the most successful business women of the state, having been for many years in active control of the largest hotel camp in the country.

In subsequent weeks, plans and arrangements were made toward a reorganization of the Curry Camping Company, announced in a January 22, 1922 press release. It stated that Foster Curry's interests had been sold to family members, Mrs. Curry would continue as president of the Company as well as manager of Camp Curry, and Robert T. Williams and Donald B. Tresidder, "exceptionally well qualified" men, would serve as assistant managers. Williams had had considerable business background, including managerial positions, but no training in resort work, whereas Tresidder knew the lower sorts of camp jobs but little else. His sole business experience had been a stint as an

Yosemite residents showed their regard for Jennie Curry by giving her a surprise party on her sixtieth birthday. *(YP&CC collection.)*

auto salesman in Indiana. Besides that, he had taught school there, and demonstrated ambition and tenacity in pursuing his medical studies. Both men were Stanford graduates and ex-Army Air Force pilots; Williams had served overseas. What truly gained them their new responsibilities was their love and loyalty toward Mother Curry, the camp, and Yosemite—and the fact that they were married to her two darling daughters didn't hurt.

Camp Curry's 1922 "Yosemite Road Guide" advertising folder, showed other changes indicating total

Assistant managers Williams and Tresidder. *(YNP collection.)*

At 8 p.m. on June 2, 1922, the regular "LET 'ER GO GALLAGHER" call echoed up, and the firefall cascaded down, but the new Stentor was calling from Stockton rather than Camp Curry, and his voice was heard by a 100,000 people all over California instead of just the 1,000 or so gathered around the traditional campfire. That night the entire Curry entertainment staff broadcast their evening program on the *Stockton Record's* KWG radio station and over loudspeakers rather than on the Camp Curry stage.

Thirty-one new bungalows, costing over $32,000, were built during the 1922 season. Only number 90 differed from the others in that it was larger and had a stone fireplace. It belonged to Rufus Green, who paid $2,135 for it, and it was reserved for his family. The Green cabin, Mother Curry's bungalow and Foster's cabin, which the Tresidders had taken over, were the only private residences at camp until a fourth non-rental house was built in 1923 for Charles Petersen, the comptroller. After he had received his Certified Public Accountant certification, Mother Curry hired him back for $5,000 a year and free housing.

Mother Curry's attention to employees was extensive but not permissive. Once, three girls from Fresno reported to work, and she assigned them all to the laundry. "But I came up to work in the dining room,' one protested. "No, dear," her new boss corrected gently, "you came up to work for Camp Curry." During the 1920s she kept personnel lists in a ledger book. Names, addresses, dates available, and possible position were noted for each year. She had to be a shrewd judge of character to adequately fill the 107 camp jobs that ranged from bookkeeper, pan washer, chocolate dipper, towel shaker, to pin setter, lifeguard, tailor, and watchman. Application forms were specific:

Applicants who are strong and willing and accustomed to work are always welcome. . . The work is hard and calls for people who are rugged. . . If you cannot carry a tray, do not apply for a dining room job. If you cannot make a bed, sweep a room and care for a bathroom exquisitely, do not apply as a maid. If you are not willing to keep the grounds clean, empty the slop-jars, and "rustle" the baggage, do not apply as porter. . . A desire to spend a summer in Yosemite is not sufficient qualifications for a position with us . . . On the other hand. . . many employees return year after year. . . The atmosphere, both climatic and

family involvement. Mary Curry Tresidder was listed as secretary and Marjorie Curry Williams as hostess. Additionally, the folder announced that Chef Kussman, Mrs. Jilson, and Glen Hood were returning. Mrs. Emily Lane would oversee the Kiddie Kamp, which had been established the previous year. Its creation had been inspired by the "What will we do with the children" plaint often voiced by Marjorie and Bob Williams. Their children, Bobbie, Jr., and tiny Marjorie Jane, were regulars at the fenced playground, whose most popular feature was a miniature train.

social, the association with interesting people, life in the open where Nature is at her best, all these give the zest to life that offsets the fatigue of hours of labor.

Often Mother Curry penned such notations as "wept, moody, untidy, crabby, not strong enough, left without notice, hikes too much, threw food, smoking, pert, smart aleck" beside the unfortunates' names. In addition, she listed employees in classes I, II, and III. Of the five young men who made her first class in 1923, two stayed on it far beyond that summer. One was Wendell Otter, who served the Company for forty-four years; the other was George Goldsworthy, who remained for thirty-six years.

Aside from Mother Curry's evaluations, she solicited opinions from department heads before rehiring seasonal help. Those who particularly appealed to her in appearance and personality were likely to be assigned jobs as waitresses and porters, but demonstrated merit brought advancement from the pantry or other more obscure jobs. Merit equated bonuses. Inserted in the ledger were laundry lists, inventories, stock required—e.g., sixty-five dozen sheets for 1923, and a page of explicit directions for maids. Today the book is a treasure trove of nuts-and-bolts information.

Mother Curry astounded a reporter from *Sunset Magazine*, who gave readers of the August 1922 issue a breathless account of her activities:

> . . . She possesses the knack of being everywhere at all times through the day. When anything needs deciding or adjusting, somehow she is on hand with the best solution.
> They all come to her; officials of the Valley for conference; stage drivers seeking a word of authority; the autoist who couldn't do the Sierras on high and who wants his carburetor adjusted immediately; the tent-girl who has misplaced two towels; poor people who haven't money enough to stay the desired day longer; the geologist who seeks a terminal moraine; the hiker, who has lost her camera on the trail and wants to borrow cold cream; the teacher collecting flowers for the school herbarium; the soprano who wishes to entertain with the "Rosary;" the man who insists on a tent to himself when hundreds are being turned away; the lady who dislikes cornmeal in her muffin; the baker whose supplies have not arrived; the waitress who has bad news from home; the man who doesn't approve of governmental polices in the park; the youth and the maid whose eyes are a little dazzled by moonlight shining in lonesome and lovely places. For each, Mrs. Curry has a swift unerring answer of gentle reasonableness, and the questioner goes away feeling that he is to be commended for

bringing the matter to light and that this is the best of all worlds. . . .

Besides these functions, she was supervising her daughters and sons-in-law, and pressuring the Park Service for more concessions, specifically a service garage instead of a mere storage garage, which was all Camp Curry was allowed. As early as January 22 she had begun her campaign with a letter to Horace Albright, then field director, in which she requested the privilege of selling gas and oil, washing cars, doing oiling, greasing, and minor repairs, adding:

> The existence of Camp Curry's splendid garage causes our guests to expect such service, and their reaction at finding they cannot obtain it is inevitably unfavorable. . . The Y.N.P. (Yosemite National Park Company) has 60 of its own cars to keep in order. Last year there were 1,500 cars on the floor of the valley at the peak of the season. With all the good will in the world, the other company cannot cope with the situation . . .

Don Tresidder and his sister, Oliene, took part in the evening entertainment at Camp Curry. *(SS collection.)*

A preserved file shows that she kept writing letters without securing the desired privileges. Moreover, Park Service officials stated that she prodded Williams and Tresidder to bring outside pressure to bear, as had her husband and son in the past. The 1923 Franchise Report claimed that her sons-in-law were inexperienced, temperate young fellows, embarrassed and intimidated by her insistence on battle and her opinion "that with the change in management, all the fighters in the Curry Camping Company were either dead or kicked out." For all her business acumen, her permissive mother's heart disturbed her usual perspective and upset family relations.

Foster's dismissal, necessary as it had been, rankled and was much in her thoughts as the financial negotiations dragged on. The settlement was complex, as partially explained in her September 18, 1922 letter to the American Surety Company.

> "The Curry Camping Company" is undergoing reorganization and will hereafter be known as the "CURRY CAMPING COMPANY." This has been for the purpose of financing a purchase of part of the stock from one stockholder by the remaining stockholders by means of issuing preferred stock, of which about $50,000 has been issued. All other conditions concerning the company remain practically the same as hitherto.

Reorganization was not completed until August 1923, partly because of governmental requirements. Despite all the problems and emotional overtones, the new management team directed Camp Curry through the most successful season in its history. Records show

By the 1920s, the Village Store had acquired storage appendages. (*Amy L. Alexander collection.*)

Population and mail volume had increased so much that a separate structure was built to house the Yosemite Valley Post Office. (*Amy L. Alexander collectiom.*)

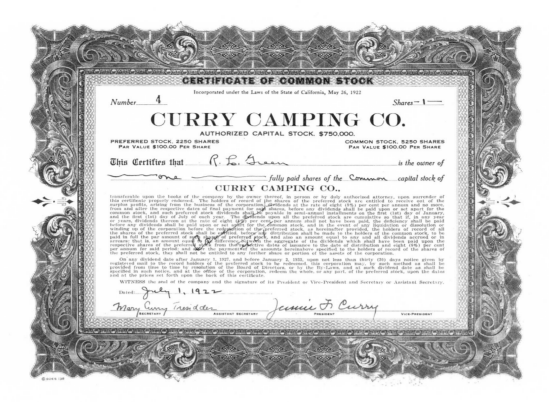

that after expenses there was a net profit of $54,000. One of the larger expenditures was "Compensation of Officers."

	Salary	Board
Jennie F. Curry, President	$12,000.00	$211.00
R. L. Green, Trustee & Dir	3,825.00	150.00
Mary C. Tresidder, Sec'y	3,350.00	150.00
Don Tresidder, Mgr	3,150.00	150.00
Marjorie C. Williams, Hostess	2,300.00	120.00
R. T. Williams, Mgr	4,200.00	120.00

Camp Curry's rolling stock consisted of six trucks, a Mercer, a Premier, a Cadillac coupe, and a Cadillac touring car. From horse and buggy to Cadillacs, from seven to 650 tents, from pennies to $12,000—Jennie Curry had reason for wonder and pride. Her character, family loyalty, and the increased and able assumption of responsibilities by Williams and Tresidder brought a spirit of unanimity to the "team" by 1923. Their forte was cooperation rather than combat, and this attitude established good rapport with local and national Park Service personnel.

Before the February 7 and 8 concessionaires' meeting with Director Mather and the new Secretary of the Interior, Albert B. Fall, Albright and W. B. Lewis pre-

pared a detailed twenty-six page "Abstract of Operations and Activities" of the Desmond enterprise, the Yosemite National Park Company, and the Curry Camping Company. On the whole, the thirteen recommendations appended to the report favored status quo for Camp Curry and expansions for the Yosemite National Park Company. The single-minded Mather insisted that the latter company proceed with the building of the long-promised modern hotel on the Valley floor.

On February 7 and 8, 1923 a polite confrontation was adjudicated by Secretary Fall in Washington, D.C. A. B. C. Dohrmann and Larry Harris represented the Yosemite National Park Company. Mrs. Curry, Don Tresidder, P. M. Lansdale, and attorney Charles R. Price were the Curry envoys. Several congressmen and Park Service officials were also present. Eyewitness Albright contended that Mrs. Curry needed no help in influencing Fall. "She had a personal approach, a charming way of expressing herself," Albright said. "Her love for Yosemite came forth with every turn. The fact of the matter is that she was pretty smart in the way she handled that. She approached Fall with the fact that she had been in the Valley for so many years, that no

Collegiate aquatic stars gave swimming and diving exhibitions in the Camp Curry "tank." (*Hensleigh Family collection.*)

one loved Yosemite more than she and her family, and they longed for the day they could be in there all year round."

Albright added that her words and appearance melted Fall, and it became a quest for Mr. Mather as to how much he could avoid giving her. On the hearing's second day, the Curry representatives showed specific, petty incidents of discrimination by the Yosemite National Park Company. For example, its employees were given free transportation on the railroads, and Curry employees weren't, and the Yosemite National Park Company information booklets did not even mention its rival. Such misrepresentation, or discrimination, seemed to surprise Dohrmann and Harris. Additionally, the 172-page transcript reveals that Don Tresidder spoke ably and made the point that Camp Curry was a substantial and complex plant with such conveniences as a bakery, a soda fountain, a studio, a bowling alley, and a factory that would produce 150 gallons of ice cream a day. "We are, sir, a community. Our obligation, Mr. Secretary, to our public is to render the people each and every form of service for which

there is sufficient public demand at Camp Curry. . . I, speaking for the second generation, looking to the future, with the great development that we know will come with the opening of the Merced Yosemite all-year road, am only asking, on behalf of the present management and the second generation, the right to share the large business that we know is coming to the park— a business which we feel will tax the capacity of every single concessionaire."

In response, Dohrmann and Harris defended their contracted right to provide services as exclusive. Harris felt that the contract allowed the Yosemite National Park Company, and no one else, to satisfy needs as they arose, but his comments, as indeed was all of the testimony, were low-keyed and without rancor.

On February 9, 1923, Fall extended Camp Curry's privileges to allow sale of gasoline and oil, minor garage repairs, building of housekeeping units, and sale of family groceries, meals, and prepared foods to guests and visitors. Jennie Curry had faced Goliath and won! Dohrmann did not take the loss gracefully, but petitioned for a rehearing, which was denied by Fall.

After that, Jennie wired her lawyer "It is a glorious victory," and redoubled her efforts to have the new activities ready for Camp Curry's opening.

Although Dohrmann was dedicated to Yosemite and the Company, his interests were diversified, embracing a multitude of companies as well as civic activities in San Francisco. At age sixty-four in 1922, his personal fortune was assured, and he enjoyed foreign travel. He could not, and did not, have an exhaustive grasp of everyday operations. That was Tom Farrow's job, but he, Dohrmann, was apologetic when he realized that there had been discrimination against Curry. Like Mrs. Curry, Dohrmann was a remarkable organizer who commanded loyalty. He was in and out of Yosemite so often and was so kind that employees at Yosemite Lodge regard him with great respect. Similarly, Mrs. Ellen Cook, manager of the Sentinel Hotel, where he stayed in the winter, was devoted to him and his family of a wife, six sons, and two daughters.

Son Bob recalled, "Dad was born a blue baby and

Sentinel manager and chef Ellen C. Cook, with business associates from Yellowstone. *(Hart N. Cook, Jr. collection.)*

never could get insurance or get out on the trails. But he saw to it that we kids had every opportunity to hike, climb, camp out, and participate in sports. Though Father's aegis, Yosemite National Park was far more than a place of surpassing beauty; to us it was a second home. My first job was picking up papers with a pointed stick. Next, I delivered telegrams, and then, when I was about fourteen, I worked up at the Tuolumne Meadows Lodge under Mrs. McCracken, who was a great boss. At the end of the summer, Father asked her, 'How did my boy do? 'Oh, fine, Mr. Dohrmann,' she answered, 'Just fine. We call him Useless around here.'"

During 1923 and 1924 the Yosemite situation wrangled on with a constant undercurrent of rivalry, discontent, charge, and counter-charge. Plans for the long-anticipated hotel stayed on blueprints, even though the construction of the All-Year-Highway up the Merced River Canyon was proceeding, with completion scheduled for the summer of 1926. In May 1923 Dohrmann sent out scores of letters to former guests, asking whether or not a hotel should be built to replace Yosemite Lodge. Unanimously, those responding, including Levi Strauss, Hall McAllister, and C. H. Crocker, were against the erection of a resort hotel. They preferred the existing rustic cabins, because of their privacy, charm, and unobtrusive sites beneath sky-reaching pine and cedar trees.

Such unison duplicated Dohrmann's own feeling that comfort and service were already provided in a friendly, homelike atmosphere. He was progressive but also a realist, and his caution was bolstered by "Desmond's folly," the basement pit and foundation of the Grizzly Hotel. In 1921, however, Dohrmann had reactivated Desmond-built buildings at Merced Lake, closed since the war, as a boys' camp. The emphasis was on sports, and the boys laid out tennis and basketball courts and a baseball diamond, on a large flat, where they were coached by college athletes. There were hiking tours, fishing, boating, swimming, and horseback riding for groups of city boys from wealthy homes. Bob Dohrmann remembered that the camp psychiatrist was the only drawback. "Mother told me that she got his report on me, and decided there was no future—she might as well shoot me!"

In 1923 the lodges at Merced Lake, Tenaya Lake, and Tuolumne Meadows became the sites of hikers' camps. Park Superintendent W. B. Lewis was the idea man, and he dispatched naturalist Carl P. Russell to find spots for other camps within reasonable walking distance from one another. By 1924 there were four

Bob Williams, Mother Curry, Secretary of the Interior Hubert Work, and National Park Service Director Stephen T. Mather, after the merger. (*J. V. Lloyd photo.*)

High Sierra Camps, which proved popular and, in altered form, exist today. They were an innovative concept and a shining example of a joint effort between the Park Service and a concessionaire to encourage visitors to, as John Muir wrote, "climb the mountains and get their good tidings."

All during 1924 there was bickering between the companies, evidenced by a mishmash of petty complaints, charges, and counter charges. W. B. Lewis, Albright, and Mather were weary of wrangling in a place so beautiful and inspiring, and gained a formidable ally in the new Secretary of Interior, Hubert Work. By late 1924 Work, an impatient man, told Mather that the rival companies would have to merge or be replaced. Albright was sent west to negotiate, and his first instruction was to Dohrmann and Harris to repay the $200,000 loan made to the company by Mather. Once that was underway, merger discussions began between the principals. "It didn't take long, and there wasn't much trouble," Albright recalled. "I thought the most remarkable suggestion made by the Yosemite National Park Company directors was that Don Tresidder be made president of the new company. That suited me fine. I liked Don and thought he had a lot of ability." Tresidder was named president and general manager, with Bob Williams, who had thought he would be number one, second in command. To his credit, Williams worked faithfully for his brother-in-law.

The title of the merged companies was the Yosemite Park and Curry Co., soon shortened to the YP&C Co., or the Curry Company. A. B. C. Dohrmann became president of the Board of Directors, whose members included Mrs. Curry, Rufus Green, Tresidder, Williams, P. W. Lansdale, I. W. Harris, A. J. Esberg, Harry Chandler, publisher of the *Los Angeles Times*, H. M. Sherman, M. H. Whittier, and J. S. Drum. The merger and the officers were announced on February 21, 1925.

The Park Service promised the new company preferential treatment, although the long-standing permits of small operators such as Best's, Degnan's Foley's, Boysen's, and Pillsbury's remained, with "the understanding that these smaller operations were not to be enlarged and were to lapse upon the death of their holders."

Mrs. Curry gave a statement to reporters.

Myself and family will be actively engaged in the management of the new company. We bespeak from our old friends a continuation of the hearty support and good will so generously accorded us in the past. Our friends will find in Yosemite the same cordial welcome and spirit of hospitality that has distinguished Camp Curry for over a quarter of a century. We are glad to be associated with a group of men, leaders in civic and state affairs throughout all California, who came into Yosemite solely to forward the development of one of California's greatest assets. We hope to form many new friendships and to cement the old and the new in a work that will merit the enduing confidence and patronage of the public.

After years of battle between rival concessionaires, Yosemite and its owners, the citizens of the United States, were the victor.

The Sentinel Hotel was festive during winter holidays. *(J. V. Lloyd photo; SS collection.)*

9   Dr. Tresidder's Practice

At the age of thirty, Dr. Donald Bertrand Tresidder, instead of treating patients, was president and general manager of a resort business. His background, family heritage, and education had been medically oriented, his goal, and indeed promise to his father, had been to become a doctor. Yet he was so challenged and satisfied with his role as resort operator that by Christmas 1925 he wrote of the business as one he loved. Despite his manifold Yosemite responsibilities and his devotion to them, Don fulfilled his internship at a San Francisco hospital during the winter months in 1927, and finished his dissertation on public health problems in national parks, primarily Yosemite. Thus he kept his filial vow and earned his M.D. degree, but he never practiced medicine.

From 1922 until 1925 Camp Curry operations had been only partly under his direction. Suddenly, after the merger in early 1925, he was in charge of the Sentinel Hotel, which had 71 guest rooms and numerous buildings; Glacier Point Hotel, with 90 guest rooms in two structures; Big Trees Lodge with 14 cabins; the High Sierra Camps; and Yosemite Lodge, hub of the merged Yosemite National Park Company. There was a total capacity (pillow count) of 1,260 guests, who were housed in 176 redwood cabins, 197 canvas cabins, and tents. A dormitory housed employees.

Tresidder was boss of various unit and store managers, the garage, transportation division, Old Village general store, meat market, print shop, warehouses, and photo studios. A less dedicated man might have fled, but he observed, studied, worked nights, listened, learned, and thrived. He had able guidance from Mother Curry and Thomas E. Farrow, the hotel manager first employed by Dohrmann in 1918. Farrow was experienced and capable but lacked the personal warmth and friendliness needed in work with the public. Contemporaries recall him as a "cold fish" but an able administrator. Mather so disliked him that he instructed directors of the merged companies that Farrow be dismissed even though he was one of the largest stockholders in the new corporation. Despite his involuntary 1925 retirement, Farrow offered to remain during the period of transition, and worked with Tresidder in the new offices of the Curry organization formerly occupied by the Yosemite National Park Company. These offices and a barbershop were in the old Cosmopolitan Building, originally a pioneer bathhouse and saloon.

A measure of Farrow's and Tresidder's worth was expressed by the latter in a handwritten letter at Christmas time 1925.

Dear Mr. Farrow:

Attached is a check for $3,000.00 which was unanimously voted to you by the Directors of the Yosemite Park and Curry Co. at the last meeting. The board took this action in recognition of the sincere, unrelenting, conscientious work performed by you since the new company came into existence. It is in no sense to be construed as a gift because you've earned it yet neither is it to be taken as a measure of your value to the new company because the Directors feel such unusual service as you have rendered cannot be purchased.

As I look back on our summer together I wonder how I ever worked next door to you for three years without ever sensing the real you. I confess that I had a wholly distorted and erroneous picture of you and felt an open mistrust and hostility.

My repentance and awakening began the first day of our meeting in Mr. Esberg's office following the consolidation. You stated then that you would serve in any capacity to the best of your ability, for a day, a week, a month or just so long as you could be of use.

You not only kept that promise in the strictest sense but you did more. I feel that you gave me a loyalty and unswerving, faithful service that no one else approached except Mother Curry. You endured a difficult and inevitably distasteful position in calm silence. You contributed more to the success of the season than any one person—and for all this I am grateful as are all the Directors.

But I personally am indebted to you for more than all this. There has gradually been revealed to me the fine human qualities of a man whom I had wholly misunderstood. You have listened sympathetically to my many perplexities—you have been very patient with my many mistakes and blunders. In spite of youth, and inexperience I have always felt that you were friendly, helpful, and anxious to see me grow up to the job. . . .

Eventually Tresidder absorbed many of Farrow's

Old Village on a summer day. Curry Company store at left; Degnan's to the right. (*H. R. Sault collection.*)

administrative capabilities which, combined with his charisma, made him an outstanding resort man. "No task, however burdensome or exacting, and no responsibility, however grave, did he fail to assume if he conceived it to be his to undertake," his friend Hil Oehlmann stated. "Don's genuine appreciation of the purposes for which the park existed extended far beyond his interest in the success of the business which he skillfully directed. And in that business his major satisfaction consisted in the part his enterprise played in serving the needs of the many thousands of guests who came here."

As Foster Curry had been, Tresidder was a great favorite with the employees, who liked his enthusiasm and friendliness. He continued his mother-in-law's policy of sponsoring Indian Field Days, and an annual employee picnic, coupled with a program of their skits and songs, and he knew most of the help by name. Women and children adored him and he could even charm irate guests. Once he escorted a late-arriving couple to the only empty tent at Camp Curry, which was next to the laundry. When they asked what all the noise was, Don answered quickly, "Oh, that's a waterfall. That's what people come here to see."

Naturally he made mistakes, and his youth, ambition, and aggressiveness earned him detractors, but they were outnumbered by supporters, especially female ones. His enthusiasms were intense, and friends enjoyed his exuberance at a good catch of fish, a sunset, or a Stanford football victory. Even after he was president of the Company, he would act as a on the bus tour to the "bear pits" where the animals feasted on

For years, Indian Field Days were an exciting annual event. *(SS collection.)*

Herbert Earl Wilson, entertainer, lecturer, author, and friend to the Indians, at Camp Curry with singer Glen Hood. *(H. E. Wilson collection.)*

garbage on a floodlit platform. His passion for Yosemite showed in his extra-curricular activities. A horseback ride astride "Pal" was usually the first order of the day. Longtime employee Florence Morris told the author that "it was a great occasion for the local children to be picked up for a short ride by 'Uncle Don.'" Both he and Mary loved and wanted children, but she could not complete pregnancies, which was a grief to them.

During the summer of 1925 they inaugurated canoeing on the Merced River, but that was soon halted by a "No Boating" edict. Earlier, Phil Gutleben revealed, Park Service officials had seriously considered a proposal to build a series of dams within the Valley so as to make the Merced placid enough for boats.

To give the firefall-less Yosemite Lodge a competitive feature, Tresidder okayed a "firedive" there. For several summers, Pete Peterson, a champion swimmer and diver, donned cotton covered coveralls just before 9:00 p.m. At that hour, when the firefall fell above Camp Curry, a match was applied to Peterson's costume, and from a twenty-foot-high platform, he made a swan dive into the Lodge pool where the spectacular flames went out with a mighty whoosh. Peterson suffered a number of burns before the act was ended. Such feats as that, and the nightly bear feeding, reflected the immaturity of both the Company and the Park Service, who supported vaudeville-type entertainment in Yosemite. "Get the people in, and keep 'em happy" was the philosophy then, partly because the Park Service needed concerned voters to pressure congressmen for funds to build roads, trails, and campgrounds.

The ebullient Tresidder was so impressed when an experienced fisherman caught a twenty-seven-inch trout weighing almost ten pounds, that he exhibited it at the nightly Camp Curry program, saying, "I would give $25 if I could catch one like this!" Jim Lloyd, information specialist for the Park, purveyed such information to the press in frequent releases, and the *Stockton Record* printed most of them. A December 6, 1926 *Record* quoted Tresidder's delight in his work: "The appeal of the job is that you are constantly meeting interesting people from all parts of the world. . . . To meet them in this place is a pleasure, and to make them enjoy, understand and see Yosemite is even a greater pleasure."

Once he had settled in as president, Tresidder offered Hil Oehlmann the job of superintendent of the commercial division. After graduation from the University of California as an economics major in 1917 and service with the Army Engineers in France, Hil had gone to work for an import-export firm in San Francisco. By 1925 he was with a merchandise brokerage firm, married and city-oriented although Yosemite's high country was always his favorite vacation site. He welcomed the opportunity of returning to Yosemite to manage all purchasing, storage, and sales. His first office was a tiny frame building in the Village where his staff consisted of a secretary, and his equipment was a typewriter, adding machine, and telephone. From the beginning, Oehlmann's appointment was beneficial to the Company for he was intelligent, experienced, tough, and single-mindedly loyal. A large 1927–31 correspondence file reveals that those qualities were leavened by humor. On July 20, 1927, for example, he

Purchasing agent Oehlmann and his air-conditioned office. *(Hil Oehlmann collection.)*

addressed a marketing firm in Merced: "While the commission houses in San Francisco are trying to sell us Merced tomatoes as being the best on the market, we received from your Association fruit about the size of apricots. . . our apricots have been arriving in a condition somewhat resembling jam."

Forecasting and stocking for visitor needs over the three major holidays, Memorial, Independence, and Labor days, was a yearly nightmare for Oehlmann. In four frantic days in July 1933, customers of the Village Store bought 6,865 loaves of bread, 18,696 pounds of meat, 47,712 quarts of milk, 4,800 dozen eggs, and 3,700 pounds of butter, not to mention mountains of ice cream, canned goods and clothes, boots, and sunglasses. After enumerating the monstrous accounts, a reporter for the *Mariposa Gazette* concluded that Oehlmann was an unsung hero "and the Lord help him if he ever over or under buys."

Besides Oehlmann and Williams, Tresidder named other strong, experienced men to his administrative team. His executive assistant was another ex-Camp Curry man, Paul Shoe, and Herman Hoss was personnel manager as well as secretary to the new company. Hoss had worked his way through college and Stanford Law School with summer jobs at Camp Curry, then served in Yosemite as U. S. Court Commissioner for several years. Bob Williams headed the traffic department, which his secretary Florence

Mabel Boysen, who ran Boysen's Studio after her husband's death, and postmaster "Alex" Alexander were mainstays of the Yosemite community.
(Amy L. Alexander collection.)

north side of the Valley. From west to east they were the Park Service's two story administrative building, the museum, which became a focal point of interpretation, Pillsbury's, Best's, and Boysen's Studios, a large post office and employee housing upstairs, and Foley's Studio. Arthur Pillsbury's Studio was the most pretentious of the new structures. Besides the customer display area, it contained a modern picture processing lab and an auditorium that could seat 450 people. Newsreels, a comedy, and a feature picture, accompanied by organ music, were presented twice a week. Unfortunately, the theater burned down in 1927, and soon afterwards the innovative but discouraged photographer sold his shop and contents to the Curry Company. Mather invited Interior Secretary Hubert Work to preside at dedicatory exercises for the new

Morris recalled, ". . . started as a very simple department but evolved into a very complicated business. Besides arranging for tour parties, we handled the solicitations of conventions, and, after they were booked, took care of their reservations for hotel or lodge accommodations, meeting places, entertainment. . . . It disseminated information to the hotel and various other departments of the Company operations—advising everyone concerned of the groups arriving in the Park."

The traffic department filed, and secured approval of, bus schedules with the California Commerce Commission and kept railroad and travel agents all over America informed of connections and rates. Williams traveled considerably to attract new business —from half a dozen people to 200 or more—while Miss Morris handled voluminous correspondence on arrangements.

For the first years after the consolidation, "the average employee didn't seem to realize that there had been a merger of the rival companies, and the competition between the Camp Curry and Yosemite Lodge continued unabated with practically no fraternization between employees of the two units," Wendell Otter observed. "It was much different in outlying units, such as Glacier Point or Tuolumne Meadows, where most of us were aware that it was all one big company."

Besides the merger, there were other significant events in Yosemite Valley in 1925, all inspired and pushed by Mather and the Park Service. Under his supervision seven attractive buildings, of wood and rock, were built in the huge semicircle on the sunny

Wendell Otter, one of Mother Curry's boys, rose from porter to a management position with the Curry Company.
(Wendell Otter collection.)

Post Office and the entire complex on April 15, 1925. That night Tresidder hosted a banquet at the Sentinel Hotel for all the dignitaries. Mather was delighted with the effects of the merger and the New (present) Yosemite Village, and promptly issued orders to have the old, ramshackled buildings razed. At the same time, he was agitating for the replacement of the dowager Sentinel Hotel, Degnan's, and the general store in the Old Village. Rome was not unbuilt in a decade, however, and his master plan was not completed for years.

Tresidder had far more than public relations and day-to-day, month-to-month operations to oversee. To secure a long-term lease with the Park Service, the Curry Company had promised to rebuild the kitchen and dining room at Camp Curry, replace the store and warehouse, modernize Yosemite Lodge, and construct a new hotel. Negotiations, plans, financing, and overall design rested on his shoulders and those of the directors who were an active group. Priority was given to the hotel, partly due to the contract, pressure from Mather, and because more accommodations would be needed for the anticipated influx of visitors arriving on the nearly completed All-Year Highway. Kenneyville was chosen as the site, and stakes were driven in by Secretary Work to mark the general placement of the hotel on April 13, 1925. While stables were still a necessary adjunct to resort operations, stage space, equipment, and equestrian populations had been drastically reduced by auto usage. Consequently the stables were moved to a smaller quarters adjacent to public campgrounds, and Kenneyville's old buildings were torn down. With a meadow to the west, forest to the east, Royal Arches towering on the north, and Half Dome and Glacier Point to the south, the cleared site was superb.

Gilbert Stanley Underwood was selected as architect, and by late 1925 preliminary plans were being studied. One of Farrow's last jobs for the merged company was to suggest alterations to make the building suitable yet economical. He thought a sixth-floor roof garden "an artificial scheme," and a separate writing room "not a direct revenue producer." Farrow's pragmatism was overruled by Mather's concept of a luxury hotel

and, ultimately, an enormous lobby, numerous public rooms, and 82 bedrooms were planned. These rooms and guest cottages, to be built later, would accommodate 400 people. Mary Curry Tresidder had a subtle but definite influence, especially in the interior decorations of the hotel, and may have suggested its name, Ahwahnee, the Indian word for "deep grassy valley."

Construction began in the spring of 1926, and progress was reported faithfully in the *Stockton Record* and *Mariposa Gazette*. Huge sugar pine trees were felled at Hazel Green, still owned by Mrs. Curry, trucked to the sawmill at Camp Curry, and cut into massive beams for the dining room. Tons of flagstone and jasper were

Arch Rock forms a picturesque tunnel above El Portal on the All-Year Highway, which opened on August 1, 1926. *(YP&CC collection.)*

Before Yosemite's winter isolation was ended with the completion of the All-Year Highway, there were festivities at the Sentinel Hotel. *(Hart N. Cook, Jr. collection.)*

quarried in Mariposa County for decorative use inside and out, and 680 tons of structural steel were hauled in.

The laying of the cornerstone took place on August 1, 1926 as part of an unprecedented two-day Diamond Jubilee Celebration of the effective discovery of Yosemite Valley in 1851.[1] Festivities had begun at 10 a.m. on July 31 with the ribbon-cutting ceremony for the All-Year Highway. Mather and California's governor, Friend Richardson, were the principal speakers, and then led an auto caravan over the unpaved new road, stopping at Briceburg and El Portal to unveil bronze plaques dedicated to the convict laborers who had built it. Indian Field Days with dances, papoose and basket shows, rides, races, and other equestrian competitions took place in Yosemite Valley that afternoon.

Many observers were late, and annoyed, because of traumatic tire troubles later described by Leo Hiestand,

garage foreman for the Curry Company at the time. On that triumphal, long-expected opening day,

> We repaired over 300 tires on cars of inbound Park visitors. Some of the cars had all four tires flattened on the new road which was covered with gravel (or tailings) from an old mine dump. The gravel contained coarse and sharp rocks, broken glass, and all kinds of scrap metal from phonographic needles to railroad spikes.
>
> We closed the shop to other work and had all our mechanics repairing tires and running service cars to pick up and deliver tires to the motorists stranded along the road between Briceburg and El Portal. We did not stop until we had all of them en route again.

In the interim before the new road was paved, sharp objects were removed by a powerful magnet. Whether paved or unpaved, the new highway was startlingly

---

1. Actually, Yosemite Valley was first seen, but not entered, by two gold miners in October 1849, but the diary kept by one of them had not been unearthed at the time of the Diamond Jubilee.

good in comparison to the other three roads entering the Park.

During the 1920s, and indeed much of the the 1930s, the chief topic of conversation among visitors was not the Park's beauties, but the terrible roads. "Did you make it up Priest Grade without boiling?" "How many flats did you have?" "Could you negotiate those hairpin turns on one try?" and "Did you catch the Control?" were common questions leading to animated discussions about the Coulterville, Big Oak Flat, and Wawona roads, which retained the grades, narrowness, roughness and dust of the stage era. All three had such precipitous, threadlike descents into the Valley that they were limited to one-way, ranger-supervised controls. Drivers planning to enter via the Big Oak Flat Road, for example, had to arrive at the Gentry Checking Station by an even hour, while out-going traffic was allowed to proceed the four miles uphill only on the odd hours. No car was allowed to exceed twelve miles per hour. Those who missed a control had to wait for at least an hour and a half, during which they fumed, fussed, picnicked, repacked cars, refilled water bags, and talked to fellow sufferers. If the last daylight control was missed, motorists had a twelve-hour delay because the road was closed all night by locked gates.

The second day of the Diamond Jubilee Celebration, August 1, was filled with events, excitement, and, presumably, exhaustion for leading participants such

Acoustical engineering could not block the thunder of Yosemite Falls, at its springtime peak, from the splendid new hotel.
(Ansel Adams photograph; YP&CC collection.)

Mother Curry spoke at the August 1, 1926 cornerstone laying of the Ahwahnee Hotel. Steve Mather and A. B. C. Dohrmann, with arms folded, are prominent among the audience. *(SS collection.)*

as Mather, Tresidder, and pageant director Garnet Holme. At 9 a.m. the Happy Isles Fish Hatchery was dedicated, at 9:45 a.m. the cornerstone was laid at the Ahwahnee Hotel, and at 10:45 a.m. a site half a mile west of the Ahwahnee was dedicated for a new $300,000 interdenominational church. (A year later an inexpensive, ruggedly attractive outdoor "Church Bowl" succeeded the grandiose plans.) That evening, after two firefalls fell simultaneously, an elaborate pageant was given depicting the 1851 discovery of Yosemite.

Of the two outstanding events affecting Yosemite in 1927, one was a dream come true, the other a nightmare. First came the trial by tourists up All-Year Highway 140. No one had envisioned how many autoists would throng in to use the winter wonderland; no one had anticipated that people would camp in, or near, their cars at a time when campgrounds were closed. After the Christmas-New Year holidays, Superintendent Lewis admitted in a report to Mather, ". . . we were not prepared to cope with the avalanche of travel." Tresidder complained that campers had broken into the office and restrooms at Camp Curry, burned wood, and strewn garbage. As winter proceeded, Yosemite residents realized that they had Detroit by the tail. Proliferation was recorded in the superintendent's monthly reports, which reveal that during January 1927, visitation jumped 690 percent from January 1926. On February 13, 1927, 875 autos entered the Valley, up from perhaps ten the previous year, and there was no room at any of the inns even though cabins at Camp Curry and Yosemite Lodge had been opened. During April of 1926, 228 people in 76 cars stayed in the public campgrounds, while in 1927, 1,744 in 425 autos used them.

On opening day of the unpaved All-Year Highway, Curry Company mechanics repaired more than 300 flat tires. *(SS collection.)*

Such an invasion presaged problems for the traditionally crowded Memorial Day weekend, but no one was prepared for how many or how varied. Tresidder's June 3 report to the Curry Company directors presented the grim story wherein beauty was submerged by mobile humanity.

Under existing circumstances, it was impossible for us to give adequate service. Tourists arrived in the Park with such rapidity that the Government lost all control of the public campers and before nightfall of the 29th the entire Stoneman Meadow was filled with camp outfits in an area where there were no toilet facilities, no water supply and no garbage arrangements. When Stoneman Meadow was filled, the campers began encroaching on Camp Curry and four actually pitched their tents opposite the Curry Garage and there they camped for two days. Campers were found cooking their meals beside the Curry swimming pool and some of them entered our kitchens and warehouses and, in fact, literally swarmed through all our various units. Neither the Government nor ourselves had a watchman force capable for handling the situation. The loss in property and good will during the period was considerable.

The line at the Curry dining room extended three and four deep from the main entrance to Mrs. Curry's bungalow. The line at the cafeteria extended from the entrance to the Curry studio. Similar conditions existed at Yosemite Lodge. The kitchen and dining room employees were on duty practically continuously from six o'clock in the morning until late at night. The front offices were literally swamped with work, as can be realized from the fact that on the 30th there were 1,202 departed from Camp Curry and 1,288 from Yosemite Lodge. This means that guests were checking out at a rate of about three a minute during the day.

The problem of labor and supplies in connection with such business is one that will probably confront the company every weekend this summer and no satisfactory solution has been reached as yet.

For example, the housecount at Camp Curry dropped from 1,430 on Sunday to 676 on Monday. At Yosemite Lodge it dropped 1,582 on Sunday to 432 on Monday. Meanwhile, the number of our employees remained at over 900. In other words, it is not possible to shrink our help when the housecount drops.

. . . Over 3,000 cars entered the park on the 28th and over 3,000 on the 29th. Mr. Lewis estimates that on Sunday, the 29th, there were 27,000 people in Yosemite Valley itself. At the Arch Rock Checking Station cars were in line from six o'clock the morning of the 28th practically continuously until the afternoon of the 29th and at times the line extended from the Checking Station to El Portal.

When the campers departed from the area where there were no suitable facilities, such as Stoneman Meadow, they left in their wake garbage, rubbish, and human excrement to such an extent as to make it difficult to walk across Stoneman Meadow. We are writing the Government setting forth the situation in connection with our operation over the weekend just past because we realize that many complaints against the service inevitably will follow. At the same time, we are calling attention to the great menace to health by permitting a repetition of camping conditions of the past weekend. If such conditions are allowed to prevail throughout the summer, the Valley may suffer some serious epidemic. The problem is largely up to the Government and we will do what we can to prevent a reoccurrence.

Tresidder felt that the opening of the Ahwahnee Hotel was one of the remedies to overcrowding, and pushed for its completion. No expense was spared in the rock exterior or interior. Art experts and historians were assigned to carry out an Indian motif in the public rooms, and their creativity resulted in a unique, harmonious, and beautiful design from mosaic floors to decorated walls. Even the elevator doors were adorned with a bead pattern. All the first floor rooms were spacious with floor-to-ceiling windows. The dining room was immense—130 feet long, 51 feet wide, and 34 feet high—and the main lounge almost as impressive in size and ornamentation. The imported artists were inspired by the environment, and they showed their enthusiasm in everything from wall hangings to the handmade drapes, friezes, tapestries, and lamps. One of the young, thrilled designers was Jeannette Dyer Spencer, who had been hired to create stained glass windows, and continued as director of the hotel's decor. Soon her architect husband, E. T. "Ted" Spencer, was appointed the company's chief architect. Both remained in these positions until 1972. So intimately were they associated with Yosemite and the hotel that their small daughter called it "My Wahnee." Their imaginative creativity and insistence on tasteful buildings inside and out, funded by the Curry Company, forecast an essential harmony between man-made structures and natural features.

Frenzied activity in furnishing, stocking, and staffing preceded the Ahwahnee's opening day, which was set for July 14, 1927. Scores of VIPs received invitations to the dedicatory banquet and complimentary night's lodging. Stephen T. Mather was one of the first to arrive and proudly inspect the product of his dreams. At 8 p.m. he welcomed 200 guests for dinner, at which he served as master of ceremonies. Short talks

Guests were delighted with both the Ahwahnee's beautiful dining room and its superb food. *(YP&CC collection.)*

were given by Mother Curry, A. B. C. Dohrmann, Harry Chandler, W. B. Lewis, Tresidder, and five others.

Mother Curry and Mary Tresidder took a conspicuous part in the festivities, but there were other behind-the-scenes women even more intimately involved with the hotel's opening and its first years. One was Mrs. Louise Temple, the hotels first manager, and a former employee of the Yosemite National Park Company. She was a big, expansive woman who strode through the building with a sharp eye for order. Another was Don Tresidder's sister, Oliene, who, in lieu of serving as his

office nurse as long planned, supported her brother in resort work, and was the Ahwahnee's first hostess.

After 1934 a third remarkable woman, Ellen Cook, former manager of the Sentinel Hotel, presided over the kitchens. Both her husband, Hart N. Cook, and their son worked for the Company. Mrs. Cook was of "Scot descent, small in stature, but mighty in management, and very positive in nature, commanding great respect . . ." her daughter-in-law commended. Don Tresidder thought so highly of her and her meals that he urged her to work long beyond retirement age. In fact, Mrs. Cook was over eighty when she finally quit in 1941, at which time she was given a year's salary in lieu of a pension. Well before she departed she trained Earl and Fred Pierson, who succeeded her as notable, long-tenured chefs. Fred, in fact, was still pleasing Ahwahnee diners when he retired in September 1974.[2]

Besides the women on the Ahwahnee staff, other career gals served the Company elsewhere. Tops among them was Louisiana Scott Foster, who joined the Curry team in 1928. Her grandfather was the distinguished and controversial Rev. William A. Scott of San Francisco, who had visited Yosemite Valley with one of the pioneer tourist parties of 1855. Lou had been raised in luxury but sought work when a family depression threatened. As a manager she was outstanding, in the opinion of employees who remembered her gentle, precise person with affection. Her "Sunday Night Specials" at the Lodge cafeteria, featuring white linen tablecloths, candlelight, and standing-rib roasts, were famous with employees and guests. Although Lou managed other units, including the Wawona Hotel and the camp at Tuolumne Meadows, Yosemite Lodge was her main bailiwick until she retired in 1940.

"Lou was a worry-wart who wanted everything just perfect which it usually was with her at the helm," Lodge hostess Midge Pittman remembered. "She always chose the food that looked like failures from the cafeteria counter to see what might be wrong. I wonder if she ever ate what she wanted!" Before she left Yosemite, Miss Foster confided to Amos Neal, who trained under her, "From now on I won't have to think, with each bit of food I take, how it will taste to a guest!"

Florence Morris began work as a secretary in the Yosemite National Park Company in 1921 and, after the merger, joined the Curry Company's traffic department, which she eventually managed, and served faithfully until she retired in 1956. Doris Schmiedell, recreation manager, and her successor, Midge Pittman, helped to entertain guests with parties, rides, barbecues, and other activities. "The best

days were mid-seasons," Miss Pittman reminisced, "when the house counts were low, but fun people came to stay for longer periods, and we dreamed up happy things to do to keep them on and on!" Another name deserves to be appended to the list of indispensable females: Lena Schweifler, wife of long-tenured barber John Schweifler. She worked for the Curry Company, and its predecessor, from 1922 until 1960, serving as

Yosemite's bosses, concessionaire Tresidder and Superintendent Lewis, in the new Ahwahnee Hotel. *(YP&CC collection.)*

2. Since then there have been numerous chefs—all good, some superior.

clerk, cafeteria checker, or whatever—and whenever needed—but she is best remembered for her years at Yosemite Lodge where she and her car, "Rosebud," were fixtures. Of course the best known and most distinguished of these topnotch women who achieved managerial status decades in advance of the women's liberation movement was Mother Curry.

From opening day on, the Ahwahnee hosted VIPs from diverse fields—Senator Hiram Johnson, publisher Harry Chandler, entertainer Will Rogers, author Gertrude Stein, producer Walt Disney, and a roster of movie stars, including Lionel and John Barrymore, Irene Dunne, Charlie Chaplin, Jean Harlow, William Powell, Charles Laughton, Shirley Temple, Greta Garbo, Humpry Bogart, Clint Eastwood, Charlton Heston, and Robert Redford. Eleanor Roosevelt stayed

Mary Curry Tresidder had a subtle hand in the Ahwahnee's interior design. *(Ansel Adams photograph.)*

Before long, Detroit's finest were known as "rubberneckers." *(SS collection.)*

at the Ahwahnee three times, John Kennedy once, and the Queen of England once. Herbert Hoover and his wife were frequent guests both before and after his presidency. His Stanford interests allied him with Don Tresidder, and the two became good friends. Ray Lyman Wilbur, Stanford's third president, was another repeat guest, and a friend of the Tresidders.

In its early years the Ahwahnee was exclusive, catering to distinguished, affluent guests. The general public was discouraged from even wandering in for a look, and employees from other units were decidedly not welcome. Hoover himself was once stopped by a uniformed doorman who disdained the ex-president's soiled fisherman's clothes. Deluxe "motor coaches" ran from Merced direct to the new hotel, then returned to Yosemite Lodge to deliver *its* guests.

"The Ahwahnee is designed quite frankly for people who know the delights of luxurious living and to whom the artistic excellence and the material comfort of their environment is important," stated an unpublished promotional blurb. David A. Curry who had begun Camp Curry to enable the common man to afford lodging, would have erupted. His widow's feelings are not known, but the director of the Park Service, whose complicated job was to run the national parks for the enjoyment of all people yet keep them unimpaired for future generations, was happy. So was

Don Tresidder, who delighted in festive occasions and wanted to mark the Ahwahnee's first Christmas with a suitable celebration. As a member of San Francisco's all-male Bohemian Club he was familiar with their Christmas "hi jinks" program, and asked a number of its singers to be in a show at the Ahwahnee.

Don hired Garnett Holme, the professional dramatist who had directed the Diamond Jubilee in 1926, to produce a special Christmas Day pageant. Inspired by Washington Irving's description of an 1812 English festival held in a Squire Bracebridge's manor, the dramatist presented the first Bracebridge Dinner on Christmas Day 1927. It was held in the Ahwahnee's baronial dining room, and was a success with the guests and host Tresidder.

After Holme's untimely death the following spring, Tresidder asked Ansel Adams and Jeannette Spencer to produce the pageant. Adams's script, based on Washington Irving's writings, and rousing ancient carols combined with liberal use of gongs and trumpets still provide an unforgettable musical treat. Ted Spencer's stage settings and his wife's costume design and Christmas windows added essential atmosphere as well as beauty. Each of the four succulent courses from peacock pie to plum pudding was introduced first to the squire and then to the diners.

At first the Bracebridge Singers were members of the Bohemian Club. They and their director, Harold Saville, were reimbursed for their performances with a week's board and room. Beginning in 1934 Eugene Fulton a professional chorale director in San Francisco, led the then all-male singers and assisted Adams. His wife, Anna-Marie, became the organist, and his two young daughters participated in the Villagers.

For over a decade, Tresidder himself was resplendent as the Squire and Mary as his demure Lady. After a stint as the Lord of Misrule, Adams juggled the job of major domo, director and photographer. His pretty wife, Virginia Best Adams, played the singing housekeeper, Fred Pierson the cook, and Herman Hoss was perfect as the parson. Mother Curry, Oliene Tresidder, the Oehlmanns and dignitaries such as Grace and Horace Albright, portrayed the Squires's family and the visiting Squire and his wife. Each year saw changes and improvements. Only floods, World War II, and the 1995 governmental shutdown have canceled the Bracebridge Dinner.

When Adams retired from the music directorship in 1973, Fulton took over, but his leadership ended after the dress rehearsal in 1978 when he collapsed and died of a heart attack. The show went on, thanks to his sorrowing wife and daughters and the stunned singers. His daughter Andrea assumed the directorship the following year, a post she still holds, leading the chorale group of men and women, singing solos herself, and annually making creative changes.

Long since, the Bracebridge Dinner's fame has spread—even to foreign countries. Currently, there are five seatings for 332 people each. Two take place on December 22, one on Christmas Eve, and two on Christmas Day itself. Despite the cost, now in the hundreds of dollars, each of the 1,660 tickets is coveted. Applications are taken between December 15 and February 15. After that date, lotteries determine who the lucky diners will be. Attending Bracebridge is a cultural and culinary experience.

During the winter of 1927–28, Tresidder had official support and guidance from Horace Albright. After W. B. Lewis suffered a heart attack in June of 1926, Arthur F. Demary took over as acting superintendent, backed ably by Ernest P. Leavitt, Lewis's assistant. Leavitt had served as chief clerk for the Army during its administration, and remained to become a career Park Service man. At that time, Albright was Mather's chief assistant and field director, and superintendent of Yellowstone National Park as well. In October of 1927,

Lou Foster in a rare moment of leisure.
(Virginia Best Adams collection.)

Mather asked him to move to Yosemite Valley as an overall superintendent. In the following months, Albright supervised the beginnings of organized winter sports and the acquisition of forest land along the western border of the Park—notably that adjacent to the Tuolumne Grove of Big Trees—and began negotiations to purchase the private land surrounding Wawona.

He and his wife, Grace, involved themselves in community affairs, and he acquainted himself thoroughly with the problems and personnel of both the Park Service and the concessionaires. "I enjoyed this association," he wrote in 1974, "and had the highest admiration for Mother Curry, Don and Mary Tresidder, and Hil Oehlmann. Don and I were horse lovers and rode almost every day. We worked together in revising trails on the floor of the Valley and planned and supervised the construction of a 'belt' trail all around the Valley following the road system, but keeping road crossings to a minimum. We encouraged horseback riding, skijoring, and interpretative work." Those 1926–28 years, with the building of the Ahwahnee, and the opening of the All-Year Highway, were exciting, significant, and important then, and to all future Yosemite development. Albright's temporary residence, coupled with his intense involvement, inspired permanent Yosemite good.

Statistics prove that, primarily due to the All-Year Highway, business increased tremendously in 1927.

	Travel	Gross Sales	Net Profit
1926	274,209	$2,388,037	$309,013
1927	490,430	$3,094,896	$463,533

The board of directors, whose members were also large stockholders, were pleased, yet wanted to expand operations. As early as 1928 they discussed purchasing the Washburn holdings at Wawona. Further, there were plans to acquire property at Lake Tahoe. Dohrmann explained "that at the time of the organization of the Yosemite National Park Company it was thought of as the center of a larger development including Lassen and Sequoia National Parks throughout the Sierras...." Harry Chandler, representing stockholders in Southern California, dissented, urging that the proper development of Yosemite holdings was the reason for investment of businessmen in his area. Despite Park Service pressure for a new store and other improvements, no definite building sites were assigned to the Company. At the executive committee meeting of June 29, 1928, quoted above, Dohrmann "emphasized the necessity of inducing the government to crystallize their plans . . . because of the fact that it was impossible for us to properly plan developments at Curry, the Lodge, or the New Village without knowing what the plan of the government is to be toward a new development for campers in the lower valley and similar possibilities."

There were several such meeting each year plus regular directors meetings, stockholders meetings, and staff gatherings, at which Tresidder presided. Beyond that when Mather, congressional members, foreign dignitaries, movie stars, or other VIPs were in the Park, Tresidder had to arrange at least a dinner to fete them. He also had to retain rapport with the supervisors of both Mariposa County, of which the Company was the largest taxpayer, and the neighboring counties of Merced, Madera, Tuolumne, and Mono.

There were scheduling conflicts with the Yosemite Valley Railroad, on which travel was declining, and a few labor confrontations. Four unit managers had been arrested in August 1927 and charged with seventy-nine violations of the eight-hour labor law for women, but after a hearing the Yosemite U. S. Court Commissioner decided that all violations were technical, time clock ones.

Tresidder had not retained rapport with his affable brother-in-law, Bob Williams, and in January 1927, after he let it be known that he favored another man as second-in-command, Williams quit to return to Illinois, where he joined his family's chicken brooder and sundries business. Mother Curry, with whom the family had lived, was upset at the rift, and even suggested departing with the Williams family, but loyalty to Yosemite and the Curry Company held her firmly in place.

Williams's successor as traffic manager was Edwin T. "Captain" Huffman of the Crocker-Huffman ranch in Merced County, who had deserted ranching to become a seaman and later a contractor. In 1911 he had begun a third career with the Yosemite transportation business. His "Horseshoe Route" boasted "In One Way —Out Another, No Scene Twice Seen," and he was the first in the field to replace stages and horses with auto stages. He owned Miami Lodge, southwest of Wawona, which was a popular resort of the 1920s and had repair garages there and at Wawona. After the merger, Huffman sold the Horseshoe Route to the Curry Company, and in 1928 began managing the traffic department. By all reports he was a salty old boy and a tough disciplinarian—brusque, forthright, droll, and legendary even in his lifetime. After phonographs and records became the rage, he was urged to utilize them rather than hiring an orchestra for the Miami

Lodge. "I couldn't do that," he said gruffly. "If I did, my wife wouldn't have anyone to flirt with!"

It was said that he fired the first man he saw each morning. Once he fired a bus driver who raced an engine instead of idling it outside the Ahwahnee Hotel. During the Great Depression his salary was cut, so he took a two-year leave, bought a yacht, and with his wife and a few friends sailed around the world. He was a pioneer aviator, one of the first men in Mariposa County to own an airplane, and inaugurated air service to Wawona. While in Yosemite he and his wife lived in the Petersen's former home at Camp Curry. Petersen had represented the Curry Company in financial matters throughout the merger, then left Yosemite to begin an accounting business, but continued taking care of Mother Curry's income tax returns until the mid-1940s. He wrote a factual article about businesses in Yosemite Valley that appeared in the June 13, 1928, *San Francisco Business* magazine, and after that, Mother Curry suggested that he do further work on area history. He did considerable research and some interviews but didn't have the time for writing. His notes, made between 1928 and 1931, were loaned to the author, who found them of great value.

In 1928 the Park Service assigned building sites for Curry employee housing in the belt of forest between the garage and the Ahwahnee. All seasonal and permanent personnel, whether maid or manager, were at that time crammed into old, uninsulated buildings at or near Yosemite Lodge or in tents at Camp Curry. The Park Service approved plans for two-story dormitories, a heating plant, and a laundry in what was named as

For years, all mail, food, furniture, and equipment was transported by these 1917 Commerce trucks, which made three to four trips daily from the El Portal railroad terminus to the Yosemite Valley Post Office. Many campers shipped tents and other gear for pickup at the post office. Jess Rust had the parcel post contract and kept the trucks in running order. The doorways were open all summer, and boarded up in winter. Assistant Postmaster Charles Michael and Postmaster Fred C. "Alex" Alexander are standing at the extreme right. (*Amy L. Alexander collection.*)

the Tecoya development. At the same time, tiny houses were built along the fringe of pines facing the Ahwahnee Meadow. One was stone, one brick, the others of wood, in an experiment to determine which building material was best suited to Yosemite's climate. Foundations were flat rocks, rooms were boxy, but, over the years, additions were made, and the structures evolved into attractive, comfortable, and still-used homes.

Park Service criteria for any structure was that it be subordinate to the environment, and screened by natural features. Pine trees and a coat of weathered gray paint effectively camouflaged "the Row." Concurrently, houses built for Park employees northwest of the New Village were simple, solid, and uniformly covered with "Park Service brown." Unfortunately, telephone and electrical poles and lines were obtrusive.

Not all of the dorms were constructed in 1928; seven cottages at the Ahwahnee, considered to be of more financial import, were under construction. About the same time, changes were being made on the top, roofless floor of the hotel. It had been planned as a roof garden and outdoor dance floor, but was not a success with guests. Don Tresidder had it roofed and envisioned it as a convention site, but that idea too was unprofitable. His sister Oliene suggested that he have rooms for himself and Mary built there, since Foster Curry's bungalow at Camp Curry, which they had occupied during summers, was entirely unsuitable for winter use. Finally a library, sun porch, two bedrooms, and two baths were built for them on the sixth floor. To this day a door knocker inscribed "Don and Mary" marks one of the rooms.

In January 1930, dynamic, long-ailing Stephen T. Mather died. National Park policy and aims were not seriously affected because Albright, his successor, had worked closely with Mather since the Park Service's inception, and, indeed, had served as acting director for months at a time during Mather's breakdowns. Albright's style was different, and he gave more

responsibilities to his subordinates, but his dedication to parks and conservation was single minded, wide, and admirable.

While the Curry expansion was going on, a new $50,000 hospital was going up north of the Tecoya area. It was built by the Park Service and operated as a concession by Dr. Hartley Dewey, who had been running the old Army-built hospital. Opening day on February 19, 1930 was marked by festivities, but the building had no name until after "Dusty" Lewis died on August 28 of that year. After that, Lewis Memorial Hospital commemorated the man who had combined capability and popularity as Yosemite's superintendent for twelve years.[3]

His successor was Charles Goff Thomson, forty-six, a tough, sharp man who had served briefly as an Army colonel and enjoyed that title. He was short and bald, with a gravelly voice and reflective nature —a man who needed time to think before making decisions. He established rapport with his assistant Jim Lloyd, and instructed him in diversionary tactics for use during the frequent conferences between Curry executives and himself. Sometimes there were guest complaints, usually on housekeeping rates; other times Tresidder wanted some concession, such as readjusting the time for the firefall because of earlier darkness. Hoss and/or Oehlmann would accompany him. After they had presented their case to Thomson, silence would ensue. Lloyd would quickly introduce some sports contest between Stanford, Hoss and Tresidder's alma mater, and the University of California, Oehlmann's school. While they argued, Thomson would stare out the window, pondering, until he made an objective decision.

Since friendly relations between the Park Service and the Curry Company were essential to the operations of the concessionaire, Tresidder soon made Thomson his friend. By the end of the 1920s Doctor Tresidder had mastered the practice of resort work and politics in the place he loved better than any other on earth.

---

3. It was a sad day in 1975 when Lewis Memorial Hospital became the Yosemite Medical Clinic. Under successive management, it still provides medical aid to employees and guests. Serious emergency cases are stabilized then flown by helicopter to a major hospital in Modesto or Fresno.

10 Mother Curry's Reign

Whether it was a summer morning in 1899 or 1936, Mother Curry was out of bed long before the sun, or her guests, were up. Accompanied by the predawn chorus of birds, she walked past the seemingly lifeless cabins and tents, enjoying the quiet, coolness, and wood odors. Each day truckloads of pine needles were brought in and spread to lay the dust, and that carpet provided a piney scent. Her first stop was the kitchen, where the chef, as many as twenty-two cooks, and numerous helpers were preparing enormous amounts of food. Camp Curry guests could consume 600 pounds of sugar, 250 pounds of butter, 1,000 pounds of flour, 354 gallons of coffee, 250 dozen eggs, four tons of milk, 1,200 to 1,500 pounds of steak, a similar amount of chops, and a mass of fresh fruit per day! Additionally, a ton of vegetables was prepared and consumed daily. These figures were enumerated in a leaflet entitled "Camp Curry Backyard Tour," which included the nitty-gritty facts that 12,000 dishes were washed per meal, and fifty garbage cans filled each day! Every morning, Mother Curry mingled with the force of seventy waiters and waitresses, complimenting, admonishing, and guiding in her gentle way. If they were shorthanded, she would set tables or stock cafeteria counters. Energetic, sports-loving Louise Logue was headwaitress, until she began managing the gift shop, and was succeeded by Ruth Van Kirk. Both were efficient and devoted to their jobs and their boss.

Mother Curry neither asked for nor accepted special service. As soon as the cafeteria and dining room doors were opened, she would slip out to stand in line like everyone else. However, there was a large, special table reserved for her and the family that was waited on by one of her "girls" or "boys"—who felt highly favored with the assignment. Instead of tips, a bonus of $25 at the end of the season was given them. At the special table

the Williams family, the Tresidders, and any other relatives, such as the Pinkerton sisters, would join her. Abbie and Jennie Pinkerton spent many summers with "Cousin Jennie."

Dining capacity in the 1920s was 725, and an additional 150 could be seated in the cafeteria. "We could now seat those 290 guests of our first season in about one-third of our present dining room," was an amused comment of Mother Curry's. In 1923 she remarked, "We have a capacity of 1,100 people comfortably which can be stretched to 1,200 uncomfortably."

By 8:30 a.m. she was at her desk to meet the head housekeeper, head chef, reservations manager, and any other staff member who needed advice, direction, or reprimand. At Camp Curry her softest word was law, her opinion was solicited by Don Tresidder and other executives on many aspects of Company management and development. She talked to rangers who were called on, at times, to quiet disturbances among guests or employees, and kept Margaret Jabes, her private secretary for twenty years, busy with letters and filing. Curry's office staff consisted of capable, friendly people whom she had hired and trained—Wendell Otter, George Oliver, Cy Wright, Bill Conrad, Charles

"Heigh ho, heigh ho, it's off to work we go. . . ." *(YP&CC collection.)*

Mother Curry knew every tent and rock in Camp Curry. *(YP&CC collection.)*

Scarborough, and her daughter Mary, who had developed a quiet competence.

Sometimes during the morning, Mother Curry would desert the office to conduct a "Backyard Tour" for interested guests, a custom established by her husband. After that she took a private tour of the camp. Guests would marvel at her memory of them and at her friendliness, while employees would work faster after her word of praise or suggestion for improvement. If a bed was ineptly made, she might remake it as an object lesson to the observant, and embarrassed, maid. On the other hand, her generosity was quick but kept quiet. If an employee needed money, especially for education, he or she could borrow from Mother Curry. Her forte was listening; her advice was serene yet succinct.

She was strict on segregation of employees. Male employees lived in a dormitory and tents in "Jungletown," while females lived on "the Terrace." "Any man who had business in the women's quarters, such as delivering suitcases or trunks," Wendell Otter said, "was instructed to call out 'man on the Terrace,' so no immodesty would be revealed to him, but calls were not as loud as they should have been on many occasions." At least one time a fresh fellow rambled on the

Terrace without giving the password and was greeted with screams that brought half the camp running. In the ensuing confusion, "brother bruin" ran off.

Several times, Mother Curry hosted weddings in her bungalow or in the ruins of the LeConte Memorial Lodge. For instance, Rufus Green's son Tom married his fiance in the latter in 1924, and, as a wedding gift, "Cousin Jennie" gave them an elaborate wedding breakfast, which even had a printed menu. Of the thirty guests, more than half were relatives. David's niece, Ida Curry, was married in Mother Curry's bungalow. In due time Ida's children and grandchildren worked at the Camp as had she and her sister Nelle. Sports stars Dink Templeton and Dick Harmon; cartoonist Feg Murray; Superior Court Judge Tom Coakley; bank president Alan Sproul; doctors Emil Holman and John Fahey; publisher and foreign ambassador Bill Lane; and many, many others worked under her, and never forgot her guidance.

Often the office staff would overhear odd exchanges between guests and clerks at the reservation counter. Once a woman registered at camp, then inquired where she could see the geysers. "Mam, the geysers are in Yellowstone National Park, not

Yosemite," the desk clerk replied. "Oh, well," she said, "where are the paint pots?" "I'm sorry, maam, they are in Yellowstone, too." At that the lost tourist glanced outside and exclaimed disgustedly, "You mean trees and rocks are all there is to see here?" Another time a man picked up a box lunch, then asked, "Now where is the Park? I want to go sit in it and eat my lunch." Mother Curry passed such anecdotes on to her guests at afternoon tea, which she held in her bungalow for relatives, old-time guests, and favored new ones, all of whom considered her invitation an honor.

Camp Curry was always first with her, and she was convinced of its complete superiority in locale, service, and history over other guest units, including the Ahwahnee Hotel. In particular, she scorned Yosemite Lodge, the former competitor, referring to its guests as "the poor things who have to stay at the Lodge."

After the merger the laundry at Camp Curry was closed and all work was done at the modern plant at Yosemite Lodge. "As superintendent of the commercial division," Hil Oehlmann recalled, "I had charge of the laundry, and, no matter how large our preseason supplies, during the peak of the season the operating units often ran short of linens, especially hand towels.

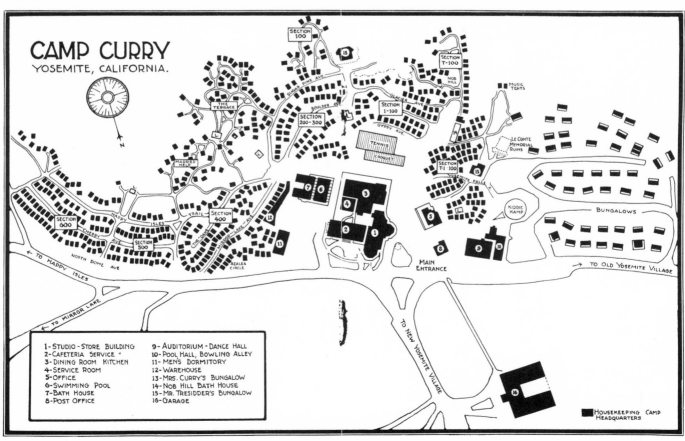

Twins Jeanette and John, David, Katherine, Ruth, and Foster Curry at Camp Baldy in 1931. *(RCB collection.)*

Frequently the Camp Curry housekeeper would call to complain of a shortage of towels, and, moments later, I would receive a call for napkins from the head waitress. Soon after I had explained the laundry's difficulties to these ladies, there would be a call from Mother Curry. 'Hil,' she always began in the sternest tone she could muster, and then I heard her story of needs. Somehow I would manage to supply the needed linens to Camp Curry, generally at the cost of adequate supplies for the Company's other units." Oehlmann also stated that Mother Curry presided at staff meetings in an Indiana hickory rocker. "She would rock gently back and forth during discussions until she had reached a decision, and then she would bring both feet down hard on the floor and state her conclusion."

As Jennie Curry trod briskly through the camp, office, shops, and varied service buildings, she was sometimes trailed by a grandchild. One of them, Marjorie Jane Williams, "adored Nana," and was greatly impressed when she or Aunt Mary would procure cookies and candies for her and her brother from the kitchen. "Camp Curry was heaven," Marjorie thought. There were large rocks, dubbed Little Half Dome and El Capitan, to climb, and the Kiddie Kamp to attend. After "graduation" from that, there was the Grizzly Club with its full schedule of cookouts, hikes, and burro rides. The Ledge Trail held endless fascination, as did the Park Service's museum. The highlight of the evening was the firefall. "Fire to fall" was a beloved family

institution; each grandson who developed a suitable voice was allowed to shout the traditional calls. Prefacing the Firefall was the highly popular entertainment at which the front row was always reserved for the children, who applauded singers, comics, and special acts such as local cowboy Al Kay, Danny Kaye, Will Rogers, and on one occasion a little-known singer named Bing Crosby. Glen Hood sang for years, and it was a sad day when Mrs. Jilson decided upon retirement. One of her most ardent fans was young Stuart Cross, grandson of Rufus Green, who always clapped madly for her.

After the firefall, guests thronged to the Pavilion to dance. Despite her Calvinistic background, and strictness with her own children, Mother Curry had been persuaded to allow dancing in camp. This horrified her aunt Vicey Elliot, a minister's conservative widow and perennial guest, who "Would look in on the nightly dancing and come back, shaking her head, saying, 'I'm afraid that Jennie will lose her seat in heaven for allowing such goings on.'" While camp guests danced, Mother Curry, relatives, and staff members were in her bungalow, playing games such as Anagrams, Monopoly, Mah-jong, and Russian Bank. Daughter Marjorie, who was becoming an expert at bridge, taught her mother to play. No matter what game was played, Mother Curry was a spirited competitor.

Beginning in January of 1927, Mother Curry had a new David to love. After a divorce from Cherry, who died in 1926, Foster Curry married Ruth Higgins, who had worked at Camp Curry. Their first child, a son, was named David A. Curry. When she heard of Foster and Ruth's marriage on June 10, 1925, Mother Curry had sent them congratulations and a check for $200, and soon reestablished close relations. Foster had lost heavily on two ill-fated airplane ventures and in running the Lebec Hotel on the Grapevine in Southern California. In 1927 he and Ruth began operating Curry's Camp Baldy in the San Gabriel Mountains, patterning it after the Yosemite business, using the "Welcome" and

"Farewell" calls, and advertising it as the "Yosemite of the South." Their management and service quickly made the place a success. Ruth helped him in every way, and, much to his mother's joy, Foster achieved control and maturity. After her mother and grandmother died, Katherine, Foster's daughter by his first marriage, lived with Ruth and Foster. She was a beautiful girl with flashing dark eyes, a big sister to David and the twins, John and Jeanette, born on May 1, 1930. Jeannette was named after her grandmother Jennie Etta. Although Foster kept his vow not to return to Yosemite, Ruth often took the children there.

When Katherine asked questions about her father's earlier troubles, Mother Curry answered, "Good forgettery." She was very close to her first grandchild, and took her on a three-week tour of Yellowstone and other western resorts in August 1926. Don Tresidder's mother and Rufus Green's wife also accompanied Mother Curry on her busman's holiday. Wherever they stayed she observed the management and services with an eye to possible adaptations at Camp Curry. Her companions noted that no matter where they registered, Mother Curry received red-carpet treatment. Often she would encounter one, two, or several staff members who had worked under her in Yosemite, and she could recall their names and when they had worked for Camp Curry.

When construction for the new cafeteria and dining room began at Camp Curry in the fall of 1928, Mrs. Curry decided that it was a good time for her to leave its supervision in Mary and Don's hands. She surprised Katherine, then sixteen, by asking, "If you could go anywhere you liked, where would it be?" "Paris," was the girl's immediate response. "All right," answered Mother Curry, "we'll go next week." Between July and October they toured Scotland, England, and the Continent. Late in 1928, the adventurous grandmother enrolled Katherine in a finishing school in Florence, Italy.

Her winter headquarters was the Hotel Gaylord in Los Angeles, where she lived with her cousins Abbie and Jennie Pinkerton. From there she could easily visit Foster, Ruth, and the Curry grandchildren. They, as well as Marjorie Jane and Bob Williams, received financial aid from "Nana" for high school and college. Part of her winter routine were the hours she spent in the Company's Los Angeles and San Francisco offices, where she interviewed and hired many college students herself, and kept a discerning eye on personnel and operations.

Ranger Jimmie Lloyd, a stylish woman, a snazzy car—a new LaSalle—and the entrance to Camp Curry. (*J. V. Lloyd collection.*)

"We could now seat those 290 guests of our first season in about one-third of our present dining room," Mother Curry remarked, after the new one opened in 1929. *(SS collection.)*

By mid-January 1929 the roof of the new dining room was on, and the crew of fifty carpenters, plumbers, and electricians was finishing the interior. Architect Ted Spencer had designed a beautiful, functional building with twelve-foot high windows and a canvas-lined ceiling. Dominating the enormous dining room was a fireplace twelve feet high and twenty-four feet wide. Robert Howard painted Indian pictographs, and Jeannette Spencer designed all the handsome metal lighting fixtures. The adjoining kitchen served both the dining room and the cafeteria, while a complete heating and refrigeration plant was housed in the basement.

To celebrate the May 12 opening of the camp and the new complex, Mother Curry collaborated with the advertising department and sent out about seventy-five complimentary invitations to publishers and automotive people. "I am giving a little dinner party Sunday evening, May 12, to some good friends of Yosemite on the occasion of the opening of the new Camp Curry dining room. . . " her letter began. Invitations entitled the recipient and spouse to a complimentary dinner, a room, and breakfast.

The dinner menu for May 12 carried the following non-culinary text:

From a humble beginning in 1899 with half a dozen tents and equipment laboriously hauled into Yosemite in a wagon, Camp Curry has steadily grown in popularity. The tradition of hospitality to which Camp Curry's success is largely due has been consistently maintained through the personal management of Mrs. D. A. Curry whose thirty-first year in Yosemite is marked by the opening of the new Dining Room and Cafeteria.[1]

May we dedicate these buildings, and the other contemplated development at Camp Curry, to those

---

1. On April 22, 1973 the dining room, cafeteria, and kitchen were destroyed by fire. Their replacements opened on May 2, 1975, and that night a fire gutted the 29-year-old gift shop and damaged another building.

lovers of Yosemite who are our old and new guests. It is their love for Yosemite and their appreciation of our efforts that have made possible the constant improvements in Camp Curry facilities.

While a publicity man's pen can be discerned in that message, so can Mrs. Curry's sincerity and dedication. When Syd Ledson's wife showed off her first tent home with a word of apology, Mother Curry admonished, "Don't be embarrassed, Helen, I venture to say I have known more of tent life than you ever have or will, and I am proud of it." Age did not quell her youthful, questing spirit. In her sixties she re-climbed the steep Ledge Trail, but from the Glacier Point Hotel telephoned for a driver to come after her. At 70 she learned to drive a car, and three years later began to play golf. According to Marjorie Williams, she did both poorly. Mother Curry's thoughtfulness was legend. Nancy Loncaric said that it was Mrs. Curry who first took the time to introduce her to the dramatic, nightly unfolding of the evening primrose blossoms. Nancy once presented her with a purple orchid on her birthday, and Mother Curry was touched. "Thank you, my dear. This is the first orchid I ever received in my life. I'm just not the type, and nobody ever thought to send me one."

During Mother Curry's long reign her character dominated the camp, but there were other noticeable individuals, both resident and transient, who were favored by her and were popular with the guests. One of them was a stocky, white-thatched man who stayed in camp all summer every year from 1919 until 1935.

His name was George C. Moore and his summer "home" was tent 127 at the foot of "Nob Hill." Once in residence, he donned a red bandanna neckerchief, cowboy-type shirt, sun-tan hiking pants encased in leather puttees, and set to work clearing his "yard." He kept the area outside his tent planted in ferns, and picturesquely fenced with weathered manzanita and staghorn lichen. There he held forth, carving manzanita canes, chatting with guests and employees, serving afternoon tea to friends, and frightening children with his gruff voice. He became so much a part of the Curry family that he attended their social events, and sometimes served as judge for the Indian Field Days events. "Uncle George," had been born in Clearfield, Pennsylvania in 1854 and had been in business there and in Philadelphia, with the exception of a couple of years spent prospecting in Alaska. Clearfield newspaper columns documented the tragedy of his life. Eleven months after his marriage, at the age of thirty-six, his wife and newborn baby had died. In 1915 Moore retired to California, and after 1919 divided his time between

Glendale and Yosemite, which he loved and where, he said, he wanted to die. On July 9, 1935, that wish was realized when he died of a heart attack in his tent.

When Kenneyville was torn down in 1926 to make way for the Ahwahnee Hotel, Herbert Sonn, the "Birdman of Yosemite," was homeless. Born in 1879 and raised in Newark, New Jersey, Sonn was a member of a distinguished scientific and artistic family. He was adventurous, traveled west in 1914, and in Yosemite Valley he found a home and career in training birds. Before long he had a workshop in Kenneyville, where he fashioned novel bird caricatures from pine cones, acorns, nuts, bark, and moss. He called them "Wild Gazoobas" and gave them titles such as "Jimmy Seekoya," "Peach-a-rilla," and "Yosemite Zip." He kept two such exotic creatures in a wire cage labeled "Something the scientists overlooked—WHISTLING KAZILLA (Pinekona Californikus)."

He sold his copyrighted pinecone birds, had postcards made of them, and sold the cards to tourists. When Kenneyville was dismantled, Sonn appealed to Mrs. Curry for a site at Camp Curry, and she allowed him a place on the western edge of camp. There, amid

"Uncle George" Moore spent seventeen summers in tent 127 at Camp Curry. *(YNP collection.)*

boulders, pines, and oaks, the slight, gentle Birdman had a tent for an office and another one for a home, tables, several bird-feeding stations, and a cleared space where people gathered to watch his twice daily bird shows. A manzanita and rock fence enclosed his camp, and the approach to the Ledge Trail bisected it. Rufus Green's grandson, Stuart Cross, says his first Yosemite job was working for the Birdman in 1936. He was twelve, and was paid an occasional quarter, for, as he wrote, "packing souvenir birds for shipment, arranging the chairs before his lectures, and sometimes raking the yard. . . ." At other times it was his duty to retrieve the ball bearings Sonn had aimed at ground squirrels with a sling shot.

Park naturalists felt that Sonn's lectures gave people an appreciation and interest in birds and conservation, and this was concurred in by Horace Albright. Onlookers watched various birds land to eat, while Sonn described their traits and their roles in bird life.

Bert Sonn, the "Birdman of Yosemite," in his camp. (*SS collection.*)

About 1932 the Birdman married a Camp Curry maid. Until he retired, in 1937, he continued to give shows and to sell bird creations and postcards at Camp Curry. In July 1934, no less a personage than Eleanor Roosevelt thrilled him with a visit and an order for pinecone birds to give to her grandchildren.

A description of Camp Curry would not be complete without brief mention of some outstanding, long-tenured employees who have not already been cited. There were the Littells—Al, who could and did do anything, and Ray, his talented wife, who composed music performed by symphonic orchestras. There was Jack Greener, the "Aussie," who was the Company printer for decades and a prize fisherman, and his wife, Ella. Also Tillie Sample, a longtime housekeeper; Art O'Donnell, head baggage porter; and sanitary engineer John Powell, an amiable little Welshman, whom Mother Curry supported when he was no longer able to work. By day, Herbert Earl Wilson was a bus-tour spieler; by night, a campfire entertainer who talked about the local Indians and their customs. He was a good friend to them, wore buckskin-fringed clothes, and held forth in a bark umacha (Indian home) near the Camp Curry gateway. There he sold copies of his small book, *The Lore and the Lure of Yosemite.*

During the 1920s Alex Beck, a dark-haired, hard-working versatile man, presided over the firefall. He loaded fuel, particularly red fir bark, in the back seat of an open touring car and drove out the narrow up-and-down trail to Glacier Point, where he laid the fire. He set it afire an hour or so before 9 p.m., then pushed it off slowly with a long-handled rake after the echoing call, "LET 'ER GO GALLAGHER," reached him.[2] One notable Fourth of July he pushed off three firefalls almost simultaneously—a big one for his wife and two smaller, flanking ones for his daughters. Mother Curry thought it would be an interesting change to have fireworks atop Half Dome, so one time Beck and another man packed up eight pounds of fireworks and strung them across the face of Half Dome.

So many people had climbed out on the Overhanging Rock or stood perilously

2. To alert Beck and to insure correct timing, a light that shone from the top of a lofty pine was switched on before the first call.

**Mother Curry was the heart of Camp Curry—universally loved, gentle yet firm.
Here she poses on the steps of the original LeConte Memorial Lodge.** *(SS collection.)*

"West Virginia Slim," an entertainer at Camp Curry, and a friend on a forbidden and forbidding "stage." (*SS collection.*)

Alex Beck at work building a fire for the firefall. (*Audrey Beck Wilson collection.*)

close to Glacier Point's edge that a large warning sign had been erected, which read:

> It is 3,000 feet to the Bottom
> And no undertaker to meet you
> TAKE NO CHANCES
> There is a difference
> Between bravery and just plain
> ORDINARY FOOLISHNESS

After gas-pipe railings were installed, the sign disappeared. Beck admitted to his family that he had been so tired of tourists "Ohing" and "Ahing" about the message, that he had stacked the sign with the fir bark, and it had became part of a firefall.

Like many employees, Beck enjoyed misleading gullible Park visitors. He perpetuated the myth that there was an elevator inside Half Dome, and when asked what a capped pipe on Glacier Point was for would answer offhandedly, "Oh, that's where they pump oil up from Camp Curry to start the fire for the firefall!" Besides tending the fire, Beck did maintenance on the Glacier Point Hotel and the adjacent Mountain House, which was utilized as a cafeteria and employee's quarters, shoveled snow off the buildings when necessary, and trod the Ledge Trail like a mountain goat. Although not a big man, he was powerful and carried weighty loads in packs on his back and over his chest. Before the Glacier Point Road was cleared of snow one year, he made two round trips a day to carry fresh food up from Camp Curry to the Mountain house were meals were fed to people who had skied, snowshoed, or hiked in.

Camp Curry's most famous ex-employee was rarely mentioned at camp, but made headlines in the fall of 1932. At that time, Foster Curry was hospitalized in Los Angeles with leukemia, and kept alive by blood transfusions. For days his illness was front-page news, and get well wishes came in from all over California. His wife and mother were with him constantly. Stirred by the unfolding tragedy, his sister, Mary Curry Tresidder, who had not seen or communicated with him since his eviction from Yosemite in 1921, telephoned to offer her blood. Ruth Curry related the messages to Foster, who answered firmly, and bitterly, "Tell her I don't want her blood, don't want to see her here, and don't want her at my funeral."

He did want to return to his still-loved Yosemite, and told his wife and mother he

Virginia Best Adams beside the warning sign at Glacier Point. *(Adams family collection.)*

four years, because she was in Indiana attending her fiftieth college reunion. Afterwards she visited the eastern states. While she was away, Mary Tresidder acted as manager. A year later, four months before she was seventy-three, Mother Curry issued a press release that read:

In order to assist me in handling the many details and exacting management of Camp Curry, I am appointing my daughter, Mary Curry Tresidder, as my assistant. For the past several years, Mrs. Tresidder has been trained under my personal supervision with the thought of perpetuating the Curry family traditions in the management of Camp Curry. I shall continue to be in close touch with activities at Camp Curry directly, and through Mrs. Tresidder.

At last the head of Pacific Coast hotel women was slowing down. On a number of occasions Margaret Jabes heard her boss say that she wanted to retire when she was seventy-five—that age was celebrated on October 12, 1936. After that, Mary Tresidder managed the camp, but Mother Curry always had a definite voice in its affairs.

That she was still active and forceful in the late 1930s and early 1940s is perhaps best testified to by Foster's son, John, who knew her well—first as grandmother, then as titular boss in those years.

My overall impression of my grandmother is one of natural leadership and vision, coupled with a true concern for the employees, the guests, and for Yosemite itself. I never saw her angry in the emotional sense, although I heard her provide "strong guidance" to me and many others. She was a very dramatic figure that people could relate to and work for . . . a magnificent grandmother. . . .

wanted his ashes pushed over with a firefall. "Oh, no Foster," his mother exclaimed, "If that were done, I could never bear to look at a firefall again!" After his death, on November 21, 1932, there was a well-attended funeral, and widespread news coverage. On June 10, 1933, the eighth anniversary of his marriage to Ruth, a small plane flew over Yosemite Valley. In it were the pilot and Ruth Curry, and as it passed over a rainbow-decorated cloud, ashes spilled from a window. Foster Curry was at peace.

That same spring Mother Curry had been absent at the opening of Camp Curry for the first time in thirty-

11　Depression Years

Between 1933 and 1939, Half Dome, El , and the other wonders of Yosemite were as unsurpassable as ever, but far fewer Americans came to view them. The Great Depression was on, and most people could barely afford necessities, let alone luxuries such as vacations. Park Service statistics show how the financial crisis affected travel.

1932	498,289
1933	296,088
1934	309,431
1935	372,317
1936	432,192
1937	481,492
1938	443,325
1939	466,552

Nineteen thirty-one was the last profitable year for Yosemite concessionaires. During 1931 the Yosemite Park and Curry Company did a $1,880,632 gross business, and boasted a $97,637 net profit after taxes. The next three years were ruinous. The figures show how drastically declining travel depressed revenue.

Year	Gross Sales	Net Profit
1932	$1,592,547	$22,250
1933	$1,243,181	$ 1,495
1934	$1,425,832	$24,097

Rooms went unrented, tents were empty, reservations desks quiet, and even cafeteria waiting lines short. Inevitably, the luxurious Ahwahnee Hotel suffered the worst decrease in registration, although the bungalows maintained satisfactory pillow counts during summer. Many wealthy Bay Area families, including the Dohrmanns, continued their custom of renting a certain cottage, regarded possessively, for weeks at a time.

Despite the Depression, the Company had to fulfill its building promises to the Park Service. Construction of a new lodge in the Mariposa Grove of Big Trees, consisting of a lounge, twelve guest rooms, cafeteria, and gift shop, cost $43,384. After completion in 1933, the old unsubstantial Desmond-era buildings and tent frames were destroyed.

In the previous year, a major property transfer, involving the Curry Company, took place within Yosemite National Park. For decades, the Wawona Basin, comprising 8,785 acres of Forest Service and privately owned land, had been a resort development surrounded by protected wilderness. Because it was the key to one-third of Yosemite's high country—and the modern Wawona Road, opening in 1933, would make it even more accessible—the Park Service pushed for its acquisition. Congress matched donated funds of $180,300 to acquire the acreage, the addition of which was authorized by President Hoover on August 13. Some homesteaders refused the option, so private ownership continues to this day, but others, notably Clarence Washburn, accepted it.

Washburn, the sole male descendant of the three long-powerful Washburn brothers, sold 2,664 acres, thirty buildings, the water system, ice pond, golf course, airfield, truck gardens, hayfields, riding stock, and forty milk cows to the government. As part of the negotiations, the Curry Company bought all the hotel furnishings and equipment from Washburn for $76,802, retained him as manager, appointed him to the Board of Directors, and began operating the unit.

As a youth, Washburn had been a champion fisherman, supplying the hotel with trout at 25¢ a pound. On one pre-limit day, he caught 297 fish! In 1911, at the age of twenty-five, he became assistant manager of the Wawona Hotel, and, after his father's death, in 1917, its manager. Under his direction, two hotel buildings, a golf course, airfield, and swimming pool were added for the enjoyment of guests, many of whom returned year after year for long stays. At the end of the 1934 season, Washburn cut all his Yosemite ties and moved to Indio, where he ran the Hotel Potter for decades.

Thereafter, managing the Wawona Hotel was a prized position among Curry staff because of its historic significance, its fine clientele, natural charm, and remoteness from general office direction. Lou Foster was one of the happy, independent managers there in the 1930s. Oliene Tresidder presided through most of the 1940s, and Cy and Agnes Wright took over in the 1950s.

Along with the Wawona enterprise, the Curry Company inherited the Gordon family. "No story about Yosemite would be complete," Hil Oehlmann stated, "without mention of Eddie Gordon, one of our

In 1932 the Curry Company acquired the furnishings and equipment, including a dairy herd, of the Wawona Hotel. *(SS collection.)*

early stage-drivers and for many years manager of the Wawona Stable in summer and caretaker of our properties there in winter. . . . I can testify to his competence and fine character."

Eddie was born in Madera, California in 1886, and, because his father and uncle were stage-drivers, he spent every summer in Wawona. At sixteen he began working as a stockman, at nineteen he became a stage driver, and at twenty-three he outfoxed a stage robber by hiding $500 under a seat cushion. From 1918 until 1968 he worked in the Wawona Stable. His knowledge of the backcountry was so encyclopedic and his manner so pleasant that he was often asked to guide people on pack trips. If hikers were lost, or once when an airplane was, he was enlisted to lead searches, and usually knew the exact area in which the lost could be found.

His wife, May, managed the Wawona Store. In time, two sons, Albert and Richie, worked for the Company, and daughter Gladys acted as the mail carrier for Wawona, where she and Albert lived. She remembers how the Tresidders would visit the Gordons and everyone ended up in the kitchen. Sometimes Don would grab an apron and join May in preparing tasty dishes.

Due to the Wawona acquisition, a new twenty-year contract had to be negotiated between the Company and the Park Service, which was signed in late November 1932. On December 8, almost before the ink was dry, fire destroyed the Company offices and many records in the historic Cosmopolitan building.

Champion fisherman Clarence Washburn managed the Wawona Hotel from 1917 till 1934. *(Mariposa County Historical Society collection.)*

Three generations of Gordons: stage-driver Tom, Gladys, and Eddie.
(*Gladys Gordon Mee collection.*)

Curry staff had been thinned, their pay reduced, and those who remained exerted maximum effort to preserve their jobs and to keep the Company going. Years later, Miles Cooper, who had joined the staff in 1928, said that the entire organization could have have been staffed by people working for nothing more than room and board. Such a measure was never considered as a remedy. In fact, college students hired as weekend help were not only paid but were housed and fed, sometimes for extra days. Tresidder, Oehlmann, and Hoss voluntarily cut their salaries for the duration.

Even before President Franklin D. Roosevelt launched the New Deal, the Curry Company introduced anti-depression moves. On March 1, 1933, twenty-five-percent reductions were announced for all tours, transportation, and lodging. In immediate response the Yosemite Valley Railroad filed a lawsuit charging the Company with unduly depressing bus rates and affecting rail competition. While Herman Hoss and the legal department fought that, Fred Black, the Company's advertising manager, whose budget was intact, was one of the busiest men in the office. His advertising campaign for 1933 included twenty-four different ads

Tresidder moved his staff onto the mezzanine floor of the Ahwahnee Hotel as a temporary measure. There he ordered budget cuts and economy measures, which extended to using both sides of pieces of paper and turning off unneeded lights.

The year 1933 began disastrously for the nation and for Yosemite residents, since budgets and payrolls had been cut for both the Park Service and the Curry Company. Late in January, heavy snow fell, and there weren't enough snow plows or maintenance men to handle it. Resourcefully, Superintendent C. G. Thomson ordered a "Shovel Day," on which sixty-five men, including rangers, Curry officers, mechanics, warehousemen, and skating instructors shoveled snow off Valley roads. Thomson said that Yosemite was uniquely useful in combating the Depression since it offered physical and spiritual outlets for unhappy people. Unfortunately, so many people lacked funds and jobs that they could not afford to seek such happiness. At one bleak time in March, there were only six guests at the Yosemite Lodge, and a total of nine in the Ahwahnee, where more than once the house count was zero. Thomson and Tresidder were besieged with letters from people complaining about the exorbitant rates, such as $4.50 a day minimum for a housekeeping cabin. After conferences, the Company offered partially furnished cabins for $1.50 a day for one person and 50 cents for each additional person.

Authoritative Charles Goff Thomson, Yosemite's superintendent from 1929 until his death in 1937, was invariably known as "Colonel."
(*J. V. Lloyd photo; YNP collection.*)

No fatalities or serious accidents occurred during the twenty-nine months required to build the 4,230-foot-long Wawona Tunnel. *(Arnold Williams photo; SS collection.)*

running in major newspapers and travel magazines. On February 7, he presented a plan of selling $10 scrip books to visitors for $8.50. Scrip books, he explained to the staff, would package riding, dancing, golf, horseback breakfasts, and "all the minor vacation items which are difficult to sell because many of them are submerged and difficult to get into the average guest's consciousness." Oehlmann, Hoss, and Goldsworthy thought the idea "worth trying," Huffman was negative, and Paul Shoe was uncertain, but the go-ahead was given. By the end of July, Black was able to report that one hundred scrip books had been sold and only one woman had demanded a refund. "Our long-stay guests," Black reported to Tresidder, "are grumbling good-naturedly at the scrip books because their children get away with more than if they had to ask for cash."

Park Service officials helped attract visitors, too. Enthusiastic weekly press releases stressed natural beauties and human activities. The biggest event of the year was the June 10 "Pageant of Progress Parade" of stages, buggies, and autos to dedicate the 4,230-foot-long Wawona Tunnel. This was presented in the parking area at the east end of the tunnel, dubbed the "new" Inspiration Point. Costumed actors and Indian dances were part of the pageant. That event terminated use of the old Wawona Road, which was completed by the Washburns in 1875, and ended controlled travel from Old Inspiration Point to the Valley floor. Motorists using the Big Oak Flat Road or the little-used Coulterville Road were still subject to traffic controls, although construction of a modern highway had begun.

During 1933, the lowest point of the Depression, the Curry Company was faced with a new financial crisis when it was sued by Marjorie and Bob Williams for $304,549. That amount was the valuation they set on their preferred stock in the Company, which they wanted to exchange for debentures or cash. After 1931 no interest could be paid on any stock, and most of the Curry directors converted their shares into bonds or cash. Williams, who badly needed capital for his Illinois business, which was facing bankruptcy, asked to do likewise, but the board refused him permission. That refusal presaged some rocky times for the Williams family, and they sued for the same settlement allowed other preferred stockholders. An out-of-court settlement failed, and the trial was delayed until November 1934. At that time the presiding judge declared a nonsuit, holding that the promise of redemption was merely a statement of intention and not a binding covenant to make the company exchange cash for stock. Although the suit had been potentially ruinous to the Curry Company, Mother Curry understood its reason, did not take it personally, and was sympathetic to the Williams family. In 1936, Williams moved to Hawaii and bought an equipment company business in which he and, later, his son, were eminently successful. Leis were flown to Yosemite for Mother Curry's birthdays, and frequent visits and letters were exchanged. Marjorie Jane attended Castilleja in Palo Alto and spent vacations in the Valley with her grandmother or Aunt Mary.

In Yosemite, the Depression and edicts from Washington, D.C. dominated life. In 1933 President Roosevelt established the Civilian Conservation Corps, an ultimately beneficial relief program, and CCC camps were set up in the Park at Wawona, Crane Flat, and Eleven Mile Meadow that year. Later, other camps were located at Tamarack Flat, near Merced Grove, at Tuolumne Meadows, Empire Meadow, and at Cascades in the western end of Yosemite Valley. The CCC boys did yeoman work developing trails, thinning woods, fighting fires, erecting cribbing to stop river erosion, and building outpost cabins and roads.

Another less salutary anti-depression scheme failed to receive federal backing. The state legislature actually urged the government to put unemployed men to work building restraining dams on the headwaters of Yosemite Creek. Fortunately the powers that be ignored the proposal, and Yosemite Falls continued unregulated by anything except weather.

All during the Depression, Superintendent Thomson and Don Tresidder cooperated with Mariposa County officials. Previously there had been division between the Park and the county; now there was unity. Employment was supervised by Frank Ewing, a son-in-law of Sovulewski, and Mariposans had priority on Yosemite jobs. There was less unemployment in Mariposa County than in any other area of the state because Yosemite National Park and federal funds created jobs. Since no unemployed head of household could live in the Park, residents found their credit excellent in Mariposa, Merced, and Fresno.

Rapport between the administrative staffs of the Park Service and the Curry Company was remarkably good considering that they stood for opposite goals. However, a 1935 Conservation Forum, inspired by Ansel Adams, highlighted the basic differences between them. At that time, the Depression-hit Tresidder argued that the "intangible values" of wilderness were not only negligible, but actually negative, since insistence upon them barred the Sierra to millions. Consider also, he urged, the plight of the operators of such public service companies as his own. Hedged in by government restrictions on one side and barred by the "intangible values" on the other, the operators could not expand or improve their facilities, and such of those who were unwilling or unable to run philanthropic institutions continually risked bankruptcy. And since the parks belonged to the people why not make their magnificent landscape value available to the world?

Even as Tresidder spoke, enraging Superintendent Thomson and shocking Adams, who had thought his friend Don to be a conservationist first and a concessionaire second, highway construction was altering the landscape as the Tioga and Big Oak Flat roads (state route 120) were being built. Eventually time and planting hid most of the scars of the well-engineered roads, and millions of people were enabled to see and enjoy the High Sierra. Compromise and bitterness usually arose from confrontations between pragmatists and preservationists. Although Tresidder deeply loved wilderness, his idealism was diminished by his knowledge that roads and services translated into visitors and revenue.

Thefts increased in the 1930s. On one occasion a band of Gypsies made a substantial haul because the low-cut blouses on the soulful-eyed women so beguiled the room clerk at Yosemite Lodge that he yielded to their insistence to "bless his money," and pulled open the cash register. While its contents were "blessed," a hand was quicker than his eye and $150 or more in five- and ten-dollar bills was removed.

In June 1934, in response to public demand, the Park Service authorized liquor sales in Yosemite. For the first time in its thirty-five year history, the Curry Company put wine, beer, and whisky on sale. Don Tresidder issued a statement that concluded, "We seek the cooperation of our employees in the attempt to make alcoholic beverages available for our guests who wish it, in such a manner as it will be as unobjectionable as possible to those who do not wish it or object to its use." Mother Curry, who abhorred drinking, objected

On June 10, 1933 a Pageant of Progress celebrated the opening of the Wawona Tunnel. *(YP&CC collection.)*

strenuously. Camp Curry remained dry, and hard liquor was not displayed at the Old Village store, although it was available upon request.

Surprisingly, although the Depression drastically reduced visitation, winter sports gave the Curry Company a financial shot in the cash register. "Winter Sports," Mary Curry Tresidder recorded, "seemed to give some hope of spreading a thin layer of guests over the lean days." Ice skating had been a recreation of the pioneers, who had skated on a pond behind the Yosemite Chapel, on Mirror Lake, or, in chill winters, on the Merced River. After the Valley roads were paved, in 1925, and the contractor moved his equipment out, a huge pit, from which gravel had been excavated,

remained at Camp 6, south of the garage. Residents soon discovered that its frozen waters made an excellent place to skate.

Haphazard skiing and snowshoeing had been practiced, particularly by the pioneer mail carriers, and, of course, children had always used sleds. It wasn't until the winter of 1917–18, however, that an organized winter sports program was begun in Yosemite Valley. Late in 1917, local snow enthusiasts cleared and smoothed an 800-foot toboggan slide west of Camp Curry, and the Park Service provided ashcan lids, sleds, and bandages to the hardy souls who slid down again and again. When the opening of the All-Year Highway ended winter isolation, hundreds of people alternatively plodded up, or careened down, the slide. After a big January 1929 weekend, the *Yosemite Sentinel* recorded that several of the six dozen new ashcan lids were worn out that day from constant use. In 1927, a carefully engineered four-track toboggan slide was built near the unprofessional one. Both slides operated to the delight of residents and guests. "A big bonfire was kept blazing at the bottom," Leroy Rust reminisced, "and there was a warming hut where they could toast their toes and buy coffee and doughnuts. Did rangers assist the operations? Hell, yes, that's all they had to do in the winters."

In 1928 the Yosemite Winter Club was formed "to encourage and develop all kinds of winter sports." It was funded by the Curry Company and joined by VIPs such as Cecil B. deMille, Harry Chandler, and A. B. C. Dohrmann. Ernst Des Baillets, a ski expert, was hired by the club (and/or the Company) as director of winter sports. Three of the most dedicated members were Mary and Don Tresidder and Horace M. Albright. Late in 1928, while Albright served briefly as acting superintendent of Yosemite, he supported winter "use" of Yosemite. "Sports" was a bad word to the Park Service. One of the first projects of the Winter Club was the establishment of the largest outdoor skating rink in the West. This was accomplished simply by flooding the Camp Curry parking lot and letting the ice build up, then repeating the process. Not only was the rink a gargantuan 60,000 square feet in size, but its setting, beneath Half Dome and Glacier Point, was superb. Instructions, skates, refreshments, lighting, bleachers, live and canned music, skating exhibitions, carnivals, hockey games, and competitions were soon sponsored by the Curry Company. From the first, the directors were supportive, and Tresidder allotted funds to hire topnotch skiing and skating instructors from Europe, then the winter sports center of the world. Twice the directors sent the Tresidders abroad to study resorts and recruit talent, and the couple envisioned their beloved Yosemite as the Switzerland of the West. Indeed, both the Yosemite Winter Club and the Yosemite Ski School were the first of their kind on the West Coast. Tresidder's and the directors' ambitions were recorded by Tresidder's wife in her manuscript, "History of Winter Sports in Yosemite":

Yosemite made a bid in 1929 for the 1932 Olympics. Horace Albright, then Director of the National Park Service, sent a wire backing it up. Great were the plans, but it was turned down. Ironically, at the time of the Olympics at Lake Placid in 1932, contestants were jumping into stacked hay, while there were 12 feet of snow along the Glacier Point Road.

In the late 1920s, dog teams, sleigh rides, and skijoring (gliding on skis harnessed behind a horse) were introduced in Yosemite. Winter Club members, colorfully attired in orange and black ski-suit uniforms, assisted visitors in all activities. Newspapers and

During the Depression, Ansel Adams worked for the Curry Company ten days each month. Many of his photographs (he hated the word `picture') were orchestrated by company executives for publicity purposes. In this one at the High Sierra Camp at Tuolumne Meadows, his wife, Virginia, is the slight figure on the path.
(YP&CC collection.)

As evidenced by the scarcity of parked cars, patronage diminished drastically at Yosemite Lodge during the Depression. (*YP&CC collection.*)

magazines carried adjective-strewn articles on Yosemite as a "Switzerland," and more and more people came to see for themselves. Snow had turned from white to gold for the Curry Company. Lodging, food, equipment, and appropriate dress were provided by their units. Since ski apparel was nonexistent in California, Company officials persuaded a few manufacturers to make suitable snow-repellant clothes, and thus Yosemite helped pioneer an important industry.

On the day of the first significant snowfall, Superintendent Thomson would proclaim "Snow Day."

Whereas, on this day we have been favored by the first opportunity of the winter season to enjoy our snow sports, I do hereby declare a general winter sports holiday.

"Come and get it!" A guest barbeque was supervised by YP&CC entertainers and staff. Left to right: Glen Hood, Midge Pittman, Al Kay, Helen Timms, Doris Schmidell, and the chef. (*Marjorie Pittman collection.*)

This four-track toboggan slide, built west of Camp Curry in 1927, thrilled thousands of visitors. In 1952, a local boy suffered a broken neck on the track; it was then closed. *(Ansel Adams photograph; YP&CC collection.)*

as you could before falling down." A "hummock" across from the near stables was cleared of brush, equipped with a ski jump, dubbed "Ski Hill," and served as headquarters of the Ski School, which was founded in 1928. Experts such as Jules Fritsch, Ernst Des Baillets, and Ralph de Pfyffer, who were Swiss, Wolfgang Greeven, a German, and Canadian-born Gordon Hooley were imported to transform human windmills into skiers.

After taking lessons and practicing on Ski Hill, Oehlmann commented that "even this breathtaking run would not satisfy the giddy enthusiasts." Explorations were made of the deep snow and varying grades beyond the north rim of the Valley. In 1929 the Snow Creek Lodge, with bunks for sixteen, was built in the shadow of Mt. Hoffman. Cabins at Tenaya Lake and Tuolumne Meadows were equipped for winter use. Yosemite pioneered in providing ski huts and initiating ski touring, but skiers were neither numerous, experienced, nor adventurous enough to truly popularize this new type of outdoor activity. During the five seasons of the Snow Creek Lodge's operation, "the deadly ski virus" infected a growing throng of residents and guests who crisscrossed the snowy slopes of Mounts Watkins and Hoffman. Mary Tresidder recorded:

> With the spring of 1934, our skiing at Snow Creek came to an end. I find from the guest register that I spent nearly three months there during the five seasons. With the construction of the Wawona Tunnel and Road and the Glacier Point Road, greater accessibility led us to the Badger Pass area. . . .

And he named a King and Queen, elected by vote, to reign over the season. To signal "Snow Day," fire sirens screamed, and residents assembled to hear the proclamation read, to salute their royally-costumed majesties, and to join a parade of sleighs, dog teams, sleds, skiers, and autos to Yosemite Lodge for celebration and refreshments. At night a ball was held in the Ahwahnee Hotel.

After a slow start, skiing became supreme among the winter whirl. At first, Mrs. Tresidder noted, ". . . for most people, skiing was a matter of standing up as long

By then ski lifts and packed-slope skiing had taken the spotlight away from touring, and enthusiasts began driving to Badger Pass. At an elevation of 7,300 feet, it was crossed by the old stage road and was only a half mile off the new road to Glacier Point. After a couple of seasons on the gentle slopes, it was decided that the mountains overshadowing Monroe Meadow to the west were better suited to skiing. Plans for runs and a lodge were designed by Ted Spencer, and approved by the Park Service as not overly injurious to scenic values. Somehow the name Badger Pass adhered to the new location, and the Badger Pass Ski Lodge was in use by mid-December 1935. At that time there was a unique "upski," forerunner of the ski lifts, consisting of two enormous, cable-pulled sleds, dubbed "Big Bertha" and "Queen Mary," which counterbalanced each other as they were drawn up. This "upski" was an unimitated original that remained in service for thirteen years. Fine ski-touring runs, several miles in length, were cleared by the Park Service. Even before the official January 5, 1936 dedication, Badger was a popular success with thousands of people infected with the "deadly ski virus." They contributed thousands of dollars to the Curry coffers, and the Company inaugurated competitive skiing contests and ski races. No sales campaign was neglected, no revenue possibilities overlooked by Tresidder and his staff in efforts to attract crowds and income. He lured such champion skiers as Hannes Schroll, Sigi Engle, and Luggi Foeger as instructors, and they imparted inspiration, drama, and foreign flavor as well as sound instruction to multitudes of people. In 1938, Charles Proctor, a New England skier and Olympic competitor, was hired to direct winter sports. He was so innovative and popular that his service with the Company continued until his retirement, in 1971.

Several residents, notably Gabrielle Sovulewski Goldsworthy and Leroy Rust, whose father was stable boss for years, became competitive skiers. Gabe won a state championship for women as did Proctor's wife, Mary.

Inevitably the new Lewis Memorial Hospital hosted numbers of hapless skiers. Dr. Avery Sturm, longtime Yosemite medical director, told the author that fractures benefited the depression-hit hospital as well as the Curry Company. "During Badger's first season," he said, "146 skiers suffered broken ankles, mostly because of poor bindings and boots, while only six had broken legs." Sturm and his predecessor, Dr. Hartley Dewey, became avid skiers as well as expert bone-setters, and Sturm began first-aid school for ski patrolmen who were rangers. From the beginning, Mary Tresidder stated, "The Park Service took full charge of injuries, first aid, patrolling of the slopes, etc." Their enthusiastic cooperation was vital.

While business was Don Tresidder's primary compulsion, he was unswervingly devoted to developing skiing as an exciting and satisfying sport. No one was more exuberant than he, gliding through the forest, "yelling and whooping for sheer ecstasy, twisting between trees, dodging branches, leaping logs. . . ." Nor was anyone more sensitive to the surrounding beauty than his wife, especially while ski-touring.

Throughout the Depression the High Sierra Camps were consistent money losers. By 1938 there were five of them: those built by Desmond at Merced Lake and Tuolumne Meadows, plus newer ones at May Lake, Glen Aulin, and Vogelsang—the latter had replaced the one at Boothe Lake. Camps at Tenaya Lake and in Little Yosemite Valley had been removed. Each one had a spectacular setting beside a tumbling stream or glacier-scooped lake. Each was delightful and demonstrated how well the public could be served by cooperation between the Park Service and a concessionaire.

Snow-melt determined the camps' opening dates, and it took Syd Ledson and his resourceful maintenance crew, aided by supply-laden pack mules, several days to open each camp. Tent frames had to be repaired, canvas put on, gravity water systems reinstalled, and steel cots and furnishings unpacked from the camp's one permanent building. After Labor Day, the process was reversed for closing up. Some groceries were left in metal cans for the "snow packing" crew. Every winter four men skied or snowshoed in to

Skijoring was popular in the Valley in the 1930s. (*YP&CC collection.*)

Merced Lake and Tuolumne Meadows, which boasted ice houses, to pile layers of snow in between the double-walled structures. Each layer had to be saturated with water so that it would freeze solid. The water was obtained by breaking the ice on the river and inducing its flow through pipes and hoses. After a layer was frozen, the procedure was repeated. Herb Ewing, an icy-fingered member of the team, recalls that workers were paid fifty cents an hour for an eight-hour day even though it might take twenty hours to reach a camp.

By 1936 the national economy was strengthening, and the Curry Company was able to finance the building commitments of its long-term contracts, primarily in the construction of employee housing, which was begun in 1928. In 1936 and 1937 two three-story dormitories and a three-story apartment house were completed in the Tecoya area between the garage and the Ahwahnee Meadow.

A sad Yosemite event was Superintendent Thomson's sudden death in March 1937. A memorial service, with Don Tresidder participating, was held at the

Except for the war years when he served overseas, Avery Sturm was Yosemite's gruff-spoken, humorous, expert doctor from 1935 until his retirement in January 1971. At that time, friends and devoted ex-patients filled the Ahwahnee Hotel dining room to fete him and his equally beloved wife, Pat.
(*Avery Sturm collection.*)

viewpoint outside the Wawona Tunnel, which had been constructed under Thomson's supervision. His successor was Lawrence C. Merriam, who served conscientiously until he was replaced by Frank A. Kittredge on August 1, 1941.

On October 3, 1937, the Mariposa Airport, built with relief funds, was dedicated. E. T. Huffman, flying a Fairchild, was one of the first to land. Bad weather elsewhere prevented the Tresidders from flying in. Don had learned to fly, bought a plane, and imbued his wife with another sports virus. In time, she too earned a pilot's license, and after that they often commuted to the Bay Area by plane.

The "pillow count" was way up during the summer of 1937, but the resultant profit vanished in the most significant event of the year, the disastrous December flood. Whenever unseasonably warm temperatures melt the snow pack above Yosemite Valley there is a threat of flood, since almost every drop of water descends into the Valley. Spring runoff can cause problems, and so can late, warm rains. There are fragmentary records of serious flooding in January 1861, November 1864, December 1867, and in the spring of 1907, but nothing drastic after that. No one in Yosemite, or in northern California, was prepared for the December 1937 storm. The results were best described by eyewitness Emil F. Ernst, Park Forester, whose article on floods appeared in the March 1952 *Yosemite Nature Notes*. It reads, in part:

> The storm responsible for the tremendous damage throughout northern California began unpretentiously in Yosemite Valley with a light rain at 9:30 a.m. on December 9. By night the rain became torrential, and within 24 hours had accumulated a total of 4.52 inches in the gauges. All the streams were swollen and the most westerly of the Cascades bridges had been swept away by 6:30 a.m. of the 10th. By 4:00 p.m. on the 11th the rain gauges showed that the total had increased to 10.86 inches . . . rain finally ceased at 2:00 a.m. on the 12th with a record total of 11.54 inches.

At the flood's peak on Saturday afternoon the 11th, over half the Valley floor was under water as the Merced River became a lake. Damage to Park Service property was later ascertained to be $271,760, while losses to the Curry Company were about $150,000. No lives were lost, but several people were injured.

Statistics do not reveal the drama, tragedy, excitement, and moments of hilarity attendant to the flood, but the author was fortunate enough to hear the reminiscences of Nancy and John Loncaric, Vickie and

**Badger Pass Ski Lodge, the "Switzerland of the West,"
opened in December 1935.** *(YP&CC collection.)*

Wendell Otter, and Lenora and Ralph dePfyffer, all of whom were involved. They told of how Old Village, adjacent to the Merced River, was soon awash, and a band of volunteers had to wade into the Chapel to rescue the organ, seat cushions, and hymn books. The most severe damage, they said, was to the store and warehouse, where water pooled several feet deep. Employees worked fast and moved much of the paper and packaged goods to the second floor, but a lot of merchandise was ruined.

While the telephones were still working, a call for Hil Oehlmann was answered by his secretary, Vickie, who said, "He'll be back in five minutes or so. Shall I have him call you?" "No," Jack Van Housen manager of the curio warehouse advised tersely, "I'm standing in water to my waist now, and if I put the phone down I might never find it again!" After the power lines were broken, candles, lamps, and limited emergency lights were used in the hotels. Since there was no auxiliary power plant at the hospital, Dr. Sturm had to operate by the light of camp lanterns.

There were only five guests at the Ahwahnee, and all of them wanted to leave, but couldn't because roads and bridges were washed out. Instead of dining in the chilled, cavernous dining room, they were served meals in front of the fireplace in the elevator lobby. Royal Arch Falls so swelled and spilled that the basement was flooded, but otherwise the hotel was dry.

Camp Curry had closed for the season, and the sixteen guests at Yosemite Lodge were deposited at the Ahwahnee before the road between them became impassible to cars. Most of the cabins at the Lodge were half full of water, and many were off their foundations and afloat. A number of them were inhabited by employees, who lost their personal belongings.

Eventually the staff of the general store, and a few employees who lived in the closed Sentinel Hotel, were told to head for higher ground, and Old Village was deserted. A couple of enterprising men decided to rescue some of the liquor in the flooded store, commandeered a rowboat, and managed to row over after dark. In their zeal, however, they so overloaded the craft that it capsized in midstream, and they had to spend the rest

Damage to roads was extreme.
(Ansel Adams photograph.)

Tent-cabins at Yosemite Lodge fared badly.
(Ansel Adams photograph.)

of the night in trees. Their discomfort was reduced by swallows from a bottle saved from the sinking ship.

When the water began to recede, a group of employees went to help clean out the warehouse. Manager Van Housen had saved a lot of valuable items, such as cameras, film, and jewelry by putting them in the loft. Unfortunately, while six feet of water still stood inside the building, some unhelpful soul opened the big back door to let the water out. Whoosh! In the resulting vacuum effect everything in the loft was sucked out on a wave. "That explained the toilet paper I saw twined in trees as far west as Bridalveil Fall," John Loncaric recalled. "What a mess! Rolls and rolls of it festooned the area."

Vickie Otter remembered that "The warehouse was a disaster, one entire box of a beautiful *Four Seasons* book by Ansel Adams had broken open, and all 400 copies were ruined—water soaked. They were all mixed up with gaudy satin pillow covers, embroidered with a scene of Yosemite, that the CCC boys loved to send to their mothers.

"Telephone lines were restrung by the 13th, and Mr. Oehlmann had me order items most needed by locals—milk, meat, Kleenex, and toilet paper. When the truck came in, I was cross because it was mostly packaged with the newspaper order for the past three days."

While much of the major flood damage was in Yosemite Valley, the rampaging Merced River had swallowed the CCC camp near Cascade Fall, swept away buildings at El Portal, and taken great chunks out of both the All-Year Highway and the railroad roadbed. While three shifts of men worked day and night to repair seventeen miles of highway, Yosemite Valley was marooned for several days. Cleanup, especially on the All-Year Highway, was not completed in time for the Bracebridge Dinner on Christmas day, so registration was low at the Ahwahnee. To fill the tables, residents were allowed in at $1.00 per person.

A day or two after the flood was over, rain began again, and a number of Indian residents, whose houses were still water-soaked, marched back into Yosemite Lodge and announced that they were going to stay for the storm's duration. Manager Lou Foster failed to persuade them to leave. "What'll I do?" she asked George Goldsworthy, the hotel division chief. "The Indians won't leave the lodge." "Give it back to 'em," was his advice.

"Lake Yosemite" was created by the December 1937 flood.
(Ansel Adams photograph.)

Despite the flood, the local economy was on the up-swing as indicated by the number of residents who bought new cars in late 1937 and 1938. Documentation of purchases was found in the Yosemite news columns that appeared weekly in the *Mariposa Gazette.* Among the dozen or so new car owners of 1937 were the Tresidders, who picked one up in Detroit. Similarly, the Curry Company purchased ten Cadillac V-8 cars, and a fleet of twelve passenger buses that were the last word in streamlined chic.

In anticipation of better days, Tresidder expanded his administrative staff, which had been depleted by the effects of the Depression and the suicide of Paul Shoe. In 1935 accountant Sterling S. Cramer had been hired as an auditor, and the following year George Oliver was retained as a transportation agent. In 1937 John Loncaric, a Fred Harvey man, was imported for unit management, and Charley Proctor came in 1938. Another important addition was businessman Harold K. Ouimet, who signed on as personnel director in July 1941. These men proved so able that they soon moved upward in the Company hierarchy, which consisted of

Tresidder, Oehlmann, Huffman, secretary-treasurer Herman Hoss, his assistant Bert Carr, cashier Herb Bartlett, publicity head Stan Plumb, and maintenance superintendent Perry Gage. Goldsworthy, Otter, and Cooper were active in the hotel division, and old-timer Jack Curran headed transportation operations.

No women served on Tresidder's executive retinue, but a number of them were managing hotel units, and others were integral to the smooth operation of the general office. Two of Sovulewski's daughters, for example, were "pillars" there: Gabe S. Goldsworthy in reservations and Mildred S. Taylor in transportation. A third sister, Grace S. Ewing, worked in the U. S. Post Office. Since salaries, except for the top men, were low, it was common for both husband and wife to work for the Company. A number of ranger's wives worked there also because the government allowed only one member of the family to be employed by the Park Service. Tresidder, Mother Curry, and Yosemite itself, inspired in these diverse personalities, male and female alike, a cohesive working force whose keynote was loyalty. Competition, tension, and confrontations were minor; cooperation and friendship prevailed.

Although there is no fixed date for the Depression's end in Yosemite, 1939 was a year of heavy travel, and 1940 a boomer in which, for the first time, the number of visitors exceeded 500,000. That figure, almost reached in 1932, had been out of sight during the remainder of the depressing 1930s, when visitation decreased by as much as 200,000.

Not only had the Depression ended, but also the era of stage roads. During the 1930s, congressional appropriations allowed the Bureau of Public Roads to build new roads through the Park, but it was 1941 before the last control stretch, on the Big Oak Flat Road, was closed. After that, skeptics said, Americans could travel faster and see less.

The year 1941 continued the tremendous surge in visitation. Over the Memorial Day and Independence Day holidays, every unit was jammed and hundreds of people were turned away. Once again the economy and Americans were on the move. Yosemite was a destination point, and facilities as well as employees were overtaxed.

Squire Tresidder of Yosemite and his Ford carriage. *(YP&CC collection.)*

12 Yosemite at War

After the Japanese attack on December 7, 1941, and America's declaration of war, the national response was one of shock, anger, and unanimity. Yosemite residents reacted accordingly. "What can we do here?" Their immediate answer then and in every one of the war years, was to oversubscribe the Red Cross War Fund quota of $1,250. Nearly 200 men and women from the Park's 1,000 or so population served in the armed forces, many with distinction. A few were killed in action.

Yosemite's new superintendent, Frank A. Kittredge, had been an officer in World War I, and took zealous command of Yosemite's World War II efforts. He organized and became chairman of a local Red Cross chapter, which sponsored the yearly fund drives, first-aid classes, a womens' Blue Jeans Fire Brigade, and knitting and sewing circles. Kittredge was a friendly, unassuming man who quickly and thoroughly acquainted himself with Park affairs and personnel as well as with the peaks, lakes, and meadows. Before he had been in office a month, he had taken extensive pack trips in the high country. Both he and his wife Catherine were well-liked and hospitable but, from the first, his strong anti-liquor stand created problems with some residents.

During the war, his primary responsibility was to guard Yosemite's natural assets. Predictably, there were those who wanted usage based on so-called wartime "necessity." Cattlemen, especially, pressured the Park Service for grazing rights, and Kittredge was at his persuasive best resisting that threat. Conservation of food was so imperative, however, that he sought and received permission from Washington to utilize land between the Curry Company's maintenance shops and school for Victory gardens. The battle against worms and blight was joined by scores of residents who planted, weeded, watered, boasted of, and consumed their produce. An electrified fence was fair protection against the worst enemy—deer. Lamon's and Hutchings' three pioneer apple orchards were pruned and sprayed, and the crop was so profuse that a cider mill was imported to preserve every last drop of juice.

In one way the war was good for Yosemite: the residents drew together. For years there had been a town-gown schism between the staffs of the Park Service and the Curry Company, largely because of the fact that the former controlled every sale and service of the latter. Park housing was in one definite area, west of the Pioneer Cemetery, while Curry people lived in the Tecoya area, east of the post office, and rarely the twain did meet. Don Tresidder was disturbed by the cleavage and decided to do something about it. When Harold Ouimet was hired to become the Company's personnel director in the spring of 1941, Tresidder instructed him to establish rapport with the Park Service. Ouimet responded by joining several social groups composed mainly of Park personnel. He helped organize a new social club of all residents, which sponsored cultural activities and the Community Fund drive. As clerk of the local school board he was well placed to represent all residents and, in 1948, as charter president of the Lions Club, he worked with employees of both the Park and the Company. In a letter to the author, Ouimet stated that "the first meeting of the club was a bleak

Ex-porter Hilmer Oehlmann was named General Manager of the Curry Company after Don Tresidder was elected President of Stanford University. *(YP&CC collection.)*

Mary and Don Tresidder at Badger Pass. *(Virginia Best Adams collection.)*

affair with clear groupings of Park Service and Company members. This soon changed, and mixing and united efforts in community activities was accepted practice." Ouimet's task was greatly aided by Superintendent Kittredge's emphasis on unison and the enthusiastic sponsorship of war causes by all. Postmaster Fred Alexander, who was neither Park nor Company, was another source of unity and the sale of war bonds, as was his assistant and eventual successor, Walter Fitzpatrick.

Within weeks after America's entrance into the war, rumors were more numerous than Yosemite bears that the Park and/or the Curry Company would close for the duration, since their existence was nonessential. By January 23, 1942, the *Yosemite Sentinel*, the new Company house organ, discounted the rumors by pointing out that travel was needed as a stimulus to morale. Rest and change were essential to the productivity of both military and civilian workers. This proved true, but not until after months of uncertainty and travel restrictions brought on by gasoline rationing. In 1941 Yosemite had 594,062 visitors. That figure was not reached again until postwar 1946. Travel statistics showed that not even the

Depression years had effected so drastic a curtailment in visitation as did the war years:

1942	332,550
1943	127,643
1944	119,515
1945	251,931

The fount of some of the dilemma was none other than the president of the Yosemite Park and Curry Company. One associate recalls that Tresidder was a pessimist whose negativism was reinforced, or possibly caused by, the Great Depression. Every spring he would assess business prospects incorrectly, direct an economy drive, and then be poorly prepared for the tourist invasion. Instead of demoralizing him, the resulting stress would be challenging, and his reactions were quick, imaginative, and decisive. His sister said that Don reacted well to stress, but couldn't abide boredom.

The basic cause of Tresidder's discouragement was the rancorous, formidable person of Harold L. Ickes, who served as Secretary of the Interior from 1933 to 1946. From the first his goals intimidated Tresidder,

During the war, NPS photographer Ralph H. Anderson and Yosemite's Ansel Adams took scores of pictures of military units that either visited or trained in the Park. Uniforms and weapons were an incongruous sight amid nature's enduring wonders. *(YNP collection.)*

as Don explained in a 1946 letter to Park Service official A. E. Demary:

> Shortly after Secretary Ickes took office in 1933 he told the park operators assembled in Washington of his conviction that in the matter of long-range policy the Government should eventually own and operate park facilities. A committee of three park operators was appointed to discuss this statement with the Secretary at great length and as a member of that committee I learned first hand from Secretary Ickes of the determined purpose behind his statement of policy.

Legislation failed to document Ickes' ideas, which were opposed to the Mather-Albright policy of private development. Tresidder stated:

> Our Company finally came to the conclusion that while its Yosemite job was less than half finished, it never could carry out the program it initially had in mind due to the radical change in attitude toward private concessions. . . . Reluctantly the Company came to the conclusion that it was in its best interest to consider the sale of its assets either to a private corporation or to the Government.

That decision was made prior to the outbreak of World War II, and certainly influenced Tresidder throughout the duration.

A third reason for Tresidder's negativism was his health. In 1939 an infection of his trachea, complicated by a bad reaction to a drug, resulted in hospitalization and a prolonged convalescence in California and Arizona resorts. Hil Oehlmann, who was acting general manager, visited him to consult on Company matters. Herman Hoss was Oehlmann's backup man. Finally, on July 18, 1941, the board of directors granted the still-ailing Tresidder a six-months leave of absence, with pay, in which to fully recover his health. At the

Not even the impact of war altered the ancient, imperturbable cliffs.
(Ansel Adams photograph.)

same time, the directors elected Mary Curry Tresidder to the board and named her as executive vice-president to assume her husband's duties.

After Pearl Harbor, Tresidder resumed the Company's presidency, but the decline in housecounts, shortage of labor, and anticipation of rationing, coupled with Ickes' attitude, solidified his pessimism. In August of 1942 he called an administrative staff meeting, during which he made a bombshell proclamation. Sterling Cramer remembers the intent of Tresidder's measured words to be, "I am president. The decision will be mine. I believe that almost no one will be able to reach Yosemite during the War what with gas rationing and travel restrictions. Therefore, I believe we should close down operations." Before that statement was fully absorbed, he began issuing equally startling directions. "Hil, you will be general manager. I suggest you make your office at the Village Store. Keep it open to serve the few people who may get in and the caretaker NPS staff. Herman, when you have closed the corporate affairs for the year and handled the annual meeting of stockholders, you are through. Ouimet, as soon as you have terminated the summer crew, you are through. . . . Huffman, you are through September 30."

Similarly, Tresidder "furloughed" traffic and advertising superintendent Stan Plumb and maintenance superintendent Perry Gage. He appointed John Loncaric as hotel division superintendent to replace George Goldsworthy, who was planning to join the Navy, and then turned to Cramer. "Sterling, someone has to keep the corporate books going. I suggest you keep your secretary and that you take a couple of rooms in 'A' dormitory for office space. We will have one of our High Sierra Camp couples live in the nearest duplex house and provide family-style meal service." ". . . If there is any comfort in unanimity." Hil Oehlmann recalled in a retrospective article about wartime problems, "we can console ourselves with the recollection that not a discordant voice was raised against the false conclusion that the Park would pass forthwith into a state of practical oblivion. Under our Company's contract with the Secretary of the Interior, we would be obliged to have accommodations available. . . ."

It was believed that a few tents and cabins would be adequate to house summer visitors, principally servicemen and war workers, while a handful of dormitory rooms would take care of occasional winter guests. Only two High Sierra Camps, those at Tuolumne Meadows and Merced Lake, would be open, the Glacier Point Hotel would close, and the Ahwahnee Hotel would be abandoned if low patronage justified such action.

It was early 1943 before most of the staff left, sadly and reluctantly, for they loved their Yosemite jobs and homes. All of them, however, relocated to good positions. For example, salty, old, ex-seadog Huffman went to work as a dock captain in a Bay Area shipyard. Their absence was felt keenly when the 1943 housecounts, composed mainly of servicemen needing rest and recuperation, overtaxed facilities and personnel. Yosemite Lodge was kept open, and busy personnel manager Ouimet, who was rehired, had to beat the bushes and the alleys for employees. "Virtually our only source of labor were the 'skid rows' of Merced and other nearby towns, so usually we were staffed by a few bums and a lot of kids," Oehlmann recorded.

Ouimet added, in a letter to the author, that "College students, formerly the nucleus of our crew, were now engaged in war activities so we had to turn to high school students who were young, immature, and inexperienced for seasonal help. Parents were often more of a problem than their sons and daughters, but we could understand their concern for progeny away from home for the first time in an area overrun with servicemen. The employment was a three-sided affair—the Company, the parents, and the students."

To ensure security, Ouimet hired counselors and instituted an intensive recreational program as well as one of job training. Naturally the youngsters tried to emulate the few oldtimers. At Camp Curry, experienced waiters could trot through the dining room balancing a tray of dishes on one hand, whereas broken crockery rewarded the young imitators. "Mother Curry's efforts to slow them down were not very successful," Ouimet remembered. "and it disturbed her no end. Eventually the diners made a game of it and applauded success rather than failure. Soon, there was a dramatic decrease in casualties. We learned to respect the intelligence and sincerity of these students, and, on the whole, they did an outstanding job." Tops among the high schoolers were youngsters imported from the Phoenix Indian School who, after their initial shyness wore off, were excellent, responsible workers. A number of men rated 4F because of minor handicaps such as a football knee were eagerly recruited. One of the most treasured 4F employees was Earl Pierson, longtime chef at Yosemite Lodge, who commanded a battery of hot stoves and did battle with an inexperienced staff and strict food rationing.

"It was extremely difficult to feed our guests and employees," Hil Oehlmann said. "I recall times when

Earl prepared food almost single-handedly, always with the spirit, `Don't worry, Boss, we'll manage it.' Harold Ouimet, as personnel manager, and I, as general manager, were often in the Lodge kitchen, and a few times even helped out with the dishwashing. Earl may still attest that turkey necks make excellent oxtail stew, but I venture that he may now confess that bean sandwiches were not very acceptable even during wartime."

Hotelman Loncaric never had to wash dishes, but filled in at stoves, waited tables, and worked on the reservation and transportation desks. He recalled a time when a truckload of chickens failed to arrive, and spaghetti, macaroni, and rice became the monotonous order of the day. He lauded Earl Pierson for working around the clock and for "creating fairly filling dishes with the judicious use of cereal and bread as entree-stretchers."

Loncaric's wartime reminiscences in the October 25, 1966 *Yosemite Sentinel* revealed more of his problems:

Chef Earl Pierson in the old Yosemite Lodge kitchen, flanked by Lee Brazitis and Wendell Otter. *(Earl Pierson collection.)*

As the noose of rationing grew tighter, the bills of fare at the Lodge and Camp Curry became skimpier, particularly in the meat line. John found himself, at one time, able to get only lamb for an extended period. Lamb was served in every possible fashion—in stew, as chops, in patties and as steaks. The regulars at the Lodge cafeteria made impolite sheep noises when they spied John. Later, when ration stamps were needed for lamb as well, poultry became the mainstay. . . .

While business could scarcely be called brisk, it did improve, John says, making the ever-growing shortage of help more vexing. Competent, or even sober, male employees were impossible to find. The hotels operated with bare-bones crews, mostly women and child labor. Laws were changed permitting youngsters to work, but only for a minimum number of hours a day. There were as many as fifty young boys in the Curry dishroom, John recollects, and they smashed about as many dishes as they washed.

Harold Ouimet, John remembers, set out in a company bus to recruit men from the nearby communities to dismantle the tents at Curry and the Lodge. (Whether the men were recruited or shanghaied, only Ouimet knows.) However, Harold arrived one early morning with a busload of men. As they stepped, bleary-eyed, from the bus John heard them ask. "Well, where are the grapes you want picked?"

In emergency situations, Loncaric asked for volunteers from the office force. At times Frances Gann and Alice Hewiston deserted their desks for ovens and helped with the baking at Yosemite Lodge, while Vickie Otter, Gabe Goldsworthy, Mil Taylor, and others pitched in to do maid work at Camp Curry. The gas station and garage there were managed by Myrtle Cuthbert, who proved that she could lube and service cars as ably as she had cooked at Big Trees Lodge before the war. Mother Curry requested some faithful old-time workers to return to Camp Curry. One of them was ex-waitress, ex-teacher Helen Mickle Sault, who had married Yosemite ranger Bert Sault, and came back to work in the summers of 1943 and 1944. Her daughter, Shirley, fourteen, cleaned dorms and tents. "My most agonizing job," she recalled, "was cooking Mother Curry's egg exactly four minutes, then carrying her breakfast to her bungalow. I wanted everything to be hot and perfect for her."

Neither labor nor gasoline shortages kept Santa Claus Tresidder from arriving on Christmas Eve. Every child in the Valley assembled in the vast Camp Curry dining room, opened specially for the occasion, to await Santa's descent down the chimney. The fireplace was subtly separated from the room by a towering screen from around which Santa bounded the moment suggestive noises in the chimney ceased. His "ho, ho, ho" and bustling presence made true believers out of the most skeptical of children, and the gifts, requested earlier by letter, were eminently satisfying. After Santa bustled off behind the screen, refreshments were served and Nancy Loncaric's "Rhythm Band" of youngsters entertained with appropriate songs. "Uncle Don" would slip in to join "Aunt Mary" and everyone was content. All arrangements and presents for both Company and Park children were taken care of by the Curry Company. In turn, the Park Service presented residents with Christmas trees cleared from the roadway or thinned from a view-obstructing thicket. The other seasonal celebration, the Bracebridge Dinner of Christmas Day, was a wartime casualty, but Santa was undeterred.

Late in January 1943, front-page news startled Yosemite residents and its devotees. Donald Bertrand Tresidder had been elected president of his beloved Stanford University. His alliance with, and support of it, had been close since his undergraduate days, while his friendship with President Wilbur, trustee Herbert Hoover, and other important alumni had grown with their visits to Yosemite, where Tresidder arranged VIP treatment for them. During his long convalescence from the throat ailment, he read extensively on theories, ideals, and development of education. In recognition of his background and interest, he was elected to the Stanford Board of Trustees in December of 1939. He was then its youngest member. By May of 1942 he was its president and actively in search of a successor to Stanford President Wilbur, who was beyond retirement age. While Tresidder was in the East interviewing candidates for the position, Stanford's ten deans petitioned that he be named president. The trustees agreed, and on January 21 unanimously elected Tresidder as Stanford's fourth leader. So it was that David Curry's

Chief Ranger Forrest Townsley smiled approval at Yosemite school children's purchase of World War II Postal Savings stamps. The children in the front row are: Donna Alexander at the desk to the left; Burleigh Johnson; Jim Ouimet; Shirley Quist; Charlie Jobe; Barbara Bertoncinni; Patty Fitzpatrick; and Joanne Stevinson seated at the right.
(Amy Leavitt Alexander collection.)

son-in-law followed Curry's hero, David Starr Jordan, in leadership.

War had diminished Tresidder's business responsibilities in Yosemite. Stanford offered challenge, prestige, and the task of making a great university greater under wartime conditions. Yosemite was his passion, but Stanford's woody, still pastoral environment was his second love, as it was his wife's. He accepted the mortarboard but at the same time retained his Yosemite "hat." Stanford's gain was not entirely Yosemite's loss, since after his inauguration on September 1, 1943, he served the Company without pay, although a house in Yosemite Valley and a car were provided for him. His duties were minimal, but the Curry directors wanted him to continue negotiations with the armed forces and the Secretary of the Interior.

Not everyone in the Valley regarded Tresidder's departure with the mingled regret and pride proclaimed in the *Yosemite Sentinel*. There were those who felt that he was aggressive and even ruthless. Others resented his intellectual aloofness, and called him the "Squire of Bracebridge." There was no middle ground; he was either loved or hated. Not even his closest associates truly understood his complex and subtle personality. Dr. Russell V. Lee, a classmate and fellow Stanford booster, admitted as much in random reminiscences of eminent Stanfordites whom he had known and treated. In the book *Stanford Mosaic*, Dr. Lee stated:

I thought at one time that I knew Donald Tresidder very well indeed. In fact, I thought I was perhaps his closest friend. But many others thought that, too. Don, handsome, laughing, cordial, had one of the most charming approaches to human relationships of anyone I ever knew. He made each person feel his intense interest in him and his ideas. But he was truly a complex man, and I believe now that no one person knew him completely. After talking to many people, he made up his own mind and had his own sense of direction from which he could not be swerved. He brought tremendous organizational changes to the president's office—a sort of general staff system replaced the old one-man personal direction. He himself became rather inaccessible, but the machinery moved very smoothly indeed.

If any man knew Don Tresidder intimately it was Hil Oehlmann, who wrote that his friend and boss combined determination, imagination, integrity, and leadership in "the framework of a warm and vibrant personality, a pervading human interest, a kind and sympathetic understanding." Oehlmann's evaluation was based on his observations of Tresidder in Yosemite, whereas Lee knew him best at Stanford.

Predictably, Oehlmann was appointed general manager, in effect the acting president of the Company. Mother Curry's handwritten letter of congratulation indicated pride:

My dear Hil:

May I congratulate you on your new position with our organization and express my pleasure that one of "my boys" has made good in such a substantial way.

It is a far cry from porter at Camp Curry to the position you now hold but you have well earned your various promotions by continuous devoted service. . .

With all good wishes,
MOTHER CURRY

Venerable Mother Curry, who had celebrated her eightieth birthday in October 1941, still wielded influence, and challenged by wartime conditions she even pitched in to help with the work at Camp Curry.

Oehlmann shouldered the responsibilities and difficulties of operating under restrictions and shortages, and by mid-September 1943 voiced optimism via the *Yosemite Sentinel*:

A year ago many felt that Yosemite had completed its last active season for the duration. Such persons visualized a period of relative inactivity in which the Park Service would continue its important function of preserving and protecting the values of Yosemite and the Company and other concessionaires would devote all their efforts toward survival. . .

One can now scarcely question the value of Yosemite's contributions to the war. There appears no longer to be the question of survival for resumption of activities after the war, but rather the problem of handling with insufficient personnel the volume of travel which will continue during the war. We feel sure that, in spite of many curtailments and restrictions, the public feeling has generally been one of high commendation for the efforts of those who have kept the Park open for needed vacations and of great hope that such efforts may continue to keep it open.

Oehlmann's integrity, loyalty, and steadfastness combined in a warm, kindly, even-tempered character. He was always a gentleman, ever a Yosemite devotee, and completely at home whether camping in forest or presiding at a board of directors meeting. His boss might try to wear two hats, but Hil wore one—that of the chief concessionaire.

Many "Uncle Sam wants you" letters were directed to eligible Yosemite men, but in 1943 the most astonishing request from Uncle Sam was issued by the U. S. Navy, which wanted the Ahwahnee Hotel for use as a convalescent hospital. In many ways the proposal was

Navy Captain Reynolds Hayden operated the USS Ahwahnee under the supervision of Yosemite's wartime superintendent, Frank A. Kittredge. *(YNP collection.)*

Guests had not left the Ahwahnee Hotel before the first sailor, a maintenance man, landed on May 30, 1943. Between that time and July 6, when the first patients arrived, the hotel's contents had to be inventoried and stored by the Company. That job was tackled by John Loncaric and Sterling Cramer. Neither man wore a uniform but both fought the little-known Battle of the Ahwahnee with valor. An account by Henry Berrey in a latter-day *Yosemite Sentinel* gave details of the engagement.

> For three months they counted, tagged, and prepared for storage outside the Park the thousands of chairs, sheets, rugs, etc. Meanwhile several navy chiefs, with eyes for comfort, had to be discouraged from rerouting easy chairs and innerspring mattresses to their quarters. When the landing operations were complete, Capt. Edmiston, USN, took charge.

According to Cramer, who knew almost every piece of furniture's serial number by heart, the bulk of it was trucked to El Portal, then loaded into several dozen freight cars for shipment to Oakland for storage. En route down the Merced River the train had a wreck and dumped several cars into the river, to the detriment of chairs and tables.

Dining room furniture was kept by the Navy for use in what must have been one of the world's most luxurious mess halls. The enormous, twenty-four-foot-high Great Lounge was turned into Ward A, where 350 or more men slept in five rows of double-tiered cots. The gift shop became a canteen, the writing room a Protestant chapel, and the bar and cocktail lounge on the mezzanine floor converted into a Catholic chapel that seated ninety. Fittingly, the Tresidder's sixth-floor apartment was headquarters for the commanding officer. On visits to the Park, the Tresidders stayed in one of the newest houses in the Tecoya "Rocky Heights" section.

In 1928, countless hours of manpower and $30,000 had been expended on landscaping and planting wildflower gardens around the Ahwahnee. They were the first casualty of the naval invasion. Where flowers had bloomed at random in clumps and banks, and meadow-like lawns had stretched, an interconnected series of barracks-type buildings was built. Eventually these excrescences housed an auditorium, a pool hall, a two-cell brig, a large washroom, a bowling alley, an enlisted mens' club, occupational therapy quarters, and hobby and craft shops. Natural beauty was sacrificed for utility and rehabilitation of human resources.

For a few months the new hospital treated neuropsychiatric patients, whose conditions worsened in the

attractive: leased to the Navy the hotel would show the Company's patriotism and also add revenue. After a series of meetings a contract was negotiated and signed, wherein the Navy filed a condemnation suit in court and deposited $55,000 yearly to cover taxes, insurance, and depreciation on the property. The Curry Company argued that the sum was insufficient, and negotiations continued spasmodically during the thirty months of the Navy's occupancy.

Probably the last major private event at the Ahwahnee was the February 27 wedding of Lt. Robert T. Williams, Jr., to Roberta Kincaid. His parents, sister, and grandmother Curry were present at the evening ceremony. Bob was the second of Mother Curry's grandchildren to marry. Katherine Curry, who had renamed herself Cherry after her deceased mother, had been the first, and had provided Mother Curry with her first great-grandchild.

face of the fortress-like cliffs. Claustrophobia was added to their other stresses. By 1944 the usage was changed and only general medical and surgical patients were admitted. These war-weary veterans wanted girls, beer, and fun and games. Their appreciation of beauty, other than in feminine form, was virtually nonexistent. One sailor summed up the patients' mood as "Yosemite is a beautiful place surrounded by solitude." In summertime the swabbies established beachheads with the female employees at Camp Curry and Yosemite Lodge. Shore patrolmen had to restrain men from worrying the girls in the Tecoya dorms and government housing areas. There were a few arrests for rape and a number for drunkenness.

As head of the hotel division, Loncaric was continually involved in trying to protect Company properties from the Navy. His holding tactics were not overly successful as recorded in a retrospective *Yosemite Sentinel* article:

The first patients at USS Ahwahnee were veterans of naval encounters near Okinawa. Despite their convalescent status, they were a lively lot, and upon release from duty at 4 p.m., were wont to take a little cheer at the Lodge bar which had about 30 stools. A hundred fifty bluejackets arrived one 4:05 p.m. and, as boys will, hoisted a few too many. When the situation became explosive and the jolly tars commenced smashing the furniture, the Lodge manger sent out a distress call for John. There was no shore patrol so Loncaric took on the mob. The fracas ended with two bartenders hors de combat, the place demolished, and the bottled booze going out by the armsful. John escaped with minor bruises.

In time, the battle of the bottle was lost by all concerned. Officers would pull rank on the enlisted men at the Yosemite Lodge bar, which inspired rebellion. More than once the bartender was attacked when he tried to close the place at 11 p.m., the official witching hour. Turnover in bartenders was frequent, and soon Superintendent Frank shut the bar down for the

On June 25, 1943, the luxurious Ahwahnee Hotel was commissioned as a Naval Hospital. Its new "guests" were nonpaying, and mostly unappreciative. One sailor commented, "I joined the Navy to see the high seas, not the High Sierra." *(Ansel Adams photograph; YNP collection.)*

duration. After that, liquor was brought in for the sailors by their visiting friends and relatives and hidden in the talus slopes north of the Ahwahnee. This whisky-on-the-rocks practice, and Naval pressure, were so great that Kittredge was forced to provide a place for sale and imbibing of alcoholic refreshments besides Degnan's, where only beer could be bought. He reluctantly ordered an area just outside the Village Store to be screened and equipped with tables and chairs. There sailors could hoist a can or a glass in what surreptitiously became known as "Frank's Place." Despite the problems caused by the Navy, Yosemite residents were proud to have veterans there and welcomed patients to local dances, movies, and parties. Coincident with the "occupation" were unexpected fringe benefits for inhabitants and the Company's till. Because of the labor scarcity, the Company could not operate the toboggan slide, so the bluejackets took it over. Families of patients and staff required housing. They were rented cabins at Yosemite Lodge, and, in season, tents and housekeeping cabins at Camp Curry, all at reduced rates. Tents brought in only $30 each a month. Still, $30 times the forty-five tents made available was money in the cash register. Several Company houses were rented to officers and their families, and the Ranger's Club served as bachelor officers' quarters. As early as September 1942, Tresidder had documented in the Yosemite Winter Club Year Book his pessimism concerning the future of winter sports.

> The boss is just as sorely perplexed as the employee. His decisions largely depend on coming events which are just as unknown to him and over which he has no control. . . Will our fleet of buses which we have conserved so conscientiously be required to transport war workers? Will mounting congestion of trains and buses necessitate strict curtailment of non-essential travel? Is recreational skiing out for the duration?

Badger did operate in the 1942–43 season, but with the approach of the next winter Oehlmann recalled that "Superintendent Kittredge suddenly made the shocking announcement that it would have to close as the Park Service had no money to keep the road open. With that news I went to Captain Hayden, the Commanding Officer, and pointed out what a wonderful recreational need it would serve for Navy and other personnel. He agreed, and the Navy kept the road open. Badger was heavily visited, too, by the airmen from Merced. I must confess that the wisdom of the decision was mildly questioned by those in charge when the usual number of broken legs, sprained ankles, etc., showed up among the navy men and flyers. But, on the whole, the Badger operation served a useful purpose and was regarded with approval. "After Doctors Dewey and Sturm left to enter military service, naval doctors and corpsmen staffed Lewis Memorial Hospital and kept it operating for civilians. On the whole the Navy's presence was a pride and a boon to Yosemite.While Navy men were in the majority, Army, Marine, and Army Air Force members also came to the Park for rest and recreation during the war. Military personnel accounted for about half of the total visitation in Yosemite in those years, and Signal Corps units trained in the Park. When the United Nations Conference was held in the spring of 1945 in San Francisco, Yosemite was their weekend goal and surely must have given the 340 American and foreign delegates needed uplift. During a walk through the Mariposa Grove of Big Trees a Frenchman commented, "I believe if we were holding our meetings here, we would have a better sense of proportion."

By its very existence, Yosemite influenced the war and peace efforts and so, by energetic and patriotic contributions, did its residents, who joyfully celebrated the war's end on August 15, 1945.

13 Yosemite at Peace

Yosemite National Park survived the war. It had not been invaded by enemy troops, American loggers, or cattle, and limited military training use had made almost no visible impact. Not even the unsightly buildings adjacent to the Ahwahnee would be permanent scars. All the priceless scenic wonders were intact at war's end, but were immediately assaulted by a peacetime invasion of servicemen and civilians seeking peace, rest, and inspiration amid the granite stability.

Gasoline rationing ended August 15, and between that time and September 8 nearly 40,000 people entered the Park. Over the three-day Labor Day holiday, 18,291 visitors filled every accommodation and overflowed the campgrounds. Many people had to sleep in their cars. Once more, reservation clerks were frantic and cafeteria waiting lines lengthy as travel during the dry, water- and bloom-shy month of September was the heaviest in history. At a time when business usually dwindled and the summer help left, the onrush overtaxed the Curry Company's facilities and manpower. On October 27, an editorial in the *Yosemite Sentinel* admonished employees that the days of occasional discourtesy caused by shortages of labor, supplies, and tempers were over. Once again the guest was always right, the customer king!

Fortunately for the Curry organization, winter slowed visitation to an easily manageable volume, and the Company was able to begin rebuilding staff and restoring services before the spring 1946 influx. George Goldsworthy returned from the service to direct the hotel division and, in time, replacements were hired to superintend both the maintenance and transportation departments. Some reorganizing was done: the secretary-treasurer position became one of Hil Oehlmann's multitudinous responsibilities, and Cramer took over as his assistant on those jobs in addition to his function as general auditor. Legal eagle Herman Hoss had opened a law firm in Palo Alto, but was retained by the Curry Company as special counsel. His analytical and objective mind enabled him to condense the most complex problem into terse, concise, and thoroughly documented sentences. This ability was manifest at the yearly conferences between the Company and the Park Service wherein rates for transportation, lodging, and

De. Tresidder at Stanford, as painted by artist Arthur Cahill. *(YNP collection.)*

meals, and any plans for building improvements, sites, equipment, or new activities were reviewed.

While peace and Curry prosperity seemed at hand, the Company's troubles were not over. To finance the higher wages needed to attract effective employees, Company officials wanted price increases on services, such as meals and rooms. Every price change had to be okayed by the government after long deliberations. The Teamsters Union began flexing its bargaining muscle, and Mariposa County was threatening to reassess properties and increase taxes. Buildings and equipment had not received proper maintenance during the war, and that had to be financed even as the Park Service demanded the improvements and new construction delayed by the war.

Most of these concerns were long-range ones involving months of study, discussion, and bargaining. On May 7, 1946, however, an unexpected problem demanded immediate attention. That day, newspaper headlines such as "Huge Yosemite Profits Bared," Curry Co. Questioned," and "Yosemite Park Concession Hit" were bombshell news, especially in California. Representative John J. Rooney, a member of the House Appropriations Committee, had inspired the headlines and news articles by charging, after a hearing of the committee, that Yosemite National Park was "run for the benefit of a concessionaire," specifically the Yosemite Park and Curry Co. That corporation, he announced, had done nearly a $3,000,000 gross business in fiscal 1945, yet paid the government only $6,100. "Is it not a fact," Rooney declaimed, "that if you did nothing but sell hot dogs and soda pop at Yosemite Park, the Federal treasury would have a better return than under this contract?"

Next the New York Congressman revealed that the Company's twenty-year concession had been granted in 1932 while Ray Lyman Wilbur, later president of Stanford University, had been Secretary of the Interior. Signer for the Company had been Don Tresidder, the succeeding Stanford president. Furthermore, Tresidder and his family owned a majority of the Company's stock. Rooney's last verbal shot was that "The government should make no private arrangements with distinguished families in California or elsewhere for its public park concessions." His statements and insinuations were reiterated to the House on May 8.

Tresidder was away, but Dr. Wilbur immediately issued a statement declaring that thousands of concessionaire contracts had been routinely signed by him, and none questioned until now. "It seems quite evident," he said,"that the whole thing is being presented on a most extreme basis, evidently with the idea of making an attack on the Department of Interior. . . . No one has seen the necessity of bringing it out for criticism before. Probably this is because last year was the first considerable profit the company has realized. . . ."

On May 10, Mrs. Tresidder talked to a reporter from the *San Francisco News* and denied that the Curry Company was operating virtually tax free or that any special grants were given it. She was quoted as saying:

> Washington stories have so far given only one-sided accounts. Under terms of the contract with the government the Curry Company has many obligations not yet disclosed. The Company must follow out any reasonable suggestion by the National Park Service to add to public enjoyment of the valley.

Further, she pointed out that building the Ahwahnee Hotel, a government idea, had taken a large investment and that the Company had operated consistently in the red until recently. "Since then," said she spiritedly, "we have averaged roughly 6 percent on our investment. I don't think that is an exorbitant return."

In Yosemite, office lights burned late as Cramer and Oehlmann gathered facts and figures for reporters. It is true, Oehlmann said, that the Company paid only $5,000 a year for its franchise, but it also paid the government about $90,000 for electricity, water, telephone, and incineration service, and paid out $207,000 in 1945 for federal, state, and county taxes. It was true that the Tresidders owned 72,490 shares of stock, Mrs. Curry 55,072 shares, and other family members 20,280 shares, yet 422 other stockholders owned a total of 192,572 shares. In the nineteen years since the merger, the Company had paid stock dividends ranging from two percent to twelve percent. No dividends had been paid between 1932 and 1936, nor in 1941, and thus the average annual return paid stockholders was 4.99 percent. In addition to his statement to the press, Oehlmann wrote Tresidder privately:

> It appears to me that the most important step is to get an Associated Press or United Press release on the other side of the story. Undoubtedly the most effective means of accomplishing this would be to have some member of Congress attack Rooney's position on the floor. . . .
>
> It is interesting to speculate whether Congressman Rooney was in any way inspired by the attorney for the Teamsters Union . . . who is a Stanford graduate and, I understand, not one of our well wishers.
>
> For such personal embarrassment as this barrage may cause Mary and you, I am deeply sorry and

Yosemite had survived the war, but peace brought a new invasion —visitors in abundance. *(SS collection.)*

hope a counter-attack can be launched which will repair some of the damage.

Tresidder *was* hurt. On June 11, he admitted so in a handwritten personal letter to Park Service Director Newton B. Drury:

Congressman Rooney's attack has set in motion more difficulties than one would expect—and the end is not yet. . . . I will say that I'm suffering more than simple personal embarrassment from the attack.

Late in May a barrage of mimeographed, unsigned postcards was received by Stanford faculty members, who reacted quickly and angrily. The anonymous message ran:

Dear Colleague:

How much longer will we accept the former manger of Curry Company—Uncle Don—as president? Is not Stanford worthy of a scholar rather than a resort manager as president? Let us stop merely expressing our disapproval and unite for action.

By that time Tresidder was fifty-two, distinguished-looking, urbane, and somewhat dissatisfied with the pressures of his job. "All I'm doing is running errands to get money . . . seeking grants, grants, to keep this thing going," he told Bob Dohrmann. Nevertheless, he loved the contact with undergraduates. "You know," he confided to Dohrmann, "Mary and I never had any children, and we've always loved them and where could you get a bigger crop than at Stanford?"

There had been talk of Tresidder moving up to high political office. His poor-boy-makes-good background, his prestigious position at Stanford, and his powerful circle of friends—Hoover, Albright, Wilbur, Henry R. Luce, Harry Chandler—fueled rumors that Tresidder must have heard and probably relished. In view of such speculation, Rooney's attack and the resultant bad press were indeed hurtful.

Earlier, Director Drury had defended the Curry Company—and thus Tresidder—in a formal statement, which a California congressman had had printed in the May 16 *Congressional Record*. Tresidder thought that defense to be pretty weak, "but then," he confessed to Drury, "I may be incapable of rational judgment in the matter." After his "kind" deed, the congressman wanted his back rubbed to the extent of having a young friend admitted to Stanford.

Tresidder replied on May 24:

> I was very glad to get your comments about —— and I am passing them along to the Registrar. Pressure for places here is terrific, but I do hope that your friend —— will be able to qualify.
>
> I deeply appreciate the statement you made concerning the Yosemite situation. Even the National Park Service did not go as far as I felt it should in giving the true facts surrounding our operations.
>
> The form of contact which our Company negotiated during the term of Dr. Wilbur was devised by Stephen T. Mather and Horace Albright in 1916. It was the fourth such contract that our Company and its predecessor companies had held, and Dr. Wilbur was not even aware of negotiations for the 1932 contract since it was more or less of a routine matter.

Assistant Secretary John J. Edwards acted for the Department.

> Even now the risks of park operations are so great that the Government could probably not induce capital to undertake the operations without the assurances which are contained in our present contracts. The monopolistic feature of the contracts was not devised by operators but was developed by the Government itself, first, in order to restrict the number of facilities to the minimum consistent with good service to the public, and next, to give the operator every reasonable assurance that he could earn a fair profit on his investment.
>
> For the thirteen years since the 1932 contract the Yosemite Company has declared in dividends an average of approximately 4.9% per annum. In view of the hazards of the business, this would seem a reasonable amount.

There were other strong men who rallied to the Curry-Tresidder cause. One was banker Philip M. Lansdale, a longtime financial advisor to the corporation. By May 20 he had prepared a three-page answer to Rooney's "findings," which he sent to Oehlmann and Tresidder. A copy may have reached Horace Albright, too, for he wrote a detailed background summation that he submitted to Tresidder, Oehlmann, and an executive of McCann-Erickson, the Curry Company's advertising agency, for review. Although Albright had been president of the United States Potash Company since 1933, his alliance with the Park Service was still close, his integrity and dedication unquestioned, and his influence great. Even before his statement reached the public, Tresidder thanked Albright:

> I cannot tell you how much I appreciate this cooperation. I think the Park Service tends to underestimate the damage that such irresponsible statements as Rooney's does. Surely their own half-hearted comments on his statements only serve to convince thoughtful people that something was wrong.

Albright submitted the many-authored statement to Senator Carl A. Hatch of New Mexico, chairman of the committee on public lands, who added a few personal notes and had it read into the June 19 *Congressional Record*. It was reasonable, had historical perspective, and cited profit-and-loss figures from 1926 through 1945. It stated, in part:

> Now what does this operating company get out of all this? Is the cost of these services—without which few of our people every would visit or enjoy Yosemite or our other national parks—is this cost too high? . . . In the year 1931, the company's net loss was nearly $100,000 ($97,636.54) and in 1933 their net

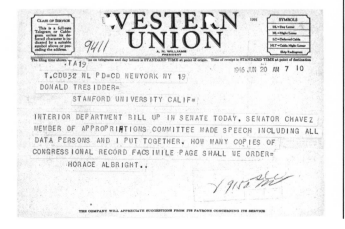

profit after taxes was only $1,495.31 on nearly $2,000,000 worth of business. Even in the last few years the company has never earned the 6 percent beyond which, under the contact, the Government recapture begins. Compare that with any hotel operation you know of, in the last 5 years.

So, in pointing out that all rates, tariffs, and charges are under the supervision and subject to the approval of the National Parks Service, I feel justified in commending that Service and the Department of the Interior, for their wisdom and watchfulness in seeing to it that the public is served at moderate and reasonable cost.

Press response, especially by a Washington, D.C. columnist and the *Los Angeles Times,* was good. Upon Tresidder's advice, Albright had 2,000 copies of Hatch's statement reprinted for distribution to newspaper editors, Stanford trustees, Curry stockholders, concessionaires, and other significant persons. Some of them were mailed from Washington, but McCann-Erickson sent out the majority, and adverse publicity ceased.

Negotiations for the sale of the Yosemite Park and Curry Co. were concurrent with the stressful situation created by Congressman Rooney. In September of 1945, forty-five representatives of the National Park Concessions, Inc., a nonprofit corporation, met with Curry and Park Service officials. Sale was the chief topic of discussion. This, Don Tresidder recorded, was at Secretary Ickes' request. Lt. Colonel Don Hummel had taken time from a 1945 leave to examine the properties with the thought of purchase by his own Lassen National Park Company, which did not make an offer. Years later, however, he served briefly as president of the Curry Company.

In 1946 the Curry Company gave an option to buy to Government Services, Inc., a nonprofit quasi-government corporation that operated government cafeterias and other services within national parks. That sale fell through when the prospective buyer was refused a $2,500,000 loan from the Reconstruction Finance Corporation. Tresidder was not sorry. Even before the option lapsed, he wrote the Government Services president, who was also associate director of the National Park Service:

We have never been able to sympathize with Secretary Ickes' policy of Government ownership of park facilities and we continue to believe the present concessions policy is in the public interest. We recognize, however, the Government's right to fix its own policies and if Secretary Julius Krug adheres to his predecessor's position with respect to park operators,

Heir apparent David A. Curry with his mother, Ruth Curry Burns. *(RCB collection.)*

we have no desire to place unnecessary obstacles in the way

If on the other hand, he reaffirms the policy formulated by Secretary Lane, our Company is eager and ready to carry out its program.

Although Krug was in favor of government ownership, Congress did not back him, and family-owned concessions, such as Curry's, continued—with less insecurity. Thereafter, Oehlmann told the author, "The consistent answer of the board of directors was that the Company was not for sale."

From 1944 on there was a new generation of Curry descendants working in the organization. One was Stuart Cross, a favorite of Mary Tresidder's because of his intellect and academic ambitions. He attended Stanford, but worked summers and holidays in Yosemite. His doctoral dissertation choice of David Starr Jordan

As did his brother Earl at the Lodge, Chef Fred Pierson delighted guests at the Ahwahnee with culinary coups. *(Pierson collection.)*

pleased Mary as did his desire to become a college teacher.

In June of 1944 the first of Foster Curry's children by his second marriage began work at the camp that Foster had been evicted from in 1921. Young David, seventeen, was no stranger to resort work, for he had spent most of his life at Camp Baldy, "The Yosemite of the South." After his father's premature death, in 1932, his mother had run the place until her remarriage to handsome, genial Edmund Burns, a movie actor, who shouldered many of the camp duties and became "Pop" to his three stepchildren. The destructive 1938 flood literally wiped out Camp Baldy in its rocky, river-cut site. But the Burns family rebuilt, slowly paid off all their creditors, and ran the place until 1948. David, John, and Jeanette helped contribute to its success, working from childhood at varied jobs.

"My association with Camp Curry began officially," David stated, "when I took a job as a shoeshine boy in the early 1940s. I soon realized I wasn't cut out for this work, for on my second day of work, my aunt Mary Tresidder, who always wore white shoes, brought in six pairs to be cleaned, and I spilled a large bottle of white polish all over them, several pairs of brown shoes, and some baggage. It took me the better

part of a week to scrub it out of everything, but this seeming adversity really worked to my advantage because it earned me the sympathy of the porters and other staff who weren't too delighted at having a Curry on their hands to train in the business. They considered me a company spy at best."

After that, Dave become a messenger boy, and in the traditionally approved fashion worked his way up to porter, desk clerk, cafeteria manager, and, eventually, manager of various company units.

Before working at camp he had spent several summers in Mother Curry's cottage, where "Nana was a kindly but firm grandmotherly type who knew a lot of fairy tales and nursery rhymes, and I still remember my surprise when I saw her other side. In dealing with the staff, as she was in admonishing or helping them, she had an entire other role, and a different kind of personality, and it was interesting to see the response, the awe and admiration, that this earned in her business relationships. . . ."

One time, Dave and his fellow porter, Lewis Butler, were careening around Camp Curry in the electrically powered delivery cart when a hat box shot off and landed at his aunt's feet. The boys stopped, appalled. "I guess I shouldn't be here," she murmured, smiling faintly, and walked away. Mother Curry thought it appropriate that David should call for the firefall, but his teenage voice wasn't completely firm, so to ensure a steady, booming call, he and Lewis shouted together "LET THE FIRE FALL." "Remember," David remarked, "I inherited my grandfather's name, but not his vocal powers." In time his baritone shouts resounded in keeping with the family tradition.

His hobbies were mountain climbing, photography, ice skating, and skiing, while his major at Stanford University was business administration. Like his "Aunt Mary," he was studious and serious though well-endowed with humor. "She helped me with loans and outright gifts at Stanford, but we never really established rapport," Dave told the author. "Her shyness made her stiff. Frequently I was invited to the President's House on campus for dinner and the food and service were excellent but none of us, including Uncle Don, had much to say to each other and I was uncomfortable." That communication gap might have been caused by the Tresidders trying not to show favoritism to a student, and certainly must have been complicated by their seeking, unconsciously or not, to find resemblances in David to his father, whom they had disliked and helped to undermine.

John Curry began work as a houseman at Camp

Curry in 1947 when he was a lanky, still-growing seventeen. At that time David was a desk clerk and "cousin" Stuart Cross was the chief clerk. "Family or not," Stuart told the author, "John would have been fired for being late to work if Dave hadn't yanked him out of bed morning after morning." Mother Curry was delighted and proud to have the third generation taking hold in the business, but careful not to show favoritism. Age and ails increasingly confined her to her bungalow, yet she was still a power and, John said," a magnificent grandmother figure, too."

John's hobby was girls! He was in and out of love half a dozen times before he married a girl who was also working in Yosemite. Even as a teenager his personality was so winning that he was compared to his Uncle Don, who regarded him with affection. John wrote the author, however, that "I don't think I was aided by the Tresidders, and I think we dedicated ourselves to an arm's length business relationship that worked very well." John's twin, Jeanette, joined her brothers in working and enjoying Yosemite activities during summer and winter vacations. Skiing was her passion and her downfall; it took her months to recover from a badly broken leg. As had her father, all of them possessed the Curry charm and personal warmth, but not his failings.

The biggest event of the postwar years was the reopening of the Ahwahnee Hotel on December 19, 1946. It had been decommissioned by the Navy a full year earlier, but months, and $400,000, were needed to rehabilitate and refurnish it. Plaster had been knocked off walls and pillars, chests smashed, and chairs shattered so thoroughly that Sterling Cramer said, "I don't think there was a chair in the dining room that had all its legs." Most of the furnishings had been stored and, when uncrated, were found to be damaged. Cramer realized "That this damaged furniture was the stuff that had been in the train derailment in 1943 and had never been repaired although the insurance carrier had paid the mover."

Lawsuits—as well as carpentry, painting, and remodeling—were the order of the year. Jeannette and Ted Spencer directed interior restoration, and saw to it that the building was returned to magnificent life. They, Cramer, and a truck full of records had their day in a San Francisco court, when the Navy contested the Company's demand for unpaid rent of $83,000 per year instead of $55,000. Eventually the federal judge allowed the Company $83,500 a year, interest on the unpaid amounts, and allowed all costs except for

Architect Ted Spencer and his designer wife, Jeannette, were vital, creative forces in the original decoration and postwar rehabilitation of the Ahwahnee Hotel. *(Both photographs by Ansel Adams.)*

replacing the wildflower garden. The battle of the Ahwahnee was won overwhelmingly by Curry.

The first look at the refurbished hotel was "For those who helped physically and spiritually with the job . . . ," stated the *Yosemite Sentinel.* "Everyone concerned has put in countless hours of worry and work—what with factory strikes, transportation difficulties and general shortages." Dick Connett, who had begun work with the Company in 1929 as a busboy, was the hotel manager, but the star of the Open House was none other than Don Tresidder. The former porter was jubilant as he greeted residents on December 19, and reestablished the Bracebridge Dinner pageant on Christmas Eve. Once more he and Mary were ensconced in their sixth floor apartment. The Squire of Bracebridge was back in his manor and all was peaceful in the Yosemite world.

The Squire of Bracebridge and his Lady. (*Ansel Adams photograph.*)

14   First Lady of Yosemite

As Glacier Point overshadowed Camp Curry, so had Mary Curry Tresidder been overshadowed and dominated all her life, first by her aggressive, bombastic father and gentle but dynamic mother, and then by her extroverted, activist husband. By nature she was shy, and their forceful personalities made her more reticent. Even her brother Foster, in some ways an insecure carbon copy of their father, had affected her. She had hated his motorcycle and his excesses, and was annoyed, if not jealous, that he was their mother's favorite and thus the one who could, and did, hurt her the most. As children and teenagers, she and her sister, Marjorie, were close and pretty and popular. Marjorie was sensitive to her older sister's needs.

From childhood Mary had an escape, an element in which she was free and independent, and that was on the trails, mountains, and passes, where she was surefooted, responsive to nature, and wholly content. In 1917 she and two other girls from Camp Curry shocked dam builders at Hetch Hetchy by their audacity at traveling without a man to help. On that trip they skinny-dipped in pools and lakes, grew lean and rugged from packing, unpacking, and tugging the pack burro, and were enchanted by the elemental, solitary beauty.

Though without feminine grace and swirling skirts, Mary had a quiet radiance. Her eyes were dark and soulful, her dark short-cropped hair curly, her even-featured face tanned. Those who hiked with her knew her shy humor, mountaineering skill, naturalist knowledge, and balanced temperament. "Boss's daughter" she might be but, she could stake a tent, gather wood for a campfire, and fry fish with competence and composure. Hil Oehlmann and Don Tresidder courted her. Don won, and he and Mary were wed in 1920 at a time when her Ph.D. degree at Yale was complete, except for the writing of her thesis. As late as 1942 she admitted that the thesis "remains on my list of unfinished business." She had started to major in Greek, her father's zesty pride, but ended with English, which she spoke and wrote with fluency and precision. One of the the sorrows of the marriage was her inability to have children. Childlessness emphasized her role as apart from the normal housewife's life. For all that, she was not a woman suffragette, neither "liberated" nor desiring to be so. Instead, she was dependent on her mother and Don for direction and strength. Although he disappointed her sorely at times, her love was abiding and forgiving.

She was drawn to children, liked to be called "Aunt Mary," and troubled herself to shop for requested gifts for "Santa Don" to hand out. However, she had absolutely no interest in casual conversation or gossip, had no ability to make small talk, and thus intimidated even her nieces and nephews by her remoteness and intellect. If she had to wait for anything she would read, since she had no curiosity in observing people in hotels or airports. Next to books, she loved, as did her husband, classical music. She was an authority on wines and gourmet foods, and enjoyed dining out with friends. For relaxation she devoured mysteries and became a Scrabble-playing addict. Friends were amazed at the appropriate verses, either serious or hilarious, she would quote or read to fit any occasion.

After towering Herman Hoss married winsome little Della Taylor, sister of author Frank J. Taylor, Mrs. Tresidder had a close friend, for Della enjoyed walking and absorbing nature lore from her diffident teacher. "My first impression was that all the trees in Yosemite were pines," Mrs. Hoss admitted. "Mary in her scholarly way and out of her deep love for nature, taught me differently." Artistic Della began interpreting the trees in sketches and, later, by using linoleum block prints. At Christmas she joined the Squire of Bracebridge's court, of which Herman was the perennially resounding parson.

Besides Della, Mrs.T, as she was known in Yosemite, attracted a small group of women friends who knew her private self. Among them were Pat Davidson, an intimate of the Rufus Green household and a Stanford employee, Adaline Fuller, wife of the Stanford trustee's president, and Lucy Butler, whose husband was a prominent attorney in San Francisco.

In contrast to Mrs. T, her close women friends had definite outgoing personalities. They admired her for her gentle, retiring self, her quiet humor, and the nature knowledge she imparted as easily as breathing. She had no personal vanity and paid scant attention to dress, makeup, or hairdos until she became first lady of Stanford. After that she took more interest, and friends

Mary Curry Tresidder.
(Ansel Adams photograph.)

Sunrise region and the area between Merced Lake and Washburn Lake. Their favorite hideaway was a semipermanent camp off the trail between the two lakes. There, near the Merced River, they assembled log rounds, a stove, tables, a tent frame, and other conveniences. There, the Oehlmanns, Minzters, Lucy Butler, Bill Janss, and others found rest and refuge amid mountain majesty.

By the mid-1930s Mary was in the grip of a new passion—skiing. After the Tresidders moved to Stanford she enumerated her hobbies of camping, riding, fishing, and flying to a reporter, adding, "but I'd rather ski than do anything else in the world." She was an experienced skier, but had to be carried off Badger's slopes more than once. Her first fracture, in March 1942, was set in plaster by Ave Sturm and in verse by Della Hoss.

> Alack, when radiance of the ski
> Is turned to plaster on ze knee!
> For I've been raised on faith in Mary
> Infallible, unbreakable, tough and wary
> Follow her and you cannot fail.
> Have faith and lustily swing your tail
> She will bend and creak but she will last
> Never that girl will wear a cast! . . .
> Sadder now, I shed a tear
> For the lost illusions of yesteryear
> I know now that the ski's the master
> And sooner or later we end in plaster. . . .

"Mary Tresidder was not what you could call a good downhill skier but she . . . was very determined and her ability was sufficient to take her where she wanted to go in any type of snow," judged winter sports director Charley Proctor. "She loved the mountains and enjoyed being in them summer or winter. Her skiing was a means to this end, not an end in itself as it is to many. . . . When we found a beautiful long slope of perfect spring snow or light powder, she would ski it with obvious pleasure and was enthusiastic but always seemed to express her feelings in her quiet way. This was much in contrast to Don Tresidder's enthusiastic reactions and expressions. He would yell and yodel when skiing down through the powder and stamp and jump in delight at the end of the run. In the late '30s and early '40s there were few lifts and no good over-the-snow vehicles. Don and Mary had some of the first snowmobiles. I recall many trips to Glacier Point and Ostrander Ski Hut when it would have been easier and quicker without the vehicles as there were constant breakdowns and repairs. . . . She enjoyed the pioneering aspect of working with these new machines."

influenced her into buying clothes that were more becoming. She was not pretty in the conventional sense, but was always distinctive and shyly pleased when complimented. Mrs. T knew and regretted her social inabilities, admitting as much in a retrospective piece written for the book *Stanford Mosaic.* "I had an unsuccessful fling at a public speaking class, and have always regretted that I didn't grit my teeth and go through with more of it. . . . I envy the girls of today the ease and fluency with which they tell of their diversified activities or preside over a group."

Much as she loved Stanford, she could never fully enjoy or relax in her official role. Whenever she could escape, she called the pilot, since her own license had lapsed, and had him fly her to the Mariposa airport in the Tresidder's four-seater plane. From the airport she would drive, or be driven, usually in a Company car, to Yosemite.

Hiking had been her first passion, horseback riding her second. Either would take her up and away from guests, employees, and her never-ending responsibilities as a hostess. As she escaped, her glad eye cataloged "the pine marching slopes" and the carpeting wildflowers she loved. She and Don were habitues of the High Sierra Camps, but also reveled in camping in the more secluded spots such as the Cathedral Pass-

Although Tresidder loved competition and sometimes entered races and events in Badger's early years, Mary never competed, but "She was always up on the slopes for the slaloms and jumping events," Proctor said, "and usually got out somewhere on the downhill race courses. After the events she had pertinent comments to make. I doubt if Mary enjoyed awarding trophies but of course did it charmingly."

Late in January of 1948, Don was scheduled to fly east on university business, so Mary invited Lucy Butler to accompany her to Yosemite for skiing. Badger Pass was virtually snowless as was Sugar Bowl, their second stop. Impulsively they drove to Alta, Utah, then a new ski area, where the fields were whiter. Mrs. T telegraphed their move to Don and her mother, and had barely gone to bed when the telephone rang and she heard the traumatic news of Don's death of a heart attack in a New York hotel. Tresidder's name was nationally known, his sudden demise broadcast. Mary was still stunned and disbelieving after the flight back to San Francisco, where she and Lucy were met by Don's sister and her husband and their good friends the Fullers, who shielded her from reporters.

Mother Curry, who had suffered a stroke the previous year, could not come up from Los Angeles but was in touch by telephone. Ed Janss and Parmer Fuller handled all the arrangements. According to a press release, funeral services were to be "strictly private and the family members earnestly request that no flowers be sent." A brief, emotional prayer service for students and faculty was given at the Stanford Church on January 29. On Sunday, February 1, a memorial service was held, during which Chancellor Wilbur gave an eloquent tribute to Tresidder.

Tributes came from Herbert Hoover, Governor Earl Warren, Ray Wilbur, Dr. Robert Gordon Sproul, then president of Stanford's arch-rival, the University of California at Berkeley, and from many other people. "All I can think of," Sproul said, "is that I have lost a dear friend, a man of gentle nature and high ideals, a colleague with whom I delighted to work." Hoover said, "His loss is national and to his friends a great sorrow." There had been serious talk of Don having a political future in Washington. Many students felt personally bereft: his open door policy and diagnostic ability with their problems had earned him their respect and affection.

No Yosemite resident felt Don's death more keenly than Hil Oehlmann, who forced himself to write two tributes, one of which appeared unsigned in the February 7 *Yosemite Sentinel*, while the other was incorporated in a eulogy by Yosemite's Reverend Glass. "We suffer," Oehlmann said," the loss of no ordinary man, but one we were proud to claim as our chief . . . a complete man, truly outstanding among his fellows." Beside the stalwart virtues of determination, imagination, leadership, and integrity, Oehlmann felt that "As an enthusiastic lover of the mountains and outdoor life, Dr. Tresidder would yield first place to no man. It was fortunate for him and for Yosemite National Park that he was able to spend half the years of his exceptionally vigorous and useful life here."

Mary Tresidder had to endure the public ceremony marked by official pomp and unofficial emotionalism, but there were no grave-side services—in fact, no grave. Instead, the following summer, friends scattered Tresidder's ashes on mountain slopes he had climbed and cherished.

At the February 28 directors meeting, Mrs. T was elected president of the Yosemite Park and Curry Co., which visibly pleased her. Oehlmann continued as vice-president and general manager, and she insisted that, to reward the differences in responsibilities, his salary be $5,000 larger than hers. He was the daily operations man while her forte lay in behind-the-scenes work. Her keen, analytical mind and lifetime of experience in

Mary Tresidder admiring one of Della Taylor Hoss's prints.
(YP&CC collection.)

From planning to partially funding, and raising the flag on opening day July 15, 1961, Mrs. T took an active part in the establishment of Sunrise High Sierra Camp. (*YP&CC collection.*)

hotel work were assets, as was her dedication to public service.

Carl P. Russell, Yosemite's superintendent from 1947 till 1952, approved of the new administration. "Under the leadership of these two capable officers," he wrote, "the Yosemite Park and Curry Company conducts a program of public service which is appreciated by the visitor and lauded by the National Park Service. In truth, the concessionaire extends a hand in partnership with the Government in conducting the Yosemite program."

Mrs. Tresidder's loyalty to old employees was commendable yet sometimes hurtful to smooth Company operations. Some of the staff considered her to be naive, but most felt that she was capable in a low-key manner. Clare Duval, Mrs. T's personal secretary for seventeen years, stated that "She was a great and gracious lady . . . very thoughtful, kind, and considerate." Dave Curry felt that "Aunt Mary had enormous integrity and a strong sense of duty and responsibility but little natural leadership ability or venturesomeness." Stuart Cross disagreed with that judgment, writing, "Mrs. T gave a strong leadership to Hil, myself, and others who were in major positions of responsibility.

She left more visible leadership in the hands of operating people, but, basically, she set the tone, the goal, and the methods of reaching them."

Although much of her time was spent in Yosemite, Mrs. T did not burn her Stanford bridges, instead they were reinforced by the trustees, who awarded her a home on the campus for her lifetime. There, for years, she was involved with the planning of a memorial for her husband, and in aiding students. Sometimes she entertained groups of Stanford girls in Yosemite; often she helped qualified undergraduates to obtain jobs there.

There was one singularly happy event in 1948, anticipated by a February letter from Mother Curry to the *Yosemite Sentinel:*

I wish to express my appreciation for all the Christmas remembrances from my friends and assure them that since my 85th birthday, I have adopted the plan of not sending Christmas cards, but I wish all my Yosemite friends a happy New Year, especially since we are entering our fiftieth anniversary year at Camp Curry, which means that I have loved Yosemite long and loyally all these years.

Indefatigable Carl P. Russell, who served Yosemite outstandingly as a Park Service naturalist, historian, superintendent, and author.
(Ralph H. Anderson photo; YNP collection.)

An anniversary celebration was in the works, and Mother Curry planned to guide and attend it. Even sorrow for her daughter didn't halt her eagerness to return to Camp Curry for its mid-May opening. Beside the surviving Pinkerton sister, a nurse lived with Mother Curry in her bungalow. Her eyesight and hearing were failing but not her mind. Tartly she advised Hil, who visited her daily, "I don't object to getting old, but I object to getting feeble!"

No matter how she felt, Mother Curry was available to Mary, Oliene, Helen Green, and Cross, who were planning the fiftieth anniversary program for June 1. She answered their questions, volunteered information, and offered suggestions for the pageant that would depict the lives of her husband, herself, and their camp. She lived for the big night, and sat wide-eyed in a wheelchair in the front row. As the drama unfolded, old songs were played, including the parody to "I'm Strong for Camp Curry," and she alternated between tears and laughter, delighted with every moment. It was narrated by a radio announcer, who had been one of her boys, two of the actresses were Sovulewski's granddaughters, and her own grandchildren participated.

After that highlight, Mother Curry's physical deterioration was rapid. She was hostess at a June 22 reunion dinner for twelve old-time women employees, including Emily Lane, Margaret Jabes, and Florence Morris, approved Stuart Cross's engagement to Lenore Oehlmann, and was always pleased with the excellent housecounts that kept Camp Curry full, but she was less and less animated.

Many well-wishers had to be turned away by the protective nurse. Camp Curry, its staff, and guests were still of paramount interest to her, however, and she asked to meet the new hostess, Kit Whitman, whose vivacious personality pleased her. "Now, Mrs. Whitman," she advised, "I want you to be sure to tell everyone of my guests how sorry I am not to meet them myself." Service and hospitality had been the keynote of her life, and she wanted the tradition carried on. For the next twenty-two years, Kit Whitman, for one, exemplified the Curry spirit while working in guest activities.

As Mother Curry persisted in her desire to die at home, Dr. Sturm checked on her there almost daily. Toward the end, her sight failed, and one day when Hil greeted her, she responded, "I don't recognize your face but I know your voice." Mrs. Tresidder summoned Marjorie and Bob Williams, who arrived from Hawaii in time to cheer Mother Curry by their presence. Soon

Neither age nor illness kept Mother Curry from attending the
50th anniversary of Camp Curry. Left to right: Jennie Pinkerton,
Will Thomson, Mary Curry Tresidder, and Jennie Curry.
(YP&CC collection.)

she lapsed into semi-consciousness, rousing once to exclaim, "David, I am coming!" Death, basically because of heart failure, occurred on October 10. Had she lived two days longer, Jennie Foster Curry would have been eighty-seven.

Again the family requested that no flowers be sent and advised that funeral services in Palo Alto would be private. Interment was alongside her husband's remains near San Francisco. A memorial service for her local friends was conducted by Dr. Glass in the Yosemite Church Bowl. Her half century of residence was infinitesimal compared to Half Dome's longevity, but many people felt as if a Yosemite landmark had disappeared.

Once more Hil Oehlmann was called upon to write memorials first for the *Yosemite Sentinel* and then for the Company's board of directors. In the latter, he stated:

As Chairman of our Board, Mrs. Curry brought to us always a strong and quiet optimism, born of her own surmounting of untold difficulties. The fund of her experience with such problems as confronted us was inexhaustible, and her wisdom was profound. Her death has broken a continuity with the past which was invaluable in our appraisal of the present.

We cannot but feel a deep sorrow at the loss of one who held so high a place in our affections. But our abiding sense will be one of gratitude for the special privilege which was ours to observe a life so complete, so useful and worthy.

Her single-sheet, handwritten will was characteristically succinct and thoughtful:

This is my last Will and Testament.

In that certain Trust known as the Jennie Foster Curry Trust I have provided for my two daughters Mary Curry Tresidder and Marjorie Curry Williams and in an additional Trust for my son Foster Curry and his estate and for my granddaughter Cherry Curry Randle (Katharine Curry).

I wish my expenses paid from available funds.

I leave the oil paintings of Mr. Curry and myself to the Yosemite Park and Curry Co. with the hope that they may be kept in the Camp Curry office.[1]

I leave the Thomas Hill painting of Yosemite at Wawona to my daughter Marjorie, and the Big Tree painting to the Yosemite Museum, or Administration Building.

I leave my personal property to my daughter Mary to be by her distributed as indicated in a letter to her.

I appoint Henry G. Hill of San Jose, California and my daughter Mary Curry my executors to serve without bonds and to sell any property needing to be sold without court order.

And any remaining amount of the estate is to be divided equally among my grandchildren.

August 1st, 1942

/S/ Jennie Foster Curry

One trust, set up in March 1921, and amended thereafter, consisted of 37,225 shares of Curry Co. stock worth $205,000 at the time of her death. Among her papers were these heartfelt words: "I leave to my adopted Camp Curry 'boys and girls' my affection, with the wish that Camp Curry, 'Mother Curry,' and Yosemite may always have a warm place in your hearts." Her place in the memories and hearts of the hundred or so persons interviewed by the author is still warm years after her death. At the 100-year celebration, June 1, 1999, several relatives, including grandsons John and David, and retired employees spoke of her with great esteem.

Once again Mrs. T had to read and reply to hundreds of letters from sympathetic persons. Another of her tasks was assuring appropriate memorials for both her mother and her husband. Ultimately two college scholarships for Yosemite students commemorated the Curry name locally, and a Jennie Foster Curry House remembered Mother Curry at Indiana University. It took years of study and plans before all of the memorials to Don Tresidder were finished. Within weeks of his death, over $600 had been contributed in his memory by local residents, and Mrs. T directed that the fund be invested in an oxygen tent for Lewis Memorial Hospital. After a decade of bureaucratic red tape, a 10,600-foot peak, one-half mile east of Tenaya Lake, was named Tresidder Peak, a particularly fitting memorial for a man who had loved mountains. At Stanford a fund drive for a campus community center was begun in 1948, but Tresidder Memorial Union, which cost $2,600,000, was not finished and dedicated until September 29, 1962. On that occasion Mrs. T was guest of honor.

Park Service Director Conrad Wirth with concessionaires Hil Oehlmann and Mary Tresidder. *(YP&CC collection.)*

1. Instead, they hung in the executive offices of the Yosemite Concessionaire.

Her passion for the high country deepened over the years and, after Don's death, her pack-trip companions were her closet women friends and usually one of her great-nieces. Their main headquarters was the Tresidder Camp between Merced and Washburn lakes. Faithful, rough-hewn stable boss Bob Barnett was their guide and packer, and his humor added to the good times they had. He referred to the women as his "Indian squaws" and they dubbed him "Chief." Once, during a snowstorm, he was looking askance at more storm clouds when Mrs. T queried, "What is Big Chief thinking?" His answer was prompt, "Big Chief thinking of wife and electric blanket."

Mrs. T knew every wildflower by its Latin name and spotted them along the trail. One time she exclaimed at the red bloom of Pride of the Mountain, and Bob, who had been quietly practicing, shot back, "You mean Penstemon newberryi, Mrs. T?"

As manager of three stables in the Park, Bob had charge of roughly 230 mules and horses, 80 donkeys, and 30 employees. In 1960 a number of the mules helped to fulfill a dream of Mrs. T's by packing in wheelbarrows, steel, lumber, and sacks of cement to a singularly lovely plateau above Long Meadow, nine miles southwest of Tuolumne Meadows. That had been a favorite campsite of the Tresidders since 1941 and, wanting to share it with others and further commemorate Don, she had worked with the Park Service and the Company to have a High Sierra Camp erected there. Eventually trails to it were constructed by the Park trail crew, and a dozen tents, a canvas dining room, and a stone kitchen were erected by the Company. Not only had she originated and spearheaded Sunrise Camp, but donated about $20,000 for building it. Reliable, creative Ted Spencer was the architect. Naturally she was guest of honor on opening day, July 15, 1961.

Mrs. T's generosity was unpublicized but well known to residents, whom she befriended in many quiet ways. Her gifts to deserving employees were large, and often she helped outstanding Valley students. Although she rarely attended church, she was a dependable contributor and financed the enlargement of the Church Bowl. As had her mother, she was quick to respond to all local fund drives and paid for such items as new curtains for the grammar school. In 1966 she donated $3,000 to have a bicycle trail built from Camp Curry to Sentinel Bridge. After the Lions Club established an annual sale of used things, she donated many good clothes, purses, and, occasionally, books. At Christmas time she was a veritable Mrs. Santa Claus without the slightest fanfare.

For years friends had urged Mrs. T to utilize her abilities and knowledge to write about her family and the Curry Company, but she responded negatively, saying that she could not handle such a formidable task objectively. To satisfy frequent requests from historians and reporters, she did write a few sketches on her mother, father, and the pioneer years at Camp Curry and Hazel Green. They were interesting, but limited and not definitive in scope.

**For years the Yosemite Stables were known as "Barnettsville,"
in honor of its long-time colorful manager, Bob Barnett.** *(Courtesy of Bob Barnett.)*

Bob Barnett—everybody's friend. *(YP&CC collection.)*

Trees were the inspiration for her first and only book, *The Trees of Yosemite,* published by Stanford University Press in 1932. It was a happy collaboration of Mrs. T's descriptive text and thirty-four linoleum block prints by Della Hoss. The book ran through several editions and was last reprinted by the Yosemite National History Association in 1963. For years Mrs. Hoss's copies of tree illustrations were used as menus at the Ahwahnee Hotel, and saved by guests as mementos.

Stephen Arno's book, *Discovering Sierra Trees,* was published in 1973. It was beautifully illustrated by Jane

Geyer, and she was particularly pleased with the warm, congratulating note from Della Hoss.

Mrs. T hoped to follow the tree book with one on Yosemite wildflowers, and made scrawled notes on scraps of paper to that end in her nearly illegible handwriting.[2] She became an expert on when, where, and what flowers would bloom. In the 1950s Henry Berrey, who was in charge of public relations, and the *Yosemite Sentinel* persuaded her to write an annual piece on the bloom and glory of spring, which he issued as a press release. Some newspapers, including the *Fresno Bee,* and, once, the *Christian Science Monitor,* published her pieces. In January 1960 the *Yosemite Sentinel,* printed in the Company's press shop, was enlarged to a four-page $8\frac{1}{2}$ x 11-inch glossy format. Berrey and editor Esther Morgenson talked Mrs. T into contributing regularly. Between 1960 and the Sentinel's demise in 1969, she wrote thirty-six features for it, the bulk of them evocative pieces bearing titles such as "Showers of Flowers," and "Farewell to Spring."

In addition, she wrote two articles on winter sports, one published in *Yosemite Nature Notes,* the other in *National Parks Magazine,* plus a couple of historical pieces for the Mariposa County Historical Society quarterly.

After 1953, a trip somewhere abroad with friends became an annual event, resulting in a great deal of pleasure and widening knowledge of the world. Wherever she wandered, Mrs. T studied resort operations, talked to managers, and sent reports back to the Curry staff on rates, accommodations, ski schools, and equipment. She felt that the ideas she garnered were part of her job as president. A fringe benefit to her excursions was the interest and travel she inspired among the administrative staff, who also gleaned ideas that aided the Company. It wasn't unusual for Mrs. T to encounter an ex-Curry employee at a foreign hotel, and she quipped, for *Yosemite Sentinel* readers, "We train 'em, Statler gets 'em."

No matter how far abroad she wandered—Spain, South America, or Japan—Yosemite drew her back and she was contentedly at home in her Ahwahnee penthouse, Camp Curry bungalow, or a High Sierra Camp.

2. Her book was completed by Dana Morgenson, long-time Curry employee and an expert on both Yosemite trails and photography. Their book *Yosemite Wildflower Trails* was published in 1975.

Mrs. T, Lucy Butler, Bob Barnett, and John Taylor at Cathedral Lake with Tresidder Peak in the background. (*Mrs. Vincent K. Butler collection.*)

15 Two Decades of Crowds The 1950s and 1960s

It was 1959 before the last of Steve Mather's objectives, the replacement of the Old Village Store, as promised in 1925, took place. During its eighty-eight years, the old store survived three major floods, eight managements, and roughly 23,000,000 customers. In March 1959 it was demolished by men and bulldozers in just 480 man hours. Replacement came none too soon. Mather had urged rebuilding in the 1920s, and crowds had made it imperative by the 1950s. On the horrendous three-day Memorial Day holiday in 1952, for example, overcrowding was so great that the doors had to be closed several times, and lengthy waiting lines established outside. A half ton of hot dogs, a truck load of potato chips, 5,000 loaves of bread, 7,000 quarts of milk, and a mile of marshmallows were bought by 43,000 visitors. Days like that prompted popular butcher and *Yosemite Sentinel* columnist Andy Koller to write, "In the winter we are either snowed in or snowed out . . . in the summer we are snowed under."

Water, however, was far more of a problem than snow. A mid-November 1950 flood inundated the store with four feet of water. Just before Christmas of 1955, heavy rains again devastated northern California and Yosemite Valley, and the All-Year "except-for-floods" Highway suffered extensive damage. Auditor Cramer reported that the Curry Company lost $45,000 in property damage, $5,000 in salvage costs, and $50,000 in lost revenue. Another casualty of the storm was the Bracebridge Dinner. As usual the river did not stay away from the Old Village Store, but filled it with fifty-two inches of water and silt. Evacuation, directed by manager Jack Ring, was recorded for the *Yosemite Sentinel* readers by Andy:

When your fearless, on the spot, Old Village reporter approached said village on the night of December 22, the commotion was so great, what with trucks coming and going, cars parked all over the place, crowds of people going in and out with their arms full of goods; at first glance it looked like an average day in the good old summer time.

An eager looking guest from Los Angeles

Andy Koller was well-known both as a butcher and a *Yosemite Sentinel* columnist. (*Vergena Koller collection.*)

wandered into the store thinking this was a last minute Christmas sale. He approached the boss and asked, "What's coming off?" Jack Ring replied, "Nothing is coming off, but at the rate the rain is coming down and the river is up, we don't want to be around when the two meet."

When the last truck load of merchandise was pulling out, our boss looked tenderly at the old store. Then, with his voice filled with emotion, asked us all to join him in a chorus of "River, Stay 'Way from My Store."

At this point Bob Cromer was heard to say, "I could just break down and cry." To which Jack replied, "Don't you dare! There's too much water around here already."

Although the sprawling new 48,000-square-foot merchandise center, consisting of market, gift shop, clothing department, restaurant, and barber and beauty shops was in use beginning January 27, 1959, it was not officially dedicated until May 9. At that time, Park Service Director Conrad L. Wirth, Yosemite

146

Superintendent John C. Preston, who succeeded Russell, Ted Spencer, Hil Oehlmann, and Mary Tresidder made appropriate remarks. Predictably, Wirth spoke of preservation while Mrs. T dealt with pragmatism:

> There has come to be a fashion of deploring the crowds who visit Yosemite. . . . Personally I like to think of the many to whom Yosemite has meant refreshment for spirit and body, and I look forward to the continuance of that recreation for thousands more.
>
> The objectives for a National Park have been stated as being both the use and the preservation of an outstanding area . . . . We (the Yosemite Park and Curry Co.) for our part are doing our best to make the phase of 'use' as painless as possible for the visitors of the future.

Much was made of the fact that the Old Village Store had been "returned to nature," but nothing was said concerning the new site, south of the Post Office, which had been bulldozed and filled when less conspicuous places had been urged by Company officials. A year earlier, Degnan's, run by two of their children and grandson-in-law Frank Donahoe, had moved into a ruggedly attractive A-frame building that housed delicatessen, bakery, restaurant, and gift shop. Of the four photography studios, Foley's, Best's, Pillsbury's, and Boysen's, erected in the new village in 1926, only Best's Studio and Foley's remained; the others had been torn down after the deaths of their originators. Best's, remodeled and rechristened the Ansel Adams Gallery, now operates under the supervision of the Adams family, while Boysen's, immediately west of the post office, is run by the Yosemite Concession Services as a commercial venture.

Although the floods of 1950 and 1955 damaged the Old Village Pavilion, which hosted dances and movies, it survived until the early 1960s, when it was destroyed by man. *(Henry Berrey photo; Jan Robinson collection.)*

Besides the $800,000 investment in the "Merchandise Center" in 1959, the Curry Company spent $700,000 in the construction of a huge new warehouse, containing storage area and maintenance shops, in an unobtrusive talus slope site north of Yosemite Village. "The $1,5000,000 is the greatest single-year expenditure in the thirty-two year history of the concession company," noted the May 7 *Sentinel*, "and reflects its enthusiastic participation in the Mission 66 program of the National Park Service."

Introduced in 1956, Mission 66 was an ambitious program of physical improvements of trails, roads, camps, and facilities in all national parks to provide maximum protection and visitor enjoyment before the Park Service's fiftieth anniversary in 1966. For Yosemite, the plan called for new structures to be provided by concessionaires: a new incinerator, a secondary facility operating base at El Portal, employee housing, and remodeling of campgrounds by the Park Service. The Curry Company's participation was, indeed, more enthusiastic and immediate than the Park Service's, but visitor revenue was more dependable than congressional funding. In the 1950s the disparity between expenditures of the Company and the Park Service for maintenance in Yosemite was large. Their investments in buildings and facilities were roughly the same, but the Company had sixty maintenance men employed to protect its investment while the Park had only ten. Mission 66 was a sorely needed rescue effort.

Anticipation of Mission 66 and partial realization of "Mission 1925" had taken place when the new Yosemite Lodge had been dedicated in June of 1956. it comprised four low redwood buildings, in which the use of glass was enormous, connected by covered walkways. Architect Spencer had planned every window to frame an outstanding scene of Yosemite Falls, cliffs, or forest. As Hil Oehlmann remarked at the open house, "Man-made structures can scarcely add to Yosemite's matchless beauty. Rather must we strive that they neither intrude upon this splendor nor seem to rival it in permanence." To that, Mrs. T added that the 1915-built lodge had endured "the vicissitudes of fires and floods, of wars and depression" as "temporary buildings," all the time providing hospitality. By 1983 the converted Army barracks north of the new Lodge were destroyed by man-controlled fire. Pine, Oak, and Cedar cottages, two-storied guest facilities, had been built in 1950, 1953, and 1955 respectively, and more such were planned, but many of the old WOBs (rooms without baths) were left to remind old-timers of D. J. Desmond's part in the area's history.

In the year 2000 the 1879-built Yosemite Chapel is the sole structure remaining in the Old Village. Two other remnants, the small concrete jail and Degnan's historic bake ovens, were moved to the Pioneer History Center in Wawona.

The Curry name was far better marked, since grandchildren played prominent parts in the Company. Bob Williams, Jr., was a director until he moved to the Philippines, after which his sister, Marjorie Williams Woods, succeeded him. Foster Curry's children had a definite role in Company activities. Both Jeanette and her husband, Bill Batchelder, worked in the Ahwahnee until 1953. David Curry's tenure was briefer. Because of his name, personality, and ability, he was the heir apparent but refused to work in the family business because, he said, "My interests run more to analysis and research rather than management, and more to the public rather than the private sector. . . ." To this end, he earned his master's in business administration at Stanford, and

Indian interpretations are a regular feature of programs sponsored by the Park Service. Lucy Ann Parker and Craig Bates are shown here demonstrating ancestral crafts and skills. *(YNP collection.)*

The present Yosemite Lodge complex was opened in June 1956.
(Ernest Braun photo; SS collection.)

went to work for Stanford Research Institute, which Don Tresidder had helped establish.

By training and inclination, John Curry was a hotel man. From the age of six or so he had worked either at Camp Baldy in Southern California or in Yosemite units; his college courses and attendance at Whitcomb Hotel School further prepared him for management. His charm and attention to guest needs made him an ideal hotel manager, as he proved at both the Lodge and the Ahwahnee. Aunt Mary, however, favored Stuart Cross, who finally deserted his professorial Stanford career for Yosemite resort management.

While he did not carry the Curry name, Cross had the Yosemite background and impeccable Green family heritage. His first Yosemite job, at age twelve, was the unremunerative one mentioned earlier with "the Birdman of Yosemite." After that he worked summers in the usual porter and upward jobs. His marriage to Lenore Oehlmann, who had grown up in the shadow of Half Dome, must have influenced him in pursuing a Yosemite hotel career. The initiative, however, came from Mrs. Tresidder, and his decision came only after a series of conferences between her and Cross. Soon he achieved a solid grasp of operations. Oehlmann was pleased, though he tried to maintain an impartial attitude toward his son-in-law. Ultimately the Crosses lived next door to the Oehlmanns on "the Row," and there were two grandsons to enliven both households.

A third up-through-the-ranks prospect was Bob Maynard, a hard-working young man who had married a Sovulewski granddaughter. Curry, Cross, and Maynard played musical units throughout the 1950s and early 1960s as they succeeded each other in managing the Lodge, Wawona, Camp Curry, and the Ahwahnee. Three other comers were Miles Cooper's son, Bill, who had been born and raised in Yosemite, Keith Whitfield, whose parents were longtime residents, and Wayne Whitman.

Although the 1950s were a time of high house-counts and long waiting lines, of weekend traffic jams and delays due to road construction, the decade was largely one of peace, plenty, and revenue. At Camp Curry summer sounds were squawking jays, splashing swimmers, the "toot toot" of the Kiddie Kamp train, and the mellow band music. At nights, "LET THE FIRE FALL" resounded, and then the dance began. Over at the old Yosemite Lodge, Wendell Otter set a record for longevity as manager from 1948 until 1956, and was proud of the fact that the Lodge was the first unit to gross $1,000,000 in a single year.

Ahwahnee guests were a less lively, more conservative lot than those at Curry and the Lodge. They liked such extra services as breakfast in bed and afternoon tea in the Great Lounge. Manager Dick Connett and hostess Kit Whitman kept them entertained with breakfast rides, beach barbecues, and special programs. Kit treated everyone from Marian Anderson and "Ike" Eisenhower to Red Skelton and Judy Garland with the same genuine charm. Program director Glenn Willard annually trained employees to be the "Valley Singers," whose concerts delighted guests and residents alike.

Although the Valley accommodations were unfailingly in demand, many people preferred to say at outlying units where crowds were rare. Big Trees Lodge in the Mariposa Grove, for instance, had a limited by enthusiastically select clientele, while the pastoral, piney charm of the Wawona Hotel attracted guests who returned year after year. Glacier Point Hotel was never a revenue producer but had its devotees, and the adjoining pioneer Mountain House provided employee housing and a cafeteria. The hotel gift shop and cafeteria were money makers, since hundreds of people visited Glacier Point daily. Those hardier souls who made the Loop Trip knew the delights, beauties, and family-style living of the High Sierra Camps. Stays at any of

them were memorable, and jobs at the camps were eagerly sought by employees. All six camps had the casual informality and the friendly spirit that had made Camp Curry famous.

Baseball was the organized sport of the 1950s. Each unit had an employee team, and competition on the school diamond was fierce. Tennis languished in favor, since many of the permanent residents took up golf. Wawona's meadow course was replete with locals on weekends, and browsing deer added handicaps. Horseback riding was always popular, and several families, including the Oehlmanns, kept stock at the "Barnettsville" stables. Mrs. T was a familiar sight astride her horse on her early morning rides. Solo sports such as hiking, fishing, and rock climbing lured guests; and most employees lived for their monthly three days in a row off when they could exhaust yet renew themselves with backpacking. Seasonal workers were paid minimum wages but derived maximum benefits. Many felt, as Amos Neal had when he first worked in Yosemite in 1928: "I should pay the Company for the privilege of working and living here!"

In 1954, visitation exceeded one million for the first time. Only 984,201 people came to Yosemite in 1955, but thereafter, a million plus came, saw, and were conquered by Yosemite's splendors and recreational possibilities. Each year they had to be fed, housed, and supplied with a variety of services that necessitated improvement and expansion of Company facilities, as planned in Mission 66.

Oehlmann was the leader in improvements, negotiating for a thirty-year-contact, which would allow the Company to gain long-term financing, and pushing for a Congressional policy bill to protect concessionaires. In May of 1963 he became president of the Yosemite Park and Curry Co. in fact as well as in action. Mrs. T moved up to chairman of the board of directors, and Stuart Cross, who had taken over as head of the hotel division in 1960, was appointed vice president. Oehlmann's worth had also been recognized by his peers, who elected him president of the Western Conference of National Park Concessionaires for eight consecutive years. His successor to that post was Don Hummel, president of the Lassen National Park Company, who said that "Oehlmann was a fighter who was particularly adroit and good at expressing himself in writing." Oehlmann and Herman Hoss took the dominant roles in participating in the concessions policy enactment, which set rights, privileges, and responsibilities for private companies in public parks. Hoss defined "possessory interests" as indistinguishable

John Foster Curry, grandson of Jennie and David Curry, possessed the Curry charm, and worked his way up from porter to hotel manager in the family business. Here he is pictured in the Ahwahnee Hotel with ex-governor Edmund Brown's brother and his wife. *(Curry family collection.)*

from "rights," and in 1965 guided the bill into Public Law 89-249.

After that triumph, Oehlmann gave credit to Hoss, Hummel, and Stuart Cross. Cross had proved himself to be Oehlmann's backup man and heir. In November 1965 his talent was recognized by the directors, who named him general manager. Although he continued as hotel division head, that job soon was likely to be available to a younger man. In January 1964 Bob Maynard left to be assistant manager of the Grand Teton Lodge Company. Immediately John Curry took over as manager of the Ahwahnee Hotel. It looked like clear sailing ahead. Two years later, to everyone's surprise, Maynard was asked to return as hotel division superintendent, which he did in September of 1966. Curry was offered another staff position, but, feeling

rebuffed, resigned and took a position with the Disney organization in their proposed development of Mineral King. By 1973 he had become president of the Sea-Pines Resort on an island off the coast of South Carolina. As both a Yosemite devotee and Company director, he continued his association with the Park, but his "Welcome" for the guests in the family tradition was missed.

In 1967, barely thirteen years after Yosemite visitation exceeded one million, two million people came, saw, enjoyed, and left more than footprints. Inevitably there was litter, petty theft, drownings, trail erosion, overcrowding of campgrounds, and occasional weekend traffic jams. Motorcyclists caused problems, especially with noise, and at times campfire smoke resembled smog. Seasonally, Yosemite Valley suffered urban ills. Employees of that period referred to the

Valley as "little Los Angeles." A significant number of bums, pot smokers, and drug pushers were included in the summer population explosion, and there were ugly confrontations between them and the rangers.

All this earned Yosemite an exaggerated bad national press, spearheaded by the *Wall Street Journal.* After that, lesser publications joined the headline chase. One radio commentator predicted that there would be nothing left worth seeing within a decade. Oehlmann responded in the August 10, 1966 *Yosemite Sentinel* by commenting that "that forecast surely represents a somewhat pessimistic view of the fragility of an area whose principal attraction is granite. The problems still exist, but seen in their proper perspective they are a result of the enjoyment of the Park, not of its shocking misuse. A more balanced picture of Yosemite would have been presented had the critics devoted some space to the efforts of the National Park Service and Yosemite Park and Curry Co. to improve conditions. . . ."

Studies and changes took place in the late 1960s. Such remedies as a one-way road system in the Valley, free shuttle buses, and an emphasis on bicycling greatly reduced traffic problems. To help alleviate overcrowding, the campgrounds were remodeled, the number of sites reduced, and the length of stay regulated. A ranger horse patrol, like the one in the 1930s, was reestablished in 1970, and became popular with visitors who besieged the men with questions about the Park.

Back in Washington, the Park Service director decided that the historic firefall was a man-made attraction that caused congestion and reduced the supply of red fir bark on dead trees. Let there be no more such light, was the edict. Henry Berrey wrote the obituary as a press release:

> The Firefall, a fancy of James McCauley's that caught on and was popular for almost a hundred years, died Thursday, January 25, 1968 in a blazing farewell.
> It was a dandy Firefall, fat and long and it ended with an exceptionally brilliant spurt, the embers lighting the cliff as they floated slowly downward. . . .
> There weren't many people around to watch. Maybe fifty. Hardly any congestion at all.

Coincident with the Park Service's innovations was a reorganization of the Curry Company that made it less of a family-oriented business. Old-timers such as Wendell Otter, George Oliver, Harold Ouimet, and John Loncaric, who had been hired by either Mother Curry or Don Tresidder, were retiring and their former responsibilities reshuffled so as to attain a more efficient, leaner focus. The architects of the changes were Oehlmann and Cross, aided by a year-long study by an accounting firm. The principal change was the creation of four, instead of one, vice-presidential positions. Stuart Cross continued as vice-president and general manager, but his duties were expanded to include supervision of all Company operations. Arthur R. Robinson was appointed vice-president in charge of administration, which meant serving as secretary, personnel manager, and labor negotiator. Affable Art Robinson had won the respect of employees and executives, first as a porter at Camp Curry and much

Free shuttle buses are a popular form of transportation and for enjoying the Park. (*Yosemite Concession Services.*)

later as a personnel man with a flair for labor negotiations.[1]

Bob Maynard was elected vice-president of operations to direct all hotels and restaurants, as well as to supervise the reservations and transportation offices. Charley Proctor became vice-president of the commercial department, a long way from his old Badger Pass skiing grounds. Indefatigable Nic Fiore, a superb skier, had succeeded him there as winter sports director. During summers, Nic supervised the High Sierra Camps.[2] Vice-president of finance was awarded to Sterling Cramer, who had been happy with an adding machine upon his arrival in 1935, and now had computers, as well as a large staff, to aid him in accounting and budgeting.

Oehlmann explained that the objectives of the new structure were to better satisfy guests, employees, stockholders, and directors. Furthermore, as set forth in 1966, a prime goal of the Company was:

> To be aware at all times that Yosemite National Park has been set aside for the use and enjoyment of the people and to express such awareness in our rendering to park visitors unfailingly courteous, cheerful, and efficient service in all our facilities.
>
> To remember that we are only temporary custodians of the corporation's welfare and that we have the responsibility to preserve for those who follow us sound physical properties, competent personnel, forward-looking policies and sensitivity to the natural beauty of the park.

That the custodial Park Service and concessionaire were succeeding in implementing changes, to allow use without abuse, was observed by no less a personage than Horace Albright, who had known every aspect of Yosemite National Park since 1915. After an April 1972 visit, in which he walked, rode buses, and talked with many visitors, he wrote, "I found Yosemite Valley as beautiful as I ever saw it, and I observed no evidence of harm to it by the thousands of people who have visited it in recent years. . . . Observing many or few people enjoy

Bicycling is another way to see the scenery in Yosemite Valley. *(YP&CC collection.)*

this beautiful place makes me very happy. I hope no new policy will discourage visitors who really want to see this exquisite part of our native landscape."

Ecology had become a healthy American syndrome, and the Park's beefed up interpretive force stressed the interrelation of man and nature. Because of his lifestyle and the philosophy that men should get the parks in their hearts so that "preservation and right use

---

1. His sudden death was a shock to the community and a great loss to the Company.
2. Nic became an icon, a living legend. At 79 in 1999, he had no plans and no reason to retire.

Only a fireplace and chimney survived the August 1969 fire that destroyed both the pioneer Mountain House and the three-story Glacier Point Hotel. *(Henry Berrey photo; YP&CC collection.)*

might be made sure," John Muir had become a kind of folk hero. His books were republished, read, quoted, and his advice followed. Although he had wandered the wilds of the world, Yosemite had ever been his passion and comfort, as he wrote in the following passage:

> Yosemite is a place of rest, a refuge from the roar and dust and weary, nervous, wasting work of the lowlands. . . . It is good for everybody no matter how benumbed with care. . . . None can escape its charms. Its natural beauty cleanses and warms like fire, and you will be willing to stay forever in one place like a tree.

There were two contemporary leading figures who wanted to stay in Yosemite forever. One was Hil Oehlmann who, in 1968 at age seventy-three, retired as president of the Curry Co. Stuart Cross was his successor, and Hil succeeded Mrs. T as chairman of the board. Characteristically, he regarded his new position as a job and worked faithfully every day. The other confirmed Yosemiteite who, like her mother before her, wanted to die in the Park, was Mary Curry Tresidder, who still served the Company as honorary chairman of the board and was known as the "First Lady of Yosemite." Until 1966 she continued her foreign travels and skiing, and made some new, younger friends. Ranger's wife Kathy Betts, who knew her well and informally, said "While we were stationed at Badger Pass, Mrs. T often had dinner with us, helped with the dishes, and talked to my boys. I was no yes man like many of her Company friends, and our friendship was basic and satisfying. Later, when we lived in the Valley, I would have lunch with her and then play Scrabble. Did I ever win? You bet I did!"

Shortly after she returned from a 1966 trip around the world with Lucy Butler, Mrs. T went home to Yosemite Valley. In March, while driving back alone from Badger, her car skidded on an icy Valley road and hit a tree. Her next *Yosemite Sentinel* piece, on April flowers, concluded ruefully, "My dispute with a P. ponderosa has kept me from my usual surveys." Besides facial cuts she suffered a broken rib, and from that time on showed her age. The next summer, after dismounting from her horse in the high country, she confessed to Bob Barnett, "I'm getting old, Bob. My knee hurts me." Bob replied, "By golly, Mrs. T, we will have to order you a new knee." "If you can get that for me," she smiled, "you might as well order me some new eyes and ears, too." Replacements were not available, so her last and least publicized trip to Merced Lake was made by helicopter. So highly was she regarded that special permission for the flight was granted by the Park superintendent, John Preston.

Mrs. T's final article in the *Yosemite Sentinel* was published June 29, 1967. Glaucoma was dimming her sight and she feared blindness. She was saddened by the 1968 extinction of the firefall, the uprooting of the famed sequoia Tunnel Tree, and the 1969 burning of the old Mountain House and the adjacent Glacier Point Hotel.

When The Shasta Telecasting Corporation wanted to buy out the Curry holdings, she was agreeable but upset, and further grieved when Shasta made tender offers at such attractive prices per share that significant amounts of Curry stock were sold. Before long, the Shasta officials owned thirty-eight percent of the Curry Company stock but had so exhausted their capital that Shasta was acquired by U. S. Natural Resources, a more aggressive concern. That takeover and the impending annihilation of the Curry Company, which had been her interest and life's work, sapped her strength and spirit. At 3:50 a.m. on October 29, 1970 a heart attack ended her life in her Ahwahnee Hotel apartment. Knowing that even trees cannot stay in place forever, she had ordered cremation, and asked faithful friends to scatter her ashes in the high country were she had known her happiest and most carefree days.

Mrs. T's death signified the end of an era in which a family business, begun by David and Jennie Curry in 1899, built on personal service and hospitality for the visitor, had long dominated Yosemite.

Nearly 30 years after the Glacier Point Hotel burned, an amphitheater with amazing views was built at the Point. It was funded by the Yosemite Fund, the Yosemite concessioner, and Bill Lane. Lane was formerly copublisher of *Sunset Magazine,* **and served as ambassador to Australia. He began his career as a high school lad working at Camp Curry.** (*Yosemite Concession Services.*)

16   Eternal Yosemite, Uncertain Future

Between 1916, when the National Park Service was organized and Yosemite's first park superintendent was appointed, and 1965, six men— Lewis, Thomson, Merriam, Kittredge, Russell, and Preston—supervised the Park's 1,189 square miles of forest, meadows, lakes, mountains, trails, roads, camps, concessions, and visitors. Interpretive work was basic to the ranger force, which was composed of naturalists and law enforcement people charged with the protection of scenery and wildlife. For decades, their work, loyalty, and dedication to Yosemite inspired respect and admiration in the visiting public.

Yosemite's image as a sylvan sanctuary ended on July 3, 1970 when several hundred authority-flaunting predominantly young people chased a band of about thirty mounted rangers out of Stoneman Meadow using rocks, bottles, and chunks of wood as weapons. The riot's aftermath was equally disruptive: outside law enforcement forces aided the reactionary, heavy-handed rangers in making hundreds of arrests, during which injuries and a bad press were incurred. After that, proliferating problems of vandalism, drugs, liquor, theft, nudism, and illegal camping confounded the unprepared and largely untrained rangers.

The protective philosophy, training, equipment, and Yosemite's law enforcement division had to be restructured under the direction of top-echelon Interior Department personnel. Congressional funding allowed an infusion of professional men and women. They introduced a diversity of visitor activities, including setting aside a campground for people intent on "doing their own thing," and placed greater emphasis on walking, bicycling, and public transportation. An attractive pedestrian mall was created out of the vast parking area fronting the Village commercial complex in order to provide additional space for interpretive programs and visitor use. Law enforcement rangers, bent on rapport, shed their hard-nosed attitudes, but were trained to use weapons such as chemical sprays. Man-made fires destroyed the government stables in 1972, the dining room at Camp Curry in 1973, and the Camp Curry garage in 1975. Order was maintained, however, and

confrontations were drastically reduced. By the mid-1980s, visitation was approaching three million, yet arrests were far below the 1970s high.

Vandalism, theft, and drug and alcohol use also increased among employees of both the Curry Company and the Park Service. Management changes, reflecting three different ownerships of the Yosemite Park & Curry Company, caused layoffs, resignations, and poor morale. Between 1970 and 1974 three men— Stuart Cross, Alan Coleman, and Don Hummel—succeeded each other in Company leadership. Coincident with the advent of Leslie Arnberger, Yosemite's eleventh superintendent, in January 1974, was the arrival of Edward C. Hardy, the Curry Company's tenth head in its seventy-five years of existence. Hardy represented the Music Corporation of America, an entertainment conglomerate, which purchased the Yosemite Park and Curry Company in August 1973.

Although MCA retained the Curry name and promised to continue the traditions of service and hospitality, there was considerable public sound and fury concerning the takeover by a Hollywood-based corporation. Several of MCA's early moves smacked of Disneyland. Historic Degnan's was renamed "The Great Yosemite Food and Beverage Company." Some people, especially residents, reacted so forcefully that the old name was returned on October 20, 1975. When the name of Camp Curry was altered to Curry Village there was little publicity and, therefore, little grumbling. Rumors of a ten-story hotel caused further uproar even though denied categorically by both the Company and the Park Service. Governmental permission for such construction would have been mandatory. The Company was allowed to build a near-replica of the Camp Curry cafeteria and dining room, but was not permitted to replace the Glacier Point Hotel. When the Company proposed replacing some of the 600 tents and old, uninsulated bungalows at Curry Village with modern, high revenue-producing units, conservationists and the press reacted with such ferocity that the request was dropped.

Much of the adverse publicity was garnered

because, at the request of a National Park Service official, Universal Studios, a subsidiary of MCA, intruded in Yosemite to film a television series presenting the problems and effectiveness of the rangers. The idea was sound, but the production offensive, since liberties, allowed by Washington, were taken with the environment, and visitor traffic was slowed or stopped during the months of filming. Again the public rose in print, and the poorly plotted, unrealistic, over-acted "Sierra" series was canceled after only a few appearances on TV.

The legions of absentee taxpaying devotees included environmentalists and hard-core Sierra Clubbers. They were so responsive and influential that the "Sierra"-tainted National Park Service director was pressured from office. Later in 1974 the Park Service's Yosemite Master Plan was so overwhelmingly opposed by the public that the Park Service shelved it. A new management plan, evolved after months of expensive but democratic participation, was not finalized until 1980. Relocation of Park Service and concessionaire facilities to areas outside Yosemite Valley was a priority of the plan. Much of that was accomplished during the 1989–1994 tenure of Yosemite Superintendent Michael J. Finley. The Curry Company moved some facilities as far away as Fresno; the Park Service moved some of its functions to El Portal.

During the conservative Republican administrations of the 1980s, drastically reduced budgets caused more problems for Yosemite. The National Park Service could not afford to hire, train, or maintain staff to properly protect the Park's resources and activities. Morale and productivity decreased as visitation, overwork, and unrealistic liability suits increased. Public donations were solicited by the Yosemite Association in a multi-million dollar campaign to implement certain facets of the management projects. The drive was enormously successful, but raised questions as to whether the government was abdicating its legal and fiscal responsibilities.

Founded in 1924, the Yosemite Natural History Association (now Yosemite Association) is a non-profit organization dedicated, its publicity states, "to the support of Yosemite National Park through a program of visitor services, publications, and membership activities." Money-raising was not a function. That problem was resolved when the Yosemite Fund was created to raise money for improvements in Yosemite. Individuals, foundations, and corporations gave overwhelmingly. By 1998 over $11 million had been raised and committed to fund 150 projects. They ranged from building new bikeways, remodeling the old Happy Isles Fish Hatchery into an eye-catching nature center, creating interpretive signs and exhibits, repairing and rerouting trails, supplying 2,000 bear-proof food-lockers for campsites, funding sorely needed research on great gray owls, mountain lions, and fire prevention, encouraging Native American oral history, and many, many more. In 1998 alone $3.76 million was raised. One of the Fund's biggest projects of the 1990s was the building of the amphitheater at Glacier Point pictured on page 155. On this, as in many jobs, National Park Service personnel and volunteers did the work.

The Fund's small staff, directed by Bob Hansen, and an enthusiastic group bolstered by volunteers, accomplish wonders. Of every dollar raised, 86 cents goes into park projects, only 14 cents into overhead. Humanitarian aid is not forgotten. After the historic flood of January 1997, an emergency flood relief campaign brought in half a million dollars. This money not only helped repair damage, but aided the employees who were flooded out of their housing and lost all their belongings. Both the Yosemite Fund and the Yosemite Association are vital to the park's well-being.

In contrast to the early negative events, the Curry Company, under the MCA and the direction of its history-minded president, Ed Hardy, funded positive goals such as the historical restoration of both the Ahwahnee and Wawona hotels. Appropriate celebrations for the Ahwahnee's 50th anniversary in 1977, its 60th in 1987, and Wawona's centennial in 1979 were sponsored by the concessionaire. It also played a large part in the 100th anniversary celebration for the Yosemite Valley Chapel in June of 1979. A popular and successful recycling program, and free shuttle buses were Curry Company innovations. Behind the scenes, upgrading of employee housing and incentive programs, such as length-of-service awards, were strongly emphasized. The Curry Company's goal, Hardy said, existed "to provide a quality guest experience while protecting the park's resources yet earning a fair profit." More and more, Hardy's idea of "fair profit" was questioned. What seemed fair in 1973 when visitation was two and a third million seemed excessive in 1993 when almost four million came and business increased proportionally. In 1992 the Yosemite Park & Curry Company grossed over $92 million and returned just three-fourths of one percent to the government. Stress and expense for both the Company and the Park Service resulted from nature's dramatic and tragic dominance in the 1980s. Floods, earthquakes, Mono winds, lightning, and rock slides caused devastation, deaths and temporary closure of all Park roads and many trails, bridges, and campgrounds.

Nature's dominance was even harsher in the 1990s. The decade began with the catastrophic forest fires of 1990, and continued with heavy snows in 1995 and a minor flood, followed by a horrendous rock slide that pulverized part of the Happy Isles area and new nature center. Before that clean-up was completed, more damage was delivered by the flood in January 1997. The year of 1999 was relatively calm but there were more slides in back of Curry Village, closing part of the camp in its hundredth year. Competing with nature, Congress and the U. S. budget crisis in 1995 caused lengthy closure of Yosemite in November and again in December. Visitation had topped four million for three years, but decreased drastically in 1998 and 1999, partly as a result of the ongoing repairs to the flood-damaged road to El Portal, and partly to the bad press associated with four brutal murders in 1999.

All these natural and political disasters affected the finances and fortune of the newest concessionaire. During Yosemite's centennial year, 1990, MCA was purchased by a Japanese conglomerate. Meanwhile, to avoid foreign control of a national park, the Curry Company had to be sold separately. There were several bidders competing to take over the 91-year-old company when its contract expired October 1, 1993. All of them sent investigative teams of hard-headed businessmen to scrutinize every facet of operation.

Delaware North Company (DNC), a billion-dollar, family-owned complex based in Delaware, specializing in food and sports services, won the bid. Once again, Yosemite's devotees erupted, since DNC had little experience running a resort.

However, Congress did not object to the choice, so National Park Service officials worked out a 15-year contract giving the government 20 percent of DNC's gross revenues each year. A new name was chosen—Yosemite Concession Services Corporation (YCS) —and a new CEO. Gary Fraker, a 16-year veteran of DNC and a member of the investigative team, was their high-energy, goal-oriented choice. It helped that he was a friendly cuss in awe of Yosemite's grandeur.

Fraker's background in food service and purchasing forecast changes in menus. Another of his goals was to solidify relations with the NPS, still another to get to know employees and their jobs. Of the 1,600 employees, (1,900 in summer) 220 of them in management, he soon saw the need for reorganizing and downsizing, but implementation was gradual. Nevertheless, the new broom's sweeping caused bitterness and controversy, especially when partial replacements came from DNC.

Improving equipment, remodeling of the Yosemite Lodge's restaurant area and the Village Store and adjoining gift shop, as well as the Curry Village gift shop, were among the early improvements. A new and attractive multi-purpose facility at Glacier Point took up a large amount of the concessionaire's capital investment fund plus great chunks of construction time— between natural disasters. During this time, particularly in 1995, people crammed in to see the waterfalls and to try the great skiing at Badger Pass.

Between 1965 when John Preston, the last long-term, forceful superintendent, left, and 1999, nine more men and one woman served short terms. They were John M. Davis, Lawrence Hadley, Wayne B. Cone, Lynn H. Thompson, Leslie P. Arnberger, Robert O. Binnewies, John M. Morehead, Michael J. Finley, Barbara (BJ) Griffin, and Stanley T. Albright, 65-year-old nephew of the illustrious Horace Albright.

Most of them had strong assistant superintendents who functioned ably as acting superintendents in the top man's absence. BJ Griffin was among that number as the first woman assistant superintendent from 1987 to 1990, and returned five years later as the first female superintendent. During the mid- and late-1990s the YNP engaged in issuing updates to the many plans to improve the 1980 Master Plan. Transportation, traffic control, roads, visitor facilities, housing, and environmental concerns for natural resources were among the items on which public input was requested. But inconsistency and cross purposes reigned.

Plan after plan was either tabled by the National Park Service or shot down by the public. In 1998, the Secretary of Interior ordered the various plans to be consolidated into one comprehensive blueprint for the future. This sounded sensible, but delayed implementation to, at least, late 2000, and probably later. In October 1999 the impatient Secretary, aware that his job and power would be over when a new president was inaugurated in 2001, picked David Mihalic as the newest superintendent. Mihalic, a 53-year-old part Cherokee Indian, was superintendent of Glacier National Park. It was a political move, meant to expedite the final formulation and implementation of major changes, particularly in Yosemite Valley. Superintendent Mihalic was expected to be superhuman to achieve these changes within a couple of years. Albright became a special assistant on Natural Resources protection to the director of the National Park Service, with an office in Yosemite.

The flood of 1997 required major repair and reconstruction of the 7.5 miles of road between the El Portal/Big Oak Flat intersection and the western boundary just east of El Portal. Revegetation and sewer repair were part of the job. Pressure from outlying communities and transportation companies to widen the road to accommodate large buses also contributed to the National Park Service decision to rebuild rather than simply repair the road. Opposition was vociferous to say the least. Completion, scheduled for early fall 2000, is dependent on nature—and on law suits. Because the Park Service had not obtained all the required environmental impact statements and had not revised its management plan, it was successfully sued in federal court. Some of the planned work, such as removal of the small diversion dam across from the intersection of highways 140 and 120 was delayed and may be eliminated. Meanwhile, night closures during tourist season and day and night closures during winter months handicap access for employees and visitors alike. Windows for travel are short, and the road rough.

As always, the precarious, unresolved balance between preservation and park usage evolves as did the glaciers—s-l-o-w-l-y. In the interim, Half Dome and all it symbolizes endures. Yosemite still attracts visitors who need bread and beds, as well as beauty, recreation, and rejuvenation.

Source Notes

Chapter 1 Notes – Welcome to Yosemite

The main sources on which this chapter was based were found in *In The Heart of the Sierras* by James M. Hutchings, 1886, "The History of Business Concessions in Yosemite National Park," by Homer W. Robinson in the June 1948 *Yosemite Nature Notes*, letters from Laurence V. Degnan, and the author's research material and earlier books: *Pioneers in Petticoats, Galen Clark, Yosemite Guardian,* and *John Muir in Yosemite*. Marjorie Cook Wilson's unpublished manuscript concerning the Sentinel Hotel, an article on Charles L. Weed by Bill and Mary Hood in the June 1959 *Yosemite Nature Notes,* and *The Big Oak Flat Road* by Irene D. Paden and Margaret E. Schlichtmann also were helpful.

Chapter 2 Notes – "All's Well!"

Documentation for this chapter exists in a four-page, handwritten memoir by Jennie Foster Curry, circa 1940, and correspondence between her and Charles H. Petersen, circa 1930, as well as his notes. Two untitled manuscripts by Mary Curry Tresidder, one written for the author November 11, 1965, gave data. Curry, Kerr, and McKee family background was supplied by Nelle Curry Manville, Bertha Lillie Curry, Ida Curry Hensleigh, Smith Curry, Dorothy Curry Johnson, and Celeste Curry McKee.

Interviews with Thomas Green, son of Rufus Green, Stuart Cross, grandson, and Pat Davidson, close friend, and letters from Marjorie Curry Williams, who read this and other chapters, added authenticity as did 1946 and 1948 interviews with Mrs. Curry recorded by Yosemite rangers.

Gertrude Thomas Bocquerza supplied information on the 1898 Thomas family camp, photos of which are in the Yosemite National Park Museum Collection. Documentation for Camp Sequoia's opening day and the subsequent career of Camp Curry exists in the *Yosemite Tourist* file, which is also safeguarded in the Yosemite National Park Research Library. Other newspapers consulted were the *Winchester Argus,* many issues of the *Redwood City Democrat,* the *Palo Alto Times* of May 7, 1917, and the March 4, 1943 *Yosemite Sentinel.*

The principal books used for background were *History of the State of California* by J. M. Guinn, 1904, *The Days of a Man* by David Starr Jordan, World Book Co., 1922, and *Stanford Mosaic,* Stanford University Press, 1962. Frank J. Taylor's article, "Mother Curry, Chairman," in *California, Magazine of Pacific Business* for January 1937 was particularly helpful.

The archives of Indiana, Harvard, and Stanford universities yielded data as did the Greensburg, Indiana, School Records, the Greensburg Public library, Ogden Public Library, Ogden City Directories, 1892–96, and Redwood City School Records.

Chapter 3 Notes – Yosemite Stentor

Before writing this chapter, I studied "Reminiscences by Jennie Foster Curry," published in *Yosemite, Saga of a Century,* Sierra Star Press, 1964, and an October 14, 1946, interview with a Park ranger, as well as articles by Mary Curry Tresidder in the March 4, 1943 *Yosemite Sentinel,* the January 1, 1962 *Mariposa Sentinel,* and the November 5, 1964 *Redwood City Tribune.*

Also of value were various issues of the *Palo Alto Times,* several editions of *Foley's Yosemite Souvenir and Guide,* plus Marjorie Cook Wilson's manuscript on the Sentinel Hotel, Fred McCauley's account in the Yosemite Research Library, a 1900 folder on Curry's Camps at Yosemite, Tahoe, and Shasta, and "The First Auto into Yosemite" by James M. Zordich, in the *Quarterly* of the Los Angeles Country Museum of National History.

The *Yosemite Tourist* file was a treasure trove, and I used Carl P. Russell's *One Hundred Years in Yosemite* extensively, as well as my own books, *Wawona's Yesterdays* and *Pioneers in Petticoats,* for background. *Sunset Magazine* for August 1922 was another good source.

Interviews with Tom Reiger, Dr. Harold C. Bradley, Hil Oehlmann, Ruth Curry Burns, Tom Green, Mary Pister, Thomas Cramer, and Eleanor Crooks supplied information and valid anecdotes.

Background on LeConte's death was found in several *Sierra Club Bulletins:* pps. 1–11, 1902; pps. 66–69, 1904; pps. 176–80, 1905; and in the June 1934 *Yosemite Nature Notes,* a tape recording made by Phil Gutleben, and notes made by Mary Curry Tresidder on identification of the rocks in the memorial cairn.

Chapter 4 Notes – Earthquake!

Once again manuscripts by Mary Curry Tresidder were invaluable. An untitled one prepared for the Palo Alto Historical Society in 1954 concerned the Currys' life in Palo Alto; another in the January 1972 *Mariposa Sentinel,* and two regarding pioneer Camp Curry, published in the March 4, 1943 and the October 15, 1965 *Yosemite Sentinel* were consulted often. Jennie Foster Curry's reminiscences in *Yosemite—Saga of a Century,* and in the August 1948 tape-recorded interview were helpful. Additionally, several letters form Marjorie Curry Williams guided my text, and I quoted figures from the file of 1908 Camp Curry invoices.

Files of the *Palo Alto Times,* the *Yosemite Tourist,* the *Yosemite Souvenir & Guide,* and the Yosemite Valley Commissioner's Reports were researched. Curry files in the Yosemite Research Library, the Palo Alto

Historical Society, Yosemite National Park travel records, and Stanford University Archives hold documentary data, as did Foster Curry's scrapbook, lent to me by his widow, Ruth Curry Burns, the *Palo Alto Times* for May 7, 1917, the August 1922 *Sunset Magazine,* and the January 1937 *California, Magazine of Pacific Business.*

Chapter 5 Notes – David and Goliath

Personal interviews with old-timers such as Dr. Emil Holman, Ruth Curry Burns, Oliene Tresidder Mintzer, Horace Albright, Marjorie Williams Woods, May Ballantyne, and Tom Green gave me background and direct quotations. Letters from Marjorie Curry Williams, Cherry (Katherine) Curry Gogerty, and Nelle Curry Manville were also helpful.

Documentation was found in the 1910–15 files of the *Yosemite Tourist,* the *Mariposa Gazette, Palo Alto Times,* and a December 12, 1914 *San Francisco Chronicle,* plus the 1913–14 Acting Superintendents Reports, "History of Yosemite National Park Business concessions" by Homer Robinson, the Concessions File in the Yosemite National Park Research Library, and *Guardians of the Yosemite* by John W. Bingaman. Additionally, I was aided by a wealth of news clippings and pictures contained in Foster Curry's scrapbook.

Muir's 1912 Yosemite visit was documented by the Wawona Hotel register, *Westways* for August 1966, and *Yosemite Nature Notes* of March 1957.

Chapter 6 Notes – David and the Park Service

This chapter was based on interviews the author had with Horace Albright, Celeste Curry McKee, longtime Yosemite postmaster Fred Alexander, Joe Desmond, Jr., Hil Oehlmann, J.V. Lloyd, and Marjorie Williams Woods.

Correspondence with Marjorie Curry Williams, Dr. John F. Fahey, and Cherry Curry Gogerty provided data. The Concessions File, Shaffer manuscript, Gutleben's taped interview, E. P. Leavitt's 1927 Report, the "Hearing of Complaint Between the Curry Camping Co. and the Yosemite National Park Co." of February 1923, the "Proceedings of the National Parks Conference, 1915," the Acting Superintendent's report for 1915, "Report on the Franchise Situation, 1923," and "Abstract of the Operations and Activities of the Curry Camping Co., 1899–1923," all preserved in the Yosemite Research Library, were studied extensively.

Quotations of Mary and Don Tresidder were copied from her September 4, 1957 letter to the editor of *National Parks Magazine,* and his article in the March 4, 1943 *Yosemite Sentinel.* Biographical material on D. J. Desmond was derived from his son, D. J. Desmond, Jr., the March 12 and 14, 1920 *Los Angeles Times,* and the March 12, 1920 *San Francisco Chronicle.*

Two meaty biographies were studied: *Steve Mather of the National Parks* by Robert Shankland, and *Wilderness Defender, Horace M. Albright and Conservation* by Donald C. Swain. *Guardians of the Yosemite* by John W. Bingaman was also helpful.

Material by Hil Oehlmann was quoted from manuscripts he wrote at my request.

Chapter 7 Notes – Foster Curry Greets You

Interviews with Oliene Tresidder Mintzer, Celeste Curry McKee, Ansel Adams, John W. Bingaman, Marjorie Williams Woods, Horace Meyer, Ruth Curry Burns, Horace Albright, and J. V. Lloyd, as well as letters from Marjorie Curry Williams and Cherry (Katherine) Curry Gogerty supplied a wealth of conflicting background on Foster Curry.

Documentation for Foster's actions and ouster was found in the March 23, 1927 "Report on the Franchise situation," and the "Abstract of the Operations and Activities of the Curry Camping Co., 1899–1923," compiled by W. B. Lewis and Horace Albright.

Interviews and correspondence with Charles H. Petersen, John Fahey, Syd Ledson, Virginia and Ansel Adams, Bob Dohrmann, and Joe Desmond, Jr., and research in financial records, the *Stentor's Call,* the *Yosemite Tourist,* and the *Mariposa Gazette* of the time gave background on other text.

Chapter 8 Notes – The Last Battles

Text was based on interviews with Horace Albright, J. V. Lloyd, Oliene T. Mintzer, C. H. Petersen, Francis P. Farquhar, Tom Green, Marjorie Williams Woods, and Bob Dohrmann, plus data in Curry Camping Co. press releases, the 1923 "Report on the Franchise Situation," Yosemite's Boys Camp brochure, a letter from A. B. Fall to Mrs. Curry, her ledger book of personnel lists, some of her correspondence, and several books, notably *One Hundred Years in Yosemite* by Carl P. Russell, *Wilderness Defender* by Donald Swain, and *Steve Mather of the National Parks* by Robert Shankland

Chapter 9 – Dr. Tresidder's Practice

Much of the material in this chapter was based on interviews with Oliene Tresidder Mintzer, Hil Oehlmann, Della Hoss Oehlmann, Francis P. Farquhar, J. V. Lloyd, Marjorie Williams Woods, Vickie and Wendell Otter, Dete and George Oliver, Nancy and John Loncaric, Stan Utter, Leroy Rust, Horace Meyer, Charles Petersen, Horace Albright, Bob Dohrmann, Jeannette and Ted Spencer, John Bingaman, Curtis Knoll, Bert Sault, Amos Neal, and Helen and Syd Ledson

I studied the Tresidder file from the Palo Alto Historical Society, and the Tresidder, Farrow, Gutleben, Ahwahnee Hotel, and Concessions files at the Yosemite Research Library, as well as *Stockton Records* and *Mariposa Gazettes* of the time. Letters from Bob Williams, Midge Pittman, and Florence Morris, and a tape recording made by Phil Gutleben were also helpful. *The Pacific Coast Record* of July 1930 contained material on Don Tresidder and Lou Foster, and family background on Miss Foster exists in the book *No Ordinary Man,* by Clifford M. Drury.

Chapter 10 Notes – Mother Curry's Reign

Almost without exception the many people I interviewed for this chapter had fond memories and high regard for Jennie Curry. Among them were Hil Oehlmann, Bob Williams, Marjorie Williams Woods, Oliene Tresidder Mintzer, Stuart Cross, Doris and Tom Green, Celeste Curry McKee, Mary Estelle Tucker Protso, Margaret Jabes, Helen Mickle Sault, Ruth Prager, Helen and Syd Ledson, Vickie and Wendell Otter, Horace Albright, Jeannette and Ted Spencer, Lucy Butler, Mrs. Curry's grandchildren, and many other ex-employees.

Documentation was found in Jennie Curry's testimony in the February 1923 "Hearing Before the Secretary of the Interior," the March 1923 "Report on the Franchise Situation," letters from Nelle Curry Manville and Cherry Curry Gogerty, postcards written by Mrs. Curry on her European trip, and "The Currys" by Mary Curry Tresidder in the March 4, 1943 *Yosemite Sentinel*. Biographical material on Herbert Sonn was supplied by Jerome E. Leavitt, Stuart Cross, and records of the Clearfield County Historical Society in Pennsylvania.

Chapter 11 Notes – Depression Years

Park Service travel statistics, the Superintendent's Monthly Reports, Curry Company financial reports, my own *Wawona's Yesterdays* and Washburn file, the *Mariposa Gazettes* of the 1930s, and biographical material in the Yosemite National Park Research Library, were my chief sources of documentation.

Material concerning Don Tresidder and Ansel Adams was derived from *The Eloquent Light,* a biography of Ansel Adams by Nancy Newhall.

Data relevant to the Williams's lawsuit was studied in case no. 15,416 in the Supreme Court of the State of California, Marjorie Curry Williams and R. T. Williams, Yosemite Park and Curry Co. Board of Directors minutes of 1933; *Mariposa Gazette*, San Francisco papers, and information given me by Bob Williams himself. Facts and human interest were given me by Hil Oehlmann, Bob Williams, Sterling Cramer, Mildred and Lawrence Taylor, Leroy Rust, Avery Sturm, the Loncarics, Otters, dePfyfers, the late John Hansen, Myrtle Cuthbert Sylvest, Herb Ewing, Gladys Gordon Mee, Amos Neal, Jim Connell, Robert Frates, and the late Bob Sargent.

Chapter 12 Notes – Yosemite at War

Valuable material was found in the 1941–68 *Yosemite Sentinels, History of the United States Naval Special Hospital,* Minutes of the Yosemite Park and Curry Co. Board of Directors, 1941–45, Monthly Reports of the Superintendent of Yosemite National Park, and wartime accounts of Oehlmann and Tresidder. The *Stanford Alumni Review* of 1948, the February 3, 1956 *Stanford Daily,* and the Tresidder file of the Palo Alto Historical Society were most helpful, as was the memoir by Dr. Russell V. Lee in the book *Stanford Mosaic,* interviews with and letters from Hil Oehlmann, Sterling Cramer, Harold K. Ouimet, John Wosky, Shirley Sault Randolph, Myrtle Cuthbert Sylvest, Vickie Otter, and Mildred Sovulewski Taylor.

Chapter 13 Notes – Yosemite at Peace

Primary sources consulted and quoted were 1945–47 Minutes of the Yosemite Park and Curry Co. Board of Directors, *Yosemite Sentinels,* contemporary news clippings regarding the Rooney attack, the *Congressional Record* for June 19, 1946, the Annual Report of the Superintendent of Yosemite National Park, 1944–47, P. M. Lansdale's financial report, yearly profit and loss figures, the June 1, 1946 *Palo Alto Times,* and letters from Tresidder, Oehlmann, and Albright in 1946.

Interviews with Sterling Cramer, Stuart Cross, Bob Dohrmann, Ruth Burns, David and John Curry, Lucy Butler, and Don Hummel gave me additional background information.

Chapter 14 Notes – First Lady of Yosemite

This chapter was based largely on may own evaluations after considerable research and interviews with Lucy Butler, Adaline Fuller, Pat Davidson, Ruth Curry Burns, David Curry, Stuart Cross, Marjorie Curry Williams, Marjorie Williams Woods, Della Hoss Oehlmann, Hil Oehlmann, Bob Barnett, Pat and Avery Sturm, Marion Woessner, Esther and Dana Morgenson, Bill Janss, Oliene T. Mintzer, Henry Berrey, Charles Proctor, Vickie and Wendell Otter, Dete and George Oliver, Alfred Glass, Clare Duval, June Dwyer, Mildred S. Taylor, Virginia Best Adams, Dick Connett, Carl Stephens, Kathy Betts, Kit Whitman, Helen and Bert Sault, Art Holmes, Jeannette and Ted Spencer, May Ballantyne, Emil Holman, John F. Fahey, Francis P. Farquhar, and Alice D. Luckhardt. Additionally, I read all the articles Mrs. T wrote for the *Yosemite Sentinel,* the *Mariposa Sentinel, The Snowflake, National Parks Magazine,* and *Stanford Mosaic.*

Chapter 15 Notes – Two Decades of Crowds

The *Yosemite Sentinels* were of great research value, as were Yosemite Park and Curry Co. records and stockholders' reports. Before writing this chapter I interviewed Andy Koller, Jack Ring, Frank Donahoe, Mary Ellen Degnan, Sterling Cramer, John and David Curry, Stuart Cross, Jan and Art Robinson, Alan Coleman, Mildred S. Taylor, Lucile and Miles Cooper, Kit Whitman, Amos Neal, Don Hummel, Hil Oehlmann, Kathy Betts, Avery Sturm, Bob Barnett, Lucy Butler, and June Dwyer.

Chapter 16 Notes – Eternal Yosemite, Uncertain Future

I consulted contemporary news articles, the 1970, 1971, and 1973 Superintendent's Annual Reports for Yosemite, and *The National Park Service* by William C. Everhart as background for my opinions on these pages. Contemporary newspaper and *Yosemite Sentinel* reports and input by Rick Vocelka aided with the updates regarding Delaware North and Yosemite Concession Services Corporation.

Index

* denotes illustration